THE DEFINITION
OF ANTI-SEMITISM

THE DEFINITION OF ANTI-SEMITISM

KENNETH L. MARCUS

OXFORD
UNIVERSITY PRESS

OXFORD
UNIVERSITY PRESS

Oxford University Press is a department of the University of
Oxford. It furthers the University's objective of excellence in research,
scholarship, and education by publishing worldwide.

Oxford   New York
Auckland   Cape Town   Dar es Salaam   Hong Kong   Karachi
Kuala Lumpur   Madrid   Melbourne   Mexico City   Nairobi
New Delhi   Shanghai   Taipei   Toronto

With offices in
Argentina   Austria   Brazil   Chile   Czech Republic   France   Greece
Guatemala   Hungary   Italy   Japan   Poland   Portugal   Singapore
South Korea   Switzerland   Thailand   Turkey   Ukraine   Vietnam

Oxford is a registered trademark of Oxford University Press
in the UK and certain other countries.

Published in the United States of America by
Oxford University Press
198 Madison Avenue, New York, NY 10016

© Oxford University Press 2015

All rights reserved. No part of this publication may be reproduced, stored in
a retrieval system, or transmitted, in any form or by any means, without the prior
permission in writing of Oxford University Press, or as expressly permitted by law,
by license, or under terms agreed with the appropriate reproduction rights organization.
Inquiries concerning reproduction outside the scope of the above should be sent to the
Rights Department, Oxford University Press, at the address above.

You must not circulate this work in any other form
and you must impose this same condition on any acquirer.

Library of Congress Cataloging-in-Publication Data
Marcus, Kenneth L.
The definition of anti-Semitism / Kenneth L. Marcus.
pages cm
Includes bibliographical references and index.
ISBN 978–0–19–937564–6 (hardback : alk. paper)   1. Antisemitism.   I. Title.
DS145.M237 2015
305.892'4—dc23
2014047350

For Anne Marcus
Educator, Trailblazer, Inspiration

CONTENTS

Acknowledgments ix

Introduction 1

1. Attitude, Behavior, and Ideology 33
2. Race and Religion 56
3. Time and Eternity 85
4. Universality and Particularity 106
5. Jewish Identity and the Figural Jew 120
6. Anti-Zionism and Anti-Semitism 146

Conclusion 191

Notes 216
Index 261

ACKNOWLEDGMENTS

KARL MARX SHREWDLY COMMENTED in his *Theses On Feuerbach* that "the philosophers have only interpreted the world, in various ways; the point is to change it." This is indeed the point of any anti-Semitism study worth reading. We study anti-Semitism in order to rid the world of its scourge. Some activists are impatient with study and would prefer to jump directly into the fray. There is something to be said for this approach. It is often best when one is solving problems that are already well understood. Unfortunately, contemporary anti-Semitism is not such a problem. This point was driven home when one prominent philanthropist offered a substantial six-figure sum of money if I would promise *not* to write this book.

This peculiar funder had no quarrel with the book's thesis. He believed however that my time, as a lawyer-scholar engaged in the battle against anti-Semitism, should be exclusively focused on the legal advocacy that occupies much of my attention as founder and president of the Louis D. Brandeis Center for Human Rights Under Law. Two other philanthropists who also prefer anonymity offered a very different assessment, however, inspiring and supporting this project. Although not Jewish, they are passionate in their commitment not to stand idly by should another catastrophe befall the Jewish people. They grasp that knowledge must be a guide to action, and they made this book possible. My gentle readers may assess which funder was correct in this respect.

My work on anti-Semitism began with my experience directing two governmental agencies, the U.S. Department of Education's Office for Civil Rights and the U.S. Commission on Civil Rights. Later, I was afforded the opportunity to reflect on these experiences during my years at the School of Public Affairs at Baruch College of the City University of New York and the Institute for Jewish and Community Research in San Francisco. Most recently, I established a home for my research and legal advocacy at the Brandeis Center in Washington, D.C. (www.brandeiscenter.com). This book has been strengthened by engagement with colleagues at all of these institutions. The Brandeis Center, which provided my home base as I prepared this volume, as well as a legal team to bring about the changes that it recommends, will benefit from the proceeds from this book.

Oxford University Press editors David McBride and Sarah Rosenthal were supportive throughout the project and provided excellent guidance. Jardena Lande generously assisted with extensive translation and interpretation of German texts, while Michael Ragozin performed similar services for Talmudic and biblical texts. Several scholars reviewed portions or interim papers in draft, including Leora Batnitzky, Steven Baum, Doron Ben-Atar, Gabriel Noah Brahm, Jr., Catherine Chatterley, Bruno Chaouat, Richard Cravatts, Karen Eltis, Lesley Klaff, Walter Reich, Alvin Rosenfeld, Asaf Romirowsky, Tammi Rossman-Benjamin, Dawinder Sidhu, Ruth Wisse, and my anonymous reviewers. Andrew Baker, David Hirsh, Christopher McCrudden, and Dina Porat all shared valuable conversation and information. Sina Arnold, Amy Elman, Manfred Gerstenfeld, Aleksandra Gliszczyńska–Grabias, David Feldman, and Kenneth Stern graciously offered unpublished manuscripts and valuable insights. Kaitlyn Boyle and Nicole Galletta provided legal research assistance.

The work benefited from participant comments and dialogue at several conferences. The Institute for the Study of Contemporary Antisemitism's (ISCA) 2014 conference on "Deciphering the New Antisemitism" at Indiana University at Bloomington provided a congenial forum for exploring the ideological aspects of contemporary anti-Semitism. My thoughts on this topic have found a place in Chapter

One. The Israel Democracy Institute's 2012 conference on "The Role of Religion in Human Rights Discourse" in Jerusalem provided a venue to explore the relationship between religion, Jewish identity, and civil rights. This later figured into Chapter Two. The ISCA's 2012 conference on the "Intellectual Sources of Anti-Semitism in Contemporary Higher Education" at Indiana University at Bloomington, which I co-convened with Alvin Rosenfeld and Tammi Rossman-Benjamin, helped me to explore the relationship between contemporary anti-Semitism and other recent intellectual trends. This would shape my thinking about ideas contained in Chapter Four. The *Journal for the Study of Anti-Semitism*'s 2012 conference at the Wiener Library in London gave me a platform to analyze the relationship between the actual lived experience of the Jewish people and the ways in which Jews are misperceived. This wound its way into Chapter Five. The International Consortium for Research on Antisemitism and Racism's 2013 conference at the Pears Institute for the Study of Antisemitism, Birkbeck College, the University of London, provided a yeasty forum for discussing the relationship between anti-discrimination law and the Boycotts, Divestment and Sanctions movement. I developed these ideas further in my keynote address for the Israel Academia Monitor's 2014 conference at Tel Aviv University, as well as in a chapter provided for Cary Nelson and Gabriel Noah Brahm, Jr.'s recent volume on *The Case Against Academic Boycotts of Israel* for Wayne State University Press. The fruits of these engagements may be seen in Chapter Six and in the Conclusion. All remaining faults remain solely my responsibility.

Stephanie Marcus, my best reader, provided love and support, as well as invaluable suggestions, while Shoshana Marcus provided companionship and inspiration.

Introduction

ONE SPRING DAY IN 2012, twenty-three-year-old Mohamed Merah walked into a Jewish day school in Toulouse. Merah, who was said to be a nice young man who got along well with everyone, took out a gun. He then proceeded to murder the defenseless local rabbi, his two young sons, aged three and six, and the seven-year-old daughter of the school's principal.[1] Merah's crime, initially misattributed to right-wing extremists, was widely condemned in France and throughout the world. But few understood what could have brought this young man to slaughter these innocent young Jews.

Some attributed the killing to liberal immigration policies, others to the influence of an international terrorist network, still others to Israel's occupation of Palestinian land and humiliation of the Palestinian people. *The New York Times* blamed personal angst as well as what it characterized as France's inability to provide immigrants with "a sense of belonging and opportunity."[2] Many commentators feared that the incident could presage violence against France's substantial immigrant population, by which they meant the North African Muslim community from which Merah came.

One word was, however, strangely absent from the most prominent reports of the Toulouse massacre. Few sophisticated commentators initially acknowledged that an obvious reason for Merah's shooting spree was anti-Semitism.[3] In fact, some writers, such as Tariq Ramadan, explicitly denied that Merah's action was anti-Semitic. Describing Merah as the victim of a social order in which he had been marginalized and disrespected, Ramadan insisted that Merah was merely "a young man adrift, imbued neither with the values of Islam, [n]or driven by racism and anti-Semitism."[4]

Ramadan's conclusion seems remarkable in light of Merah's own explicit statement that it was necessary to shoot Jewish children in order "to avenge Palestinian children." Merah's supporters seem to understand the anti-Jewish character of his actions full well. For example, the media in Algeria, the land from which his family had emigrated, hailed him as a hero. One Arab blogger reported on a typical conversation at an Algerian barbershop in the immediate wake of the murders:

> While the television anchor was speaking, one of the barbershop employees said, "He is a hero! Well done!" I couldn't believe my ears and I couldn't help exploding. I asked him, "What the hell did you just say?" . . . I said to him, "They're kids!" He replied, "They're Jews!" I said in an angrier voice, "They are (bleep) kids!" . . . He said, "Didn't you see what they did to the kids in Gaza?" . . . I asked, "What kind of an excuse is this? Just because you think they targeted kids, you go and kill kids? Doesn't this make you just as bad as you claim they are?" He said again, "They're Jews! They deserve that!"[5]

While Merah's French child victims had no apparent connection to the situation in Gaza, their Jewishness made them culpable for the supposed crimes of other Jews, which in turn made them fair targets.

Although some Western commentators predicted that the Toulouse tragedy would trigger a backlash against Muslims in France, the following weeks and months witnessed instead more anti-Jewish incidents. During the ten days following the massacre, more than 90 anti-Jewish incidents were reported across the country. Over the months of March and April, the French interior ministry recorded 148 anti-Semitic incidents, including 43 violent crimes.[6] If French commentators could not predict this outbreak, it is because they failed to understand the nature and context of Merah's actions. The reluctance of Western observers to acknowledge Jew-hatred by its proper name is sometimes perplexing, but it recurs throughout the world, especially when the perpetrators are themselves members of persecuted groups or when the State of Israel is even remotely implicated.

This reluctance can be seen closer to home as well. As this volume was going to press, the Obama White House struggled over whether to describe the January 2015 shooting at a French kosher deli as anti-Semitic.[7] In an interview with an online news site, President Barack Obama commented that Americans were right to be concerned "when you've got a bunch of violent, vicious zealots who behead people or randomly shoot a bunch of folks in a deli in Paris." Commentators immediately pointed out that the victims of the kosher deli attack were not selected at random. They were chosen because the murderer understood that a kosher market provided a good opportunity to kill Jews. The killer himself said at the time, "I have sixteen hostages and I have killed four, and I targeted them because they were Jewish."[8] Administration officials turned President Obama's offhand gaffe into a major blunder when they defended his error rather than correcting it. White House spokesman Josh Earnest argued that those killed in the deli "were not targeted by name." Similarly, State Department spokesperson Jen Psaki insisted, "There were not all victims of one background or one nationality." In fact, as reporters quickly noted, the victims at Hyper Cacher were all Jewish.[9] The kerfuffle could easily have been avoided. The administration had previously recognized that the deli murders were anti-Semitic, as French authorities also acknowledged. The White House later confirmed this position, and both Earnest and Psaki fell into line. Nevertheless, some in the Jewish community were disquieted by the administration's difficulty in identifying what should have been an obvious case of anti-Semitism.

Such challenges are now commonplace, especially on American university campuses. For the title of its March 2, 2012, editorial, the staff of the *Harvard Crimson* wrote that a controversial then-upcoming Harvard conference on the so-called "one-state solution" to the Israel-Palestine conflict was "*Deeply Wrong, But Not Anti-Semitic.*" Expressing its "strong reservations" about the conferees' politics, the *Crimson* staff nevertheless concluded—in response to contrary accusations that had circulated in the media—that there was "no evidence that discussion at this conference expresses antipathy towards Jews as a people, which is the definition of anti-Semitism." Since neither the conference nor the discussion had yet taken place, the staff's conclusion was unassailable: there was no evidence. The *Crimson*'s prejudgment of the affair suggests however that any amount of evidence would have been beside the point. What is most interesting though, in this particular editorial, is the *Crimson*'s bland assumption that "anti-Semitism" has a clear and unequivocal definition, that the definition can be stated simply, and that it is "antipathy towards Jews as a people." In fact, it is hardly clear that the concept of anti-Semitism today has any generally shared meaning much less that its meaning is what the *Crimson* staff assumes.

This lack of shared meaning can be seen in the controversy that German Nobel laureate Günter Grass touched off with a poem that appeared just before Easter in the newspaper, *Süddeutsche Zeitung*. The poem, spoken in the voice of an aged German, decries Germany's sale of a nuclear submarine to Israel and proposes international control of the controversy between Israel and Iran over Iran's nuclear program. The poem purports to present "What Must Be Said" about Israel in the face of a powerful taboo backed by the "verdict of anti-Semitism" and enforced by "forceful punishment."[10] More dramatically, the poem accuses Israel of planning a preemptive nuclear strike against Iran that could lead not only to the extermination of the Iranian people, but also to the endangerment of world peace, and potentially to the end of all life.

Grass's singular condemnation of Israel drew considerable attention in light not only of his celebrity but also of his long-known former membership in Hitler youth and his 2006 admission that he had spent the last six decades covering up his war-time service in the German Waffen SS.[11] Many commentators, including Israeli Prime Minister Benjamin Netanyahu, interpreted Grass's poem as confirmation of his long-suspected anti-Semitism.[12] Nevertheless, countless voices also rose to defend Grass's poem. For example, one Jewish writer argued that "only a twisted mind would find it anti-Semitic or even anti-Zionist.[13] Another writer denounced "the despicable campaign" against Grass, castigating criticisms of his poem as "the prelude to a war-mongering campaign" that endangers not only Iran but also the entire world.[14]

Indeed, Josef Joffe, editor of Hamburg's *Die Zeit*, noted that the many German newspapers that had been critical of Grass's poem were flooded with thousands of letters, and roughly 90% of them supported Mr. Grass.[15]

Understandably, the poem has been cited as evidence that serious commentators do not have "a shared understanding" of the meaning of anti-Semitism.[16] A widely discussed article in *Commentary* magazine made this point: "Almost 70 years after the Holocaust, the prospect that a definition of anti-Semitism, as understood by its victims, might one day emerge uncontested seems as remote as ever."[17] One can debate whether the term should be defined from the perspective of the victims, from the perspective of reasonable observers, or from some other vantage point. To the extent that the question is raised in legal controversies, different legal systems will rely upon different perspectives. Regardless of the perspective from which anti-Semitism is defined, however, the *Commentary* observation is accurate: we do not have a shared definition of anti-Semitism. While some courts have assumed that anti-Semitism is too well understood to require definition, others have bemoaned that the term is "too imprecise to be defined."[18]

Indeed, even the effort to understand anti-Semitism has become politically sensitive in the Western world. In spring 2012, for example, more than 1,000 English teenagers took a standardized examination in religious studies which required them to "[e]xplain, briefly, why some people are prejudiced against Jews." The test triggered a national controversy in the United Kingdom, as politicians and representatives of England's Jewish community queued up to chastise the Assessment and Qualifications Alliance for its insensitivity in preparing the test. Michael Gove, the British Education Minister, led the charge. "To suggest that anti-Semitism can ever be explained, rather than condemned," he proclaimed, "is insensitive and, frankly, bizarre. AQA needs to explain how and why this question was included in an exam paper."[19]

However Defined or Characterized

Yet it is precisely this "insensitive and, frankly, bizarre" project which must be undertaken for anti-Semitism to be understood and addressed.

If anti-Semitism is to be addressed, it must be explained; and if it is to be explained, it must first be defined. Since at least 1879, the term "anti-Semitism" has been repeatedly, variously, and contradictorily defined and redefined in scores of lexicons, encyclopedia, and other reference works, as well as scholarly books and monographs. Despite these efforts, the question of definition is now more unsettled than at any previous time. Indeed, the definitional issue has arisen as the central question in the contemporary study of anti-Semitism, much as etiology was the central question for the generation that emerged in the immediate aftermath of the Holocaust. Definitional controversies, while always present in the study and discourse surrounding anti-Semitism, have increased in the years following the onset of the Second Intifada, because scholars, practitioners, and activists need a generally accepted means of distinguishing between anti-Semitism and the various offenses that are directed at Israel or at Jews who support Israel but that do not merit that designation. This is true today for the same reason that it has long been true: because definitions are fraught with ideological assumptions that divide schools of thought.

Some readers may be inclined to dismiss definitional questions as a matter of arbitrary linguistic conventions that may be selected, revised, or replaced at will and with little consequence; but this misunderstands the problem.[20] Depending on how anti-Semitism is defined, certain elements are either shrouded or revealed. Consider, for example, the *dictum* with which Walter Laqueur opens his otherwise estimable volume on *The Changing Face of Antisemitism*: "*However defined or categorized*, antisemitism, Judeophobia, or the hatred and suspicion of the Jews has appeared throughout history and in many parts of the world with various degrees of intensity."[21] In fact, the opposite is true. Depending on how the term is defined, large swaths of it—from the medieval blood libel to the expulsion of Jews from England to the Spanish inquisition—have disappeared from the history of anti-Semitism because they are defined out of existence. For example, when anti-Semitism is defined (as Hannah Arendt urged) as a specifically nineteenth-century European ideology, these periods *disappear* from the long history of this phenomenon. By contrast, when anti-Semitism is defined (as traditional Jewish texts suggest) as an eternal condition, they *reappear*, together with a host of ancient quarrels that many historians would prefer to describe instead as ethnic or tribal conflicts or xenophobia. Similarly, the Toulouse massacre and the Günter Grass poem either appear in or disappear from the history of anti-Semitism depending on how the term is defined. If we perceive that anti-Semitism has "changed its face" at a particular time, it is because we have defined its body in a manner which allows for such transformations.

These definitional questions have been given urgency by the recent surge in anti-Semitic activity throughout the Middle East, Europe, and elsewhere. The July 29, 2014, cover article of *Newseek* magazine bears the foreboding title, "Exodus: Why Europe's Jews Are Fleeing Once Again." The article reviews the current crisis facing European Jews:

> One weekend in May seemed to epitomise the darkness. On May 24th a gunman pulled out a Kalashnikov assault rifle at the Jewish Museum in Brussels and opened fire, killing four people. The next day the results of the elections to the European parliament showed a surge in support for extreme-rightparties in France, Greece, Hungary and Germany. The National Front in France won the election, which many fear could be a precursor to eventually taking power in a national election.
>
> Perhaps the most shocking result was the surge in support for Golden Dawn in Greece. The party, which has been described as openly neo-Nazi, won almost 10% of the vote, bringing it three members of the European parliament.[22]

The Anti-Defamation League has estimated that over a billion adults now "harbor anti-Semitic attitudes," based on a survey conducted between July 2013 and February 2014.[23] This is fully a quarter of the world's adult population. Moreover, it is based on survey data gathered before the Gaza conflict of 2014, which has exacerbated anti-Jewish sentiments in many parts of the world. One can quibble with the ADL's methodology, but it is not far-fetched. ADL considers a person to be anti-Semitic if they give a positive response to six out of eleven survey questions like these: "Jews are responsible for most of the world's wars," "People hate Jews because of the way Jews behave," and "Jews have too much control over the United States government."

Consider the magnitude of this finding. In 2012, according to the Kantor Center for the Study of Contemporary European Jewry at Tel Aviv University, there were 686 reported incidents of physical violence, direct threats and major acts of vandalism against Jews and Jewish institutions worldwide, representing an increase of approximately 30 percent over the prior year.[24] This included 43 armed attacks; 6 cases of arson; 166 direct threats to Jewish lives, and 373 cases of vandalism. Worse, these figures may understate the problem. According to the European Union's Fundamental Rights Agency, 64% of European Jews who have experienced physical violence or threats do not report even the most serious incident. If this holds true for Jews elsewhere, the actual incident rate is approximately three times higher than reported, reaching 2,000 serious incidents annually.

Even the adjusted figures suggest that Jews and Jewish institutions are enduring only one serious anti-Semitic incident per 500,000 anti-Semites annually. This means that in any given year, the overwhelming majority of anti-Semites are not acting on their aversions. Their reasons may be lack of opportunity, want of courage, fear of consequence, or adherence to convention. Economists call this "pent-up demand." As the post-Holocaust taboo against anti-Semitism erodes, the ramifications are troubling. Suppose that one in ten thousand anti-Semites should physically harm or threaten Jews or Jewish institutions in a given year. Under this scenario, serious anti-Semitic incidents would increase to 100,000 per year, even if anti-Semitic attitudes remain constant. In other words, things can get much worse.

While the United States has seen far less of this problem, it is not fully insulated from global trends.[25] According to the 2013–2014 ADL survey, twenty-one million American adults, or 9% of the adult population, harbor anti-Semitic attitudes.[26] In percentage terms, this is little more than a third of the extent of anti-Semitism in the world at large. Nevertheless, it is a sobering finding for a country that has generally resisted the worst anti-Semitic sentiments circulating elsewhere in the world. Over the last dozen years, anti-Semitic incidents have significantly worsened on many American university campuses, with the worst problems identified at California public institutions. Despite the existing data, some influential writers insist that "anti-Semitism is just a myth."[27] Others find it everywhere. The problem is partly definitional.

Some commentators seem intent upon defining anti-Semitism out of existence, while others define it widely enough to make it ubiquitous.

The U.S. Department of State has acknowledged with some understatement that, "a widely accepted definition of antisemitism can be useful in setting the parameters of the issue. Such a definition also helps to identify the statistics that are needed and focuses attention on the issues that policy initiatives should address."[28] Similarly, just a few years ago the European Union's human rights agency bemoaned the absence of an adequate, standardized definition of anti-Semitism, observing that "The basic premise for a valid monitoring and analysis of a phenomenon is an adequate definition."[29] Beyond monitoring and evaluation, the choice of definition also has profound implications for policy-making. As philosopher Alain Badiou has observed, the most effective response to anti-Semitism will differ, for example, if it is defined as a specific manifestation of a more general social phenomenon, such as ethnic prejudice, or whether it framed as an entirely *sui generis* condition.[30] The former understanding may suggest the appropriateness of multi-cultural educational plans, for example, while the latter would indicate the need for more culturally specific responses. But the problem is even larger than Badiou perceives. Under some definitions of anti-Semitism, Jew-hatred is now an urgent problem requiring forceful and immediate response in many parts of the world, including several American university campuses. Under other definitions, however, including ones that Badiou would likely accept, it is barely perceptible in most of the Western world. Such chasmic differences have been the impetus for renewed efforts to formulate an appropriate definition of anti-Semitism.

These definitional efforts have been complicated by the disreputable origins of the word, the discredited sources of its etymology, the diverse manifestations of the concept, and the contested politics of its applications.[31] Leo Strauss called it "a most improper term," vowing (as some others have) never to use the word.[32] To be sure, "anti-Semitism" is hardly the most embattled term in the academy, and there is little clamor to remove the term from the names of the few distinguished research institutions that study the associated phenomenon. Nevertheless, it is unquestionably problematic. First, the term "anti-Semitism" was initially popularized by an ardent anti-Semite,

Wilhelm Marr, who used the word in order to provide his racial ideology with a scientific patina which could distinguish it from the religious bigotries that he disdained. Taken literally (as opposition to the political strivings of a Semitic race) the term is not only misleading but contaminated with the erroneous presuppositions of the German racists who used it to give credibility to their ideology.[33] Second, despite this disreputable origin, speakers of other Semitic languages, especially Arabs, have also claimed the term.[34] This is awkward, since the term has historically been used to describe an anti-Jewish animus, rather than an animus against all "Semites." This relatively recent political contestation over the word has led to confusion and controversy. Third, the effort to properly define anti-Semitism has been further complicated by the fact that such efforts have invariably served the intellectual, theological, or methodological needs of their drafters. This has been true since at least the 1870s, although the intellectual stakes have evolved over time. Fourth, since the term has been deployed for political and other purposes over the generations, its definitions have tended to reflect the political circumstances in which the definitions have been produced. These definitions initially served the interests of those who sought to advance anti-Semitism but also later served those who have attempted to combat it.[35] In some cases, this is blunt and explicit, as has been said of the refusal of Turkish Jews to acknowledge the presence of anti-Semitism in Turkey, lest it disrupt the delicate geopolitics of the region.[36] Despite the difficulties, the task is important, not only because definitional clarity is required for the term to be understood, but also because conceptual sophistication is needed for the associated problem to be resolved.

Anti-Semitism Denial and Exaggeration

Since the Holocaust, anti-Semitism in Western countries has tended to be tacit, covert, and coded, much like anti-black racism during this period.[37] As the American Psychological Association (APA) has cogently observed, in its important Resolution on Anti-Semitic and Anti-Jewish Prejudice, much anti-Semitism today takes a form "in which actual bias against Jews is denied while prejudiced attitudes exist and discriminatory statements or acts are engaged in.[38] While anti-black racism has tended to be coded in cultural terms, postwar anti-Semitism has been articulated in terms of opposition to Israel. Thus, the APA has announced, this unconscious anti-Semitic prejudice "may be asserted in the context of discourse regarding the actions of the government of Israel, thus further disguising the anti-Semitic nature of the discourse."[39] This anti-Semitism may be disguised even from those who engage in anti-Semitic discourse themselves, many of whom insist that they are free of anti-Semitic inclinations. As the APA has instructed, this denial is characteristic of "modern" or "new" anti-Semitism, a worldview or family of worldviews "in which actual bias against Jews is denied while prejudiced attitudes exist and discriminatory statements or acts are engaged in."[40]

Since the early 1950s, the demonic characteristics that avowed anti-Semites previously ascribed to Jews have been transferred to "international Zionism."[41] Anti-Zionism has provided anti-Semites with the freedom, the right, perhaps even the duty to assail Jews in ways that would otherwise provoke outrage in the wake of the Nazi regime.[42] This subterfuge has led to myriad arguments over the meaning of anti-Semitism, just as there are similar arguments over the meaning of racism. Nowadays virtually everyone is opposed to anti-Semitism although no one agrees about what it means to be anti-Semitic. Indeed, it may be argued that virtually every anti-Semite today is also a professed enemy of anti-Semitism.[43] In this respect, anti-Semitism is the reverse of democracy, which everyone professes to embrace, although each has a different sense of what that word means.[44]

Anti-Semitism is often denied even when it is palpably present. There may be many reasons for this, ranging from ignorance to malice to overcompensation for instances in which Jews are perceived as having cried wolf.[45] During the early years of this century, many French pundits not only denied the measurable spike in violent anti-Jewish incidents that was then occurring, but insisted that French Jews were "playing with fire" by *even mentioning* anti-Semitism.[46] Indeed, Jewish victims of anti-Semitism are so often smeared for bringing allegations in "bad faith" that the gambit now has a name, *to wit*: the "Livingstone Formulation." This "formulation" is named for former London mayor Ken Livingstone, who argued that Jews often allege anti-Semitism disingenuously, when their true motive is to suppress criticism of Israeli treatment of Palestinian Arabs.⁴⁷ (Livingstone argued this point in 2005, ignoring the 41% surge in anti-Semitic incidents that had occurred the prior year in London under his mayoralty.⁴⁸) Moreover, in some cases, Jews are reluctant to raise issues that may complicate intergroup relations. This phenomenon can be seen, for example, in the agonized 2006 response to the murdered Ilan Halimi, a young Jewish man, in Paris, an event that will be discussed in the next chapter. At the time, historian Esther Benbassa, an expert on Jews in Muslim lands, argued that labeling the crime "anti-Semitic" would hamper relations between Jews and Arabs in France.⁴⁹ On California university campuses, Jewish leaders frequently resist speaking out against anti-Semitism for precisely the same reason.

At the same time, anti-Semitism is as prone to exaggeration as any other form of prejudice, and Jews (like other historically persecuted groups) sometimes perceive danger when it is not present. Harvard Yiddishist Ruth Wisse opens her volume on Jewish humor with a joke that encapsulates the tendency of some Jews to perceive mortal dangers where others do not:

> Four Europeans go hiking together and get terribly lost.
> First they run out of food, then out of water.
> "I'm so thirsty," says the Englishman. "I must have tea!"
> "I'm so thirsty," says the Frenchman. "I must have wine."
> "I'm so thirsty," says the German. "I must have beer."
> "I'm so thirsty," says the Jew. "I must have diabetes."⁵⁰

The joke appears to be about a Jewish tendency to assume the worst. But it may equally be about accurate Jewish perceptions of the dark problems that lurk behind simple explanations. In other words, a lot may turn on whether the Jew does in fact have diabetes. As Wisse puts it, "the joke may 'know' what happened to the Jews of Europe and may assume that a Jew in European company is entitled to worry about his prospects of survival."⁵¹ On the other hand, it is also possible that the Jew has both diabetes and paranoia. Approximately one-third of those San Francisco Bay Area Jews questioned in 1985 stated that a Jewish person could not be elected to Congress from the Bay Area, citing anti-Semitism as the reason. At the time, three of the area's four congressional representatives—as well as both of the state's senators and the mayor of San Francisco—were all well known to be Jews. (The area's population was approximately 97 percent non-Jewish at the time.)[52] Such exaggerations have further complicated intelligent use of the term. As Dutch public intellectual Ian Buruma has remarked, "this particular whistle has been blown so often and with such shrillness that exaggerated anxiety sometimes impairs serious discussion."[53]

In some cases, exaggerated claims of anti-Semitism have complicated international relations. In early 2014, for example, U.S. Secretary of State John Kerry ruffled many feathers when he declared: "For Israel there's an increasing legitimization campaign that has been building up. People are very sensitive to it. There is talk of boycotts and other kinds of things. Today's status quo absolutely, to a certainty, I promise you 100 percent, cannot be maintained. It's not sustainable. It's illusionary."[54] Several Israeli leaders, sensing an implied threat, immediately labeled these comments as anti-Semitic. Naftali Bennett, a member of Israel's cabinet, protested, "We expect of our friends in the world to stand by our side against the attempts to impose an anti-Semitic boycott on Israel, and not to be their mouthpiece." Another Israeli politician was blunter, insisting that Kerry's pressure on Israeli Prime Minister Benjamin Netanyahu "may have anti-Semitic undertones."[55] One leader of Israel's settlement movement was still more direct, arguing that Kerry's statement was "an anti-Semitic move."[56]

In response to these allegations, Kerry's brother Cameron insisted that his brother's good faith could not be called into question, reminding the Israeli public that the Kerry family (previously known as the "Kohns") had hidden Jewish roots and a history of persecution that was part of his brother's "DNA."[57] In this case, both sides were wrong. Kerry may have given Israelis reason to be concerned by a statement that appeared under some interpretations to legitimize the anti-Israel boycotts (an interpretation that Kerry later disavowed). Moreover, the notion that one's Jewish "DNA," even if revealed only in middle age, may insulate one against charges of anti-Semitism, may be the *reductio ad absurdum* of the argument that one cannot be both Jewish and anti-Semitic. Nevertheless, there are far too many innocent interpretations of Kerry's remarks to infer any sort of prejudice. Indeed, Kerry's statement may well reflect only the concern, shared by some in the liberal Jewish American community, that Israel's current policy toward Palestinian Arabs is unsustainable in light of gathering international pressure.

Because of such interpretive difficulties, anti-Semitism tends to proceed in two stages. First, the incident occurs, whether as assault, insult, or provocation. Then, in the second stage, disputants argue about whether the incident was really anti-Semitic or whether the Jewish complainants are instead trying to smear and silence the innocent. Often the accuser is punished for the very act of alleging bias. "The minute you say anti-Semitism," as artist Yaakov Kirschen has observed, "you are delegitimized. . . . If I say 'anti-Semitic,' nobody looks at that . . . They look at me and say, 'Oh, you are saying it's anti-Semitic. That means you must be right-wing."[58] Ironically, the Yale Interdisciplinary Initiative for the Study of Antisemitism (YIISA), where Kirschen was artist-in-residence at the time that he delivered these remarks, was abruptly closed and its director terminated the following year, for reasons that may be related to the Initiative's boldness in addressing contemporary anti-Semitism.[59] While Yale's reasons for shuttering YIISA remain shrouded in mystery, the closure was announced in the wake of allegations that YIISA was using anti-Semitism claims to advance a pro-Israel (or pro-*Likud*) political agenda. In other words, YIISA was embattled over the Livingstone Formulation. To that extent, the very forum at which Kirschen spoke may have been delegitimized through a second-stage process of precisely the sort that he was describing.

Some anti-Semitism scholars have argued, quite incorrectly, that this two-stage process is unique to anti-Semitism: "In this as in many other respects," one scholar argues, "anti-Semitism differs from other forms of racism. There is no serious dispute about the nature of racism; racist events are rarely ambiguous in their form. Anti-Semitism is different; or it has become different. It now needs to be *explained*."[60] In fact, anti-Semitism is not at all unlike other forms of prejudice *in this respect*, since other forms of prejudice (including racism) are also said to unfold in two stages: first in deed and then in interpretation. In her classic study, Elizabeth Young-Bruehl explained that "Prejudices manifested in slurs, acts of discrimination, attacks, are followed by prejudices—not necessarily the same ones—manifested in rationalizations, self-serving descriptions, denials, commentaries, often ones designed to discredit the victims' truthfulness or belittle their pain."[61] Young-Bruehl explains that prejudices have histories, and the second stage commonly involves an argument about the first. In the second stage, interpretive or theoretical prejudices or bias can serve the rawer forms of prejudice that motivated the first.[62] "Like the disinformation that protects codes, the interpretive vocabulary swirling around each and every publicized episode of prejudice promotes a kind of dis-education that prevents understanding."[63] To be sure, this dis-education has distinctive features in the case of anti-Semitism. To the usual laundry list of reasons for second-stage controversies, the debate over contemporary anti-Semitism adds another significant contributor. In recent years, many dovish Jewish and Israeli political activists have tended to minimize the extent of recent anti-Semitism for fear that attention to this issue could discourage peaceful overtures between Israel and the Arab world. This tendency has rightly been criticized for intellectual dishonesty as well as for a tendency to promote political self-delusion, but it is remarkably resilient.[64]

Several examples may be given of this second-stage anti-Semitism. One prominent example is the Italian libel case surrounding parliamentarian Fiamma Nirenstein.[65] In 2008, cartoonist Vauro Senesi published a caricature of Fiamma Nirenstein that depicted her, in classic anti-Semitic fashion, as a hook-nosed monster adorned with fascist symbols and a Star of David. When journalist Giuseppe Caldarola called out Senesi for anti-Semitism, Senesi sued. The case went rather badly for Caldarola. The judge saw the cartoonist, rather than the politician, as the victim. Judge Emanuela Attur fined Caladrola 25,000 euros (nearly $33,000) for libeling Senesi. In an April 2012 verdict, Judge Attur announced that Senesi could not be accused of anti-Semitism in light of his "profound commitment to humanitarian causes" in third world countries. The case is no less significant for the absurdity of Attur's *non sequitur*. In the twenty-first century, anti-Semitism is as often associated with the radical left wing as with the extreme right; moreover, it can be found as frequently among anti-racism advocates as among white supremacists. But what is more interesting than the Italian judge's ignorance is his determination that anti-Semites should be protected from those who properly identify them as such.

A few months before the verdict came out, a similar controversy brewed in Washington, D.C. Several commentators publicly criticized blog comments by staff members of the Center for American Progress, a think tank with close ties to the Obama administration.[66] The CAP staffers had questioned the loyalty of those American Jews who steadfastly support the State of Israel. In one example, CAP staff dubbed these Jews as "Israel firsters," using language that reminded some readers of historical accusations that Jews harbor "dual loyalty." This initial controversy was quickly eclipsed by another drama in which those who accused CAP of anti-Semitism were themselves accused of inappropriately invoking that label. Ironically, the only person to lose his position was the researcher who had brought CAP's controversial comments to light. Josh Block, a research fellow at the Truman National Security Project, another think tank, was terminated for claiming that some of the CAP writings were anti-Semitic. As in the Nirenstein case, the only real punishment was inflicted on the person who spoke out against anti-Semitism, rather than on those who arguably gave voice to it.

In February 2012, a professor asked a Jewish undergraduate student at a mid-Atlantic university to defend her views on Israel and the Middle East, which differed significantly from his own. The student froze up, feeling that she was "put on the spot." Later that day, she emailed the professor a letter from Middle East scholar Denis MacEoin that she felt expressed her point of view. Towards the end of his mildly written letter, prepared on the occasion of the Edinburgh University Student Association's vote on an academic boycott of Israel, MacEoin wrote, that "students . . . are not at university . . . to be tricked into anti-Semitism by punishing one country among all the countries of the world, which happens to be the only Jewish state." The professor, enraged to receive this letter, insisted that the student not send him "these kinds of emails" anymore. The student apologized, insisting that she did not intend to give offense. Rejecting the student's apology, the professor insisted, "calling someone anti-Semitic is harassment. You don't get to apologize for it; you get to meet with the Dean to explain it, because it's a violation of the Student Code of Conduct."

The European Union and State Department Definitions

In response to myriad controversies over the meaning of anti-Semitism, a few prominent definitions have emerged over the last decade in Europe and one in the United States. In its first effort to establish a workable definition of anti-Semitism, the European Union focused on the mindset or ideology that motivates anti-Semitic conduct. As we will see in Chapter One, there are important benefits that may be gleaned by focusing on the ideas, myths, images, and misperceptions underlying what may otherwise appear to be incomprehensible actions. On the other hand, as the European Union quickly learned to its detriment, such definitions also have real practical drawbacks. In its first effort to develop an official, transnational working definition of anti-Semitism, the European Union's human rights agency, then known as the European Monitoring Centre on Racism and Xenophobia (EUMC), botched the job badly. Although its aim was to develop a practically useful definitional tool, the EUMC focused on the anti-Semitic mindset, rather than the forms of conduct in which anti-Semites engage. Their initial effort at a definition is closely tied to traditional stereotypes or social constructions of what it means to be "the Jew." Specifically, it provides that "anti-Israel or antizionist attitudes and expression[s] are in those cases antisemitic, where Israel is seen as being representative of 'the Jew', i.e., as a representative of the traits attributed to the antisemitic construction of 'the Jew.'" In other words, the old European Union definition defined anti-Semitism in terms of a particular malignant conception of what it means to be Jewish. This is a theoretically interesting approach, because it is based on a sophisticated academic analysis of the nature of anti-Semitism.

For practical purposes, the old EUMC definition turned out to be useless. This can be seen in a troubling question that arose from their definition, as even EUMC officials recognized at the time: "But what if the opposite is the case and Jews are perceived as representatives of Israel?"[67] In that case, if Jews are persecuted based on others' hatred of Israel, then this definition would provide that the perpetrators are not anti-Semitic unless their animus "is based on the underlying perception of Israel as 'the Jew.'"[68] To the extent that this is not the case, then those who adopt this definition "would have to consider hostility toward Jews as 'Israelis' as *not* [emphasis in original] genuinely antisemitic, because this hostility is not based on the antisemitic stereotyping of Jews."[69] This stereotype-based definition, although influential, is deeply flawed (at least as a practical instrument) because it excludes even extreme anti-Jewish actions which are not motivated by a particular view of "the Jew." As Kenneth Stern explained, "if a Jew was attacked on the streets of Paris because the perpetrator viewed Israelis as conspiratorial, money grubbing, greasy or slimy, and then saw the Jew before him as a substitute for that Israeli—this was antisemitism. However, if someone was upset with Israeli policy and then attacked that same Jew in Paris as a surrogate for Israel or Israelis—this was not antisemitism."[70] If regulators adopt this sort of definition, they may disregard even brazen assaults on Jewish students if these attacks are thought to be proxy battles against the Jewish state.

The weakness of such definitions can be seen from the immediate aftermath to the European Union's adoption. Much to the European regulators' embarrassment, a Montreal Jewish elementary school was firebombed five days after the report containing this proposed definition was issued. The attacker left a note that said that the explosion was intended to avenge Israel's assassination of an alleged terrorist leader. This presumably would not constitute anti-Semitism according to the European Union's definition. In Stern's example, this would be equivalent to "declaring the lynching of a young African American man in the 1960s racist if the motivating factor was a belief that blacks were shiftless or lazy or were destroying the white gene pool, but not if the same victim was swinging from the same magnolia tree and the murderer was motivated by dislike of the Voting Rights Act of 1964."[71]

The European Union wisely abandoned this definition of anti-Semitism, formulating (but not officially adopting) a working definition of anti-Semitism that is focused more on conduct than on perceptions. On January 28, 2005, the European Union's Fundamental Rights Agency (then known as the "EUMC") established a definition of anti-Semitism that is notable for its explicit recognition that anti-Semitism "could also target the State of Israel, conceived as a Jewish collectivity."[72] This so-called International Working Definition reflects its joint development by governmental officials and others who were concerned to combat a particular outbreak of anti-Jewish incidents in Europe. Historian Dina Porat argues that the EUMC's International Working Definition was fundamentally different from prior definitions as a matter of origin and process.[73] The myriad definitions formulated between 1879 and 2005 were, by and large, the work of individual scholars and writers, many of whom were commissioned to do so by the editors of encyclopedias and other volumes. The EUMC's definition, by contrast, was the negotiated joint product of teams of scholars, government officials, and representatives of civil rights and community organizations. Like all of its predecessors, this definition reflected its time, its place, and its social and political environment. The crafters of the Working Definition however were very consciously reacting to the very specific historical context of their time, namely, the rise of a "new anti-Semitism" worldwide at the time of the Second Intifada. For this reason, it is not a theoretical or academic work, like most of its predecessors, but rather a practical tool for government officials and civil rights activists to use in identifying anti-Semitism.[74]

The Working Definition provides several examples of anti-Semitism in public life, the media, schools, the workplace, and religious institutions that relate to this collectivity, including the following.[75] They include, for example, making "mendacious, dehumanizing, demonizing, or stereotypical" claims about Jews as a collectivity; charging Jews individually as a people with inventing or exaggerating the Holocaust; or accusing Jews of double-loyalty with respect to Israel. These examples reflect the EUMC's insight that the putatively political or anti-Israeli cast of much anti-Israelism shrouds significant continuities with antecedent forms of the "longest hatred." In addition, the Working Definition provides several more explicit examples of how anti-Semitism can be manifested, when context is taken fully into account, with respect to the State of Israel. These include denying Jewish people a right to self-determination; applying double-standards by expecting from Israel a behavior not expected of any other state; applying the images and symbols of traditional anti-Semitism (e.g., the blood libel) to Israel; comparing contemporary Israeli policy to that of the Nazis; or holding Jews collectively responsible for actions of the state of Israel. The EUMC emphasizes, as do virtually all commentators, that criticism of Israel similar to that leveled against other countries does not constitute a form of anti-Semitism.[76] Indeed, virtually all commentators agree that criticism of Israel is not a form of anti-Semitism per se.

This International Working Definition has been widely applauded and enormously influential. The definition has been adopted by the U.S. Department of State, the U.S. Commission on Civil Rights, the Organization for Security and Co-operation in Europe, and other agencies. The Inter-Parliamentary Coalition for Combating Antisemitism, an international body composed of legislators from dozens of countries, has urged public officials to endorse the definition. For example, the Inter-Parliamentary Coalition's London Declaration urged that governments "must expand the use of the EUMC 'working definition' of anti-Semitism" for national and international regulatory purposes and law enforcement training. More specifically, the coalition's Ottawa Protocol, which this author participated in drafting, admonishes universities to "use the EUMC Working Definition of Antisemitism as a basis for education, training and orientation."[77]

At the same time, the Working Definition has had its share of critics, as should be expected of any serious intergovernmental effort to address this difficult subject. In 2011, the United Kingdom's University and College Union (UCU), a trade union of English university professors, considered a motion to disassociate itself from the EUMC definition. The UCU had long been accused of anti-Semitism based in part on its prior, heated debates over an unsuccessful effort by some delegates to adopt a motion to boycott Israeli academic institutions. The UCU motion rejected the EUMC definition based on a belief that it "confuses criticism of Israeli government policy and actions with genuine anti-Semitism" and is used "to silence debate about Israel and Palestine" on university campuses. The UCU motion was itself widely criticized, and some accused the union of attempting to extricate itself from accusations of anti-Semitism by changing the definition of the term. This triggered a lively controversy that engulfed not only the English academic and Jewish communities, but also Jewish, human rights, and higher education groups throughout Europe and worldwide.[78]

In the United States, the meaning and application of the Working Definition have been contested even among those who support it. In 2011, Kenneth Stern, who was then the top anti-Semitism expert at the

American Jewish Committee, drew intense criticism when he co-authored a widely circulated statement with Cary Nelson, then-president of the American Association of University Professors.[79] Stern and Nelson argued that the Working Definition was being invoked by complainants in federal civil rights cases before the United States Department of Education's Office for Civil Rights (OCR) to censor speech that is critical of Israel.[80] Jonathan Tobin, then-editor of *Commentary* magazine, responded that Stern and Nelson had staked out a position on the definition of anti-Semitism that "makes it unlikely that Title VI of the Civil Rights Act will ever be applied to protect Jews from anti-Semitism on college campuses."[81] Several other commentators chastised Stern and Nelson for distorting the definition of anti-Semitism, the extent of campus anti-Semitism, and the nature of Title VI challenges at OCR. In response to the controversy, Stern's boss, AJC Executive Director David Harris, repudiated Stern and Nelson's article as "ill-advised" and wrote that it should not ever have been released.[82] Nevertheless, the AAUP in fact has continued to stand behind the statement. Meanwhile, controversies continue to mount, both at the University of California and elsewhere throughout the world, over incidents that some observers consider to be deeply anti-Semitic.

In response to highly publicized incidents of anti-Semitism and racism throughout the University of California system, Chancellor Mark Yudof established a system-wide University of California President's Advisory Council on Campus Climate, Culture, & Inclusion.[83] In July 2012, committee members Richard "Rick" D. Barton and Alice Huffman issued the fact-finding team's report and recommendations on campus anti-Semitism.[84] Huffman is president of the California NAACP, while Barton is a lay leader of the Anti-Defamation League. Since then-chancellor Yudof had handpicked the committee's members, some activists had doubted that the committee's report would challenge the status quo. In fact, Barton and Huffman delivered a detailed, substantive, balanced, and powerful assessment of both good and bad conditions for Jewish students at the University of California.

The Barton-Huffman report contains several wise recommendations. Most importantly, it urges university officials to adopt a clear definition of anti-Semitism like the International Working Definition. Describing the Working Definition in detail, the committee urged the university to work with outside organizations to promote education around the definition of anti-Semitism and, in particular, the relationship between anti-Semitism and hostility toward Israel. Unfortunately, the report also overreached somewhat, urging university officials to ban all hate speech on University of California campuses. Critics immediately focused on the proposed hate speech ban, correctly arguing that it would violate the First Amendment as interpreted by the U.S. Supreme Court. As controversy ensued, most of the committee's other recommendations were largely forgotten, including its important pending recommendation about the definition of anti-Semitism.

Shortly afterward, the California Assembly passed a nonbinding resolution reinforcing some of the campus climate committee's recommendations. On August 28, 2012, the Assembly approved without debate a resolution urging California public universities to combat campus anti-Semitism.[85] House Resolution 35, authored by Assemblywoman Linda Halderman, detailed a wide range of anti-Jewish incidents in California public higher education and admonished that the problem requires additional serious attention from university administrators. In its most important recommendation, the state assembly urged California public university administrators to use a proper definition of anti-Semitism, such as the International Working Definition, to guide campus discussions and educational programs for combating anti-Semitism on their campuses. Unfortunately, the resolution also includes some language that would arguably offend First Amendment limitations.[86] Predictably enough, activists assailed the questionable provision, building a chorus of voices in opposition to the resolution as a whole. The assembly's important and lawful recommendations were largely ignored in the resulting hubbub surrounding a small portion of the resolution, much as the Campus Climate Committee's key recommendations had been lost.

The greatest blow to the Working Definition was inflicted by the agency that produced in. In 2013, the Fundamental Rights Agency quietly removed the Working Definition from its website, together with other "non-papers," during a remodeling of the site.[87] The agency insisted that there were no legal implications to its actions, emphasizing that the Working Definition had never been officially sanctioned within the European Union. Blanca Tapia, the FRA's spokesperson, infamously dodged the issue, insisting that, "We are not aware of any official definition [of anti-Semitism]."[88] Under pressure from Jewish communal organizations, such as the Simon Wiesenthal Center, Blanca maintained that, "The agency does not need to develop its own definition of anti-Semitism in order to research these issues."[89] Blanca's comment is belied by statements that the FRA's predecessor had made about why such a definition is sorely needed.

While the European definition of anti-Semitism is now more uncertain than ever, the situation is different in the United States. In 2010, the U.S. State Department definition, which draws heavily on the International Working Definition, made some elements of Natan Sharansky's famous so-called 3-D Definition of anti-Semitism (which we will discuss later on) more explicit.[90] The State Department's definition is now the federal government's authoritative current statement on the issue, although the government has not yet applied it to domestic cases. The State Department definition borrows the EUMC's Working Definition of anti-Semitism as "a certain perception of Jews, which may be expressed as hatred toward Jews. Rhetorical and physical manifestations of anti-Semitism are directed toward Jewish or non-Jewish individuals and/or their property, toward Jewish community institutions and religious facilities."[91] The definition then provides several specific contemporary examples of anti-Semitic hostility that may properly be characterized as anti-Semitic, discussed in greater length in Chapter Six. These examples are also largely consistent with the International Working Definition, adding only a couple of improvements. While the State Department's definition has received relatively little public attention, it is now much more important that the Working Definition, at least in the United States, because it is an official statement of government policy. Unfortunately, since the definition was issued by the State Department, rather than by a domestic agency, the United States has thus far utilized the definition only to assess incidents that occur outside its borders. Ultimately, this is an unsustainable position, since an incident cannot be anti-Semitic if it occurs in France, Egypt, or Venezuela but not if it happens in California or New York. The State Department definition will come into its own when it is recognized inside of United States borders as well as outside.

American Civil Rights Enforcement

In the American domestic sphere, these issues have had an especial currency in the unsteady efforts of federal civil rights officials to determine the point, if any, at which protests against the State of Israel on university campuses cross the line into anti-Semitic harassment or a hostile environment for Jewish students. Just a few years ago, OCR was able to avoid such thorny questions, because it took the position that Jews were not a group that the statutes within its jurisdiction were enacted to protect. The OCR's statutes prohibited discrimination against students in federally funded educational programs and activities, including most colleges and universities, on the basis of race, color, national origin, sex, age, disability, or even membership in certain patriotic youth organizations. In an unusual anomaly for American civil rights law, these statutes did not mention religion.[92]

This lacuna forced federal investigators to answer two questions under politically charged conditions that are familiar to Jewish studies but unfamiliar to civil rights law. The first question is "What does it mean to be Jewish?" More specifically, are Jews members of a group that is properly protected under a federal civil rights law (Title VI of the Civil Rights Act of 1964) that speaks of race, color, and national origin but not religion? For many years, OCR answered this question in the negative. In 2004, during the first George W. Bush administration, I headed OCR and established a new policy that changed course, taking the affirmative position. In other words, I announced that OCR would henceforth extend to Jewish students the same protections already enjoyed by African American, Hispanic, and Muslim students, at least to the extent that they faced discrimination based on their ethnicity or ancestry. Shortly after I left the agency, however, my successors in the second George W. Bush administration abandoned this policy, reverting to the older line from roughly 2005 until 2010. My first book, *Jewish Identity and Civil Rights in America*, explained in 2010 why the affirmative answer was correct after all and that, for purposes of extending civil rights protections, Jews fall as squarely within the ambit of Title VI as virtually any other group.[93] Shortly after that volume's publication, the Obama Education and Justice Departments accepted this answer and pledged that they would, once again, apply that statute to protect Jewish students against harassment and hostile environments.[94]

The second question is, "What is anti-Semitism?" Now that OCR has decided that it will enforce federal civil rights law against anti-Semitism, it must decide what anti-Semitism is. Unfortunately, it must do so in an environment in which this question is both intellectually and politically contested. This can be seen in one of OCR's most controversial cases. In that case, which I directed OCR investigators to open in 2004, the Zionist Organization of America (ZOA) alleged in extraordinary detail that University of California at Irvine university administrators had permitted a hostile environment toward Jewish students to form. During the ensuing investigation, Jewish students reported being threatened with beatings for wearing t-shirts that express a love of Israel.[95] They spoke of being called "you f—ing Jew" and told to go "back to Russia," and that they would "burn in hell." They heard Jews and Zionists described as a "cancer" and Zionism as a "disease," by lecturers who insisted that Jews "control the government." One lecturer said, "If you have any questions why we're in Iraq, ask the Jews in the audience." University administrators reportedly sat in the audience and said nothing. Flyers advertising Jewish events, such as Shabbat (Sabbath) dinners, were quickly removed and replaced with flyers equating the Star of David with a swastika, Zionism with Nazism, and Ariel Sharon with Adolf Hitler.

In the face of this treatment, Jewish Irvine students reported to OCR investigators the remarkable and disturbing toll taken on their emotional well-being, their education, their ability to use campus facilities, and in some cases their ability to endure continued studies at Irvine. One girl describe herself as "a pretty tough girl," but complained that it was "emotionally distressing" to experience what she found at Irvine. Another, who emphasized that she is not a campus activist, said that anti-Israel incidents affected all Jewish students even if a student did not take a political position on Israel. One young man transferred out of Irvine because he felt he could not be fully Jewish while studying on this campus. When OCR asked him to elaborate, he explained that he felt unwelcome and discriminated against. Another man said that he felt that he had to leave the university because he did not feel safe. It was, he said, like "living in a Jewish ghetto—I could go only where

Jews are." Given the campus climate at Irvine, many students stopped identifying themselves as Jewish, for example, by wearing Jewish clothing, displaying Jewish symbols, attending Jewish events, or participating in Jewish organizations. One male student said that he no longer tells people he is Jewish because of the stereotypes that were perpetuated at campus lectures, in posters, on signs, and elsewhere. Like some other Irvine students, he also stopped wearing anything that would identify him as Jewish. A young woman stopped wearing a shirt to school that would have identified her as Jewish; other students told her they would tuck Star of David necklaces under their shirts so that they would not be seen. Another student's fraternity brothers told him that they are uncomfortable with his wearing symbols of Israel. At least one student was afraid to let people to know of his association with Hillel House, the campus Jewish students' community center. Another student said she tries to avoid all events about Israel because she finds them too upsetting.

Given this evidence, including testimony from many students covering incidents over a span of years, OCR's San Francisco staff unsurprisingly found that Jewish students at Irvine faced a hostile environment. Their preliminary finding was that there was indeed a hostile environment toward Jewish students at that campus of the University of California.[96] This finding was however reversed by headquarters officials who were determined not to exercise OCR jurisdiction against any complaint of anti-Jewish discrimination. In other words, the case was dismissed because senior federal officials did not want to deal with anti-Semitism under any circumstances. This unfortunate situation appeared to be resolved in late 2010, just a few months after *Jewish Identity* was published, by the Obama administration's announcement that it would embrace the policy that I had written six years before, under which OCR would prosecute discrimination that is based on Jewish ethnicity or ancestry. Nevertheless, OCR officials remain stymied by the second question: What is anti-Semitism? To the consternation of OCR officials, ZOA had alleged many incidents that relate to Israel, and most of the misconduct appeared motivated by hatred of that state. To be sure, ZOA also alleged that Jewish students were physically as well as verbally harassed, shoved, threatened, and otherwise abused.[97] But this begs the question as to whether they were harassed because they were Jews or because they were supporters of Israel. To some, it may be sufficient to observe that their persecutors called them "dirty Jew" and "fucking Jew" and told to "go back to Russia."[98] For federal investigators, though, it has been unclear whether these derogations were given on account of the victims' Jewish ethnicity, as opposed to their support for Israel. In August 2013 OCR issued a series of opinions affirming its prior dismissal of the Irvine case, dismissing a companion Irvine case, and dismissing separate anti-Semitism cases filed against the University of California at Berkeley and Santa Cruz. In a brief, cursory decision, Deputy Assistant Secretary Sandra Battle affirmed the agency's prior dismissal of the *Irvine* case without providing any reasoning or analysis. By all appearances, the question of anti-Semitism has been too much for OCR to handle—and will likely remain so until the agency adopts a meaningful definition of anti-Semitism such as the State Department definition.

The Movement to Boycott, Divest from, and Sanction Israel

In recent years, the question of the definition of anti-Semitism has been most hotly debated in connection with the movement to boycott, divest from, and sanction Israel (BDS). Israeli Prime Minister Benjamin Netanyahu, for example, argues that Western advocates of anti-Israel boycotts are "classical anti-Semites in modern garb."[99] He reasons that today's boycotters resemble those who previously boycotted Jewish businesses and that the BDS movement has singled out the Jewish state for unique criticism. The Anti-Defamation League also argues that BDS is anti-Semitic, although its reasoning is different. The ADL National Director Abraham Foxman has argued that the BDS campaign is anti-Semitic because it supports the Palestinian right of return, and this position could threaten the Jewish character of the State of Israel.[100] Others deny this, arguing that BDS is not anti-Semitic. Indeed, the website of the U.S. Campaign for the Academic Boycott of Israel goes so far as to argue that calling BDS anti-Semitic is itself anti-Semitic. That group reasons that the BDS campaign does not equate Zionism with the entire Jewish people as do those who falsely accuse them.[101]

Some commentators prefer to avoid the anti-Semitism question altogether. To some readers, the question may seem rude, counter-productive, or poorly framed. The very inquiry raises hackles and may impede the search for common ground. Worse, the debate can quickly coarsen into an exchange of aspersions. And then one tends to lose sight of important issues, such as the facts underlying the various claims made by Israel's defenders and critics, or the possible solutions to conflicts bedeviling Israel and its neighbors. Moreover, if one identifies a movement as anti-Semitic, then one is vulnerable to various counter-charges. For example, one will be accused of exaggerating one's claims, or crying wolf, or improperly playing a race card. In some cases, one will be subjected to the so-called "Livingstone Formulation," as we have seen. All of these risks may be averted by avoiding the question of anti-Semitism and focusing instead on lower-stakes arguments against BDS, such as its hypocrisy, false claims, or violations of academic freedom.

As we will see, however, the question must be asked if we are to properly address the dangers that this movement poses. As a political and human rights campaign, the BDS campaign appears at first blush not to be a form of discrimination. The use of boycotts to advance legitimate political objectives has been well established since American patriots boycotted British goods in the years leading up to the Revolutionary War. But the line between political movements and psychological prejudice may be more permeable than it seems, as modern anti-Semitism emerged as a nineteenth-century political ideology and movement. Nor would this be the first time that a systematic boycott of the Jewish people was rationalized as a response to alleged Jewish crimes. Indeed, such justifications have been a distinctive characteristic of anti-Jewish boycotts since 1933. When seen in historical perspective, the BDS campaign is the latest in a series of efforts to resist the normalization of the Jewish people. But determining whether BDS is anti-Semitic is a difficult question requiring more than historical research.

Moreover, in order to determine how best to address BDS, one must know if the appearance of human rights advocacy masks a form of bigotry. If it is only the former, then it may be fully addressed by arguments regarding the validity and veracity of its claims. It would be appropriate to conduct debates between those who favor BDS and those who oppose it as, for example, *The New York Times* and *Los Angeles Review of Books* have done in their respective pages. But if it is the latter, then it is no more a matter of proper debate than, for example, the putative inferiority of certain racial groups. To focus only on the truth or falsity of its claims, while ignoring the question of prejudice, would be as inappropriate as to examine, for example, the accuracy of claims historically made about the physical ugliness or bodily odors supposedly associated with many minorities (including Jews). The proper inquiry is to ask why these groups have been construed, during certain times and places, with particular stereotypical appearances, sounds, or odors, rather than to nose around to discern whether the racist assumptions are in fact correct.

In similar fashion, questions about academic freedom loom larger or smaller depending on the answer to this fundamental question. If BDS is not anti-Semitic, than one might properly ask whether BDS, as applied to academic institutions and scholars, advances or retards the scope of academic freedom. But if BDS *is* anti-Semitic, then its damage to academic freedom would be, at least by some standards of value, a matter of secondary importance. When the American Studies Association (ASA) endorsed a boycott of Israeli academic institutions, scores of institutions, including over two hundred and fifty university presidents, distanced themselves from the ASA's actions. Some did so in strong language. But almost all framed their argument in terms of the ASA's encroachment upon the sphere protected by the doctrine of academic freedom. This criticism has great resonance within academic communities. Moreover, it incurs little political cost, in the sense that exaggerated claims of academic freedom rarely elicit stinging rebukes. Nevertheless, if BDS is anti-Semitic, then criticizing it for its violations of academic freedom have something of a busting-Al-Capone-for-tax-evasion quality to them. That is to say, the arguments may prevail, but they are rather beside the point.

Matryoshka Questions

This book will explore the various ways in which anti-Semitism has been defined, demonstrate the weaknesses in prior efforts, develop a new definition of anti-Semitism, and suggest some implications for efforts to combat this ancient phenomenon. To open up the question of the definition of anti-Semitism is to encounter one puzzle after another, each opening into the next like a set of Russian nesting dolls.

To begin with, are we defining an attitude, a form of conduct, or an ideology or pathology? The old EUMC's definition, which focused on the ideology of anti-Semitism, yielded interesting insights into the nature of anti-Semitism, but it was less practically useful. The U.S. State Department definition and the International Working Definition focus instead on conduct, which has made them more practically useful but less theoretically sophisticated. Some disagreements about definitions of anti-Semitism turn out to be based on different views about how these definitions should be used. In Chapter One, we will see that different definitions serve different purposes, and it is entirely appropriate to develop different definitions for different purposes. In order to address specific controversies, such as the cases that have bedeviled OCR, it is better to utilize conduct-based definitions such as the U.S. State Department definition. For broader academic and theoretical purposes however, we need definitions that grasp the intellectual character of anti-Semitism.

Is anti-Semitism a racial ideology or a religious prejudice? As we have seen, OCR investigators have stumbled over whether particular anti-Semitic incidents are ethnic, religious, racial, or political. In some legal contexts, this question has been decisive, because racial and national origin discrimination may be treated very differently than religious discrimination. The distinction matters in other ways too. Some writers distinguish between racial and religious animus in order to understand the virulent hatreds that developed alongside modern conceptions of race. It is difficult to speak meaningfully about racial discrimination, because the very concept of "race" is based on various controversial assumptions. The concept of "religion" is also more complicated and difficult than we may assume. In Chapter Two, we will see that "racial" and "religious" anti-Semitism are different articulations of the same underlying phenomenon, rather than separate kinds of hate.

Is anti-Semitism a discrete phenomenon or a manifestation of a more universal trend? Some commentators incorrectly assume that certain features of anti-Semitism, such as its tendency toward second-stage prejudice, are unique. This prevents them from understanding the commonalities among forms of prejudice or learning from the lessons that researchers have drawn from the study of other forms of animus. Other commentators assume that anti-Semitism is merely a specific manifestation of another animus, such as hatred of the other. This prevents them from grasping unusual aspects of anti-Semitism, such as its close and complicated relationship to hostility against the State of Israel. In Chapter Three, we will see that a proper study of anti-Semitism must observe its subject in both its commonalities and uniqueness. Moreover, we will see that anti-Semitism has a peculiar relationship to other ideological elements that must be understood if its unusual nature is to be grasped.

Is anti-Semitism a product of particular sociohistorical conditions or a more persistent condition? Some writers argue that anti-Semitism has been, by and large, a unitary phenomenon over hundreds or thousands of years. This approach allows them to perceive both continuities and evolution of Jew-hatred over long periods of time. Others insist that this view is ahistoric, since it fails to appreciate the very different ways in which Jews (and everything else) have been perceived in widely different periods and cultures. This approach encourages a deeper understanding of the cultural particularities of specific anti-Jewish incidents and events. In Chapter Four, we will see neither view is entirely adequate. Anti-Semitism can best be observed in its continuities and discontinuities, its evolutions and disruptions. In some cases, what appears to be continuity is in fact a form of repetition. That is to say, similar situations may recur in different cultures either because they arise from the same underlying impulse or because they continue the same persistent trend.

Is anti-Semitism a response to Jewish behavior or to a mythical notion of what it means to be Jewish? Some argue that anti-Semitism should be defined as hostility against Jews "as Jews." That is to say, they emphasize that harm to Jewish people may not be anti-Semitic if the perpetrator is not acting on the victim's Jewishness. This observation is helpful for explaining why some actions that harm Jews are not anti-Semitic. At the same time, this approach can lead to various conundrums about what it means to be Jewish. Others emphasize that anti-Semitism is not hostility against actual Jewishness but is instead based on a false idea of what it means to be Jewish. In other words, they maintain that it is hostility against Jews as "not Jews." This approach, which underlies many definitions of anti-Semitism, can help us to understand how Jews are misperceived. At the same time, this approach also rests on various theoretical oversimplifications. In Chapter Five, we will see that anti-Semitism is not so much based on a particular perception of "the Jew" as on a process by which false perceptions arise.

Each of these questions has important ramifications for the meaning of anti-Semitism. Around each a separate debate has raged, and all must be resolved in order to fully grasp the issues posed by Muhamed Merah's crimes, Günter Grass's poems, the University of California's incidents, and the Office for Civil Rights' investigations. And behind all of them is the large lurking question of contemporary anti-Semitism: When is it proper to characterize hostility toward Israel as "anti-Semitic"? There are two diametrically opposed responses to the Israel questions. The *Webster's Third International* position is that anti-Semitism can mean any "opposition to Zionism" or even "sympathy with opponents of the state of Israel," simply because Israel is the Jewish State.[102] The University and College Union (UCU) view is that no opposition to Israel is anti-Semitic, because Israel is separate from the Jewish people.[103] As we will see in Chapter Six, both positions are wrong. All available evidence indicates that some hostility to Israel is anti-Semitic while others are not.

The question then is how to distinguish between those forms of hostility to Israel that are anti-Semitic from those that are not. For practical purposes, some existing conduct-based (or "praxeological") definitions provide workable means of doing so. In broader terms, there are four grounds on which anti-Israel hostility may properly be considered anti-Semitic, which I will identify as the *Intentionality, Tacitness, Memetics*, and *Ethnic Trait* principles. In a nutshell, we will see that hostility to Israel is anti-Semitic when it is based on conscious hostility toward Jews (Intentionality), unconscious hostility (Tacitness), transmission of negatively coded cultural myths, images or stereotypes (Memetics), or irrational ethnic trait discrimination (Ethnic Traits). In other words, anti-Israel hostility is anti-Semitic if it is consciously motivated by anti-Jewish prejudice, driven by unconscious anti-Semitism, immersed in a climate of opinion that is increasingly hostile to Jewish people, or engaged in irrational ethnic trait discrimination.

I

Attitude, Behavior, and Ideology

THE TOULOUSE MASSACRE, WITH which we opened this volume, was hardly the first nor even the most notorious incident of anti-Jewish violence that France has lately seen. Six years earlier, on January 21, 2006, a group calling itself *Les Barbares* (the "Barbarians") had kidnapped a young Jewish Frenchman named Ilan Halimi, tortured him over a period of three weeks, and then dumped his beaten body in a wooded area near a train station. Halimi crawled to the station, naked and bleeding from at least four stab wounds to his throat, his hands bound and adhesive tape covering his mouth and eyes, with acid burns covering 60% of his body, and died.[1]

The French police initially insisted that anti-Semitism was not the motive, even after one suspect told investigators that Halimi had been targeted because he was a Jew.[2] Officials assumed instead that the Barbarians had selected a Jewish victim only because Jews were more likely to be able to pay their ransom demands. "The truth is that these hoodlums first of all acted for villainous and sordid reasons—money—but they had the belief, and I quote, 'that Jews have money,'" France's then–interior minister and future president Nicolas Sarkozy explained.[3] *Les Barbares*' leader, Youssuf Fofana, denied anti-Jewish prejudice, insisting that he had chosen a Jew because Jews are rich. French authorities revised their position only when another suspect confessed that the Barbarians had burned Halimi on his forehead with a cigarette because he was a Jew.

Halimi's mother would later write that French police never suspected her son's kidnappers would kill the young man, partly because they would not acknowledge the anti-Semitic character of the crime. "The police were completely off the mark," Ruth Halimi complained. "They thought they were dealing with classic bandits, but these people were beyond the norm."[4] The Barbarians' motive should not have been mysterious. The kidnappers had demanded ransom from Halimi's parents, telling them to "go and get it from your synagogue."[5] Later they contacted a rabbi, telling him, "We have a Jew."[6]

In fairness, there were plausible reasons to doubt that anti-Semitism was involved.[7] To begin with, it was not immediately obvious that Halimi's killers hated Jews, rather than merely eying them as potentially lucrative targets. That is to say, it was not clear whether the Barbarians harbored anti-Jewish attitudes. Moreover, it was not clear whether they maintained any of the traditionally stereotypical views of Jews other than that they have money. In short, the authorities did not know whether they acted on a stereotype of "the Jew" as greedy, conspiratorial, corrupt, clannish, or materialistic, much less a more virulent conception of Judaism as a cosmic evil. In other words, they may or may not have maintained an *ideology* of anti-Semitism and its accompanying perceptions of "the *Jew*."

Nevertheless, they had clearly selected their victim *as a Jew*, and they killed him for this reason. Putting aside attitudes and ideology, the Barbarians were unquestionably taking anti-Jewish actions. But by failing to identify the crime as anti-Semitic, the authorities had made a hash of their investigation. By denying the Barbarians' anti-Semitism, the police failed to grasp the nature of the crime, its probable motivations, its urgent dangers, or its likely outcome. As in the Toulouse massacre, they were also unable to grasp the broader danger to the Jewish community. In retrospect, we now know that the Barbarians were indeed motivated by deeper antagonism toward Jews than they admitted at the time. Years later, the Barbarians' leader would be caught making anti-Semitic videos while in prison and sentenced to additional time for inciting racial hatred.[8]

Attitude, Conduct, Ideology, and Pathology

The bewildering array of definitions of anti-Semitism—and the resulting difficulty in understanding cases like Ilan Halimi's—arises because people are trying to define different phenomena. To some, anti-Semitism is an attitude, to others a form of conduct, and to still others an ideology or pathology. The differences reflect the varying qualities that people find most important or troublesome about anti-Semitism: the way that anti-Semites feel about Jews, the things they do to Jews, or the mindset that makes them think and act as they do. Each approach illuminates a different aspect of the same underlying social problem. But they are not equally adept at the various tasks to which they are put, such as determining whether a victim such as Halimi has been subjected to a hate crime.

The Mad Passion

Intuitively, the definition of anti-Semitism seems obvious. Anti-Semitism, according to the common-sense definition, is "the hatred of Jews."[9] This simple definition squares with the interchangeable use of the synonym "Jew-hatred" and fits with Tolstoy's saying that "Anti-Semitism is a mad passion."[10] (Following Tolstoy, Jean-Paul Sartre similarly proclaimed that anti-Semitism "is first of all a *passion*."[11]) Indeed, scholar Carole Nuriel of the Anti-Defamation League has gone so far as to pronounce that "there is *no doubt* about a common element in all definitions: the feeling of *hate* motivating all antisemitic acts and beliefs."[12] This definition has the merit of simplicity. If there is a vice in this virtue, it is that the "hatred-of-Jews" definition has been dismissed as a redundancy.[13] As we shall see, however, the matter is rather more doubt*ful* than this simple definition suggests.

If Tolstoy and the ADL are right, then any particular incident could be deemed anti-Semitic if it reflects a hatred of Jews. For example, the French police finally understood the Barbarians were acting from anti-Semitism when the Barbarians burned Halimi with a cigarette, because this was clearly motivated by Jew-hatred. On the other hand, hatred may be difficult to discern in some situations that are said to be anti-Semitic. Hostility to Israel is sometimes explained as a form of animus against the Jewish state as a "collective Jew." The connection may be undeniable when age-old anti-Jewish stereotypes and defamations are used to portray the Jewish state. In 2002 students at San Francisco State University circulated a flyer that featured a picture of a dead baby on a can accompanied by the words, "Palestinian Children Meat—Slaughtered According to Jewish Rites under American license."[14] This was a clear invocation of the so-called "blood libel." Since the Middle Ages, anti-Semites have repeatedly accused Jews of ritually murdering gentile babies, often specifying that the victims' blood would be baked into *matzah* for the Passover *seder* meal.[15] Despite such connections, many critics of Israel insist that they bear no animosity toward Jews. Although some protestations may be self-deceptive or self-serving, it is hard to maintain that anything like hatred of Jews can be discerned in all of the virulent criticism that is directed at the State of Israel.

There are many forms of distaste, and it is not obvious that the term "anti-Semitism" should be reserved exclusively for those that manifest in hate. The German language, offering richer resources than English for describing the many ways in which one might dislike the Jewish people, distinguishes between hatred of Jews (*judenhass*) and the lesser animosities or aversions to which Jews are also subject (*juden-abneigung*).[16] The question here, in effect, is whether the term "anti-Semitism" should include *juden-abneigung* as well as *judenhass*. While Jew-hatred is a plausible starting-point for any definition of anti-Semitism, it is not in fact common to all definitions. For example, one influential writer, perhaps more attuned to the cooler forms of disdain, defines anti-Semitism instead as "the *resentment* of Jews."[17] This is a rather different emotional response. Intuitively, the definition should not be crafted so narrowly as to exclude those like English diplomat Harold Nicolson who cringe at racial hatred but simply do not like the Chosen People. In a crisp formulation of this position, Nicolson famously declared: "Although I loathe anti-Semitism, I do dislike Jews."[18] Nicolson's statement is internally consistent if the anti-Semitism that he despises is limited to hatred of Jews, while his own distaste simmers on a lower burner. Those who strongly dislike Jews should be considered anti-Semites even if they reject anything that can properly be described as hatred.

So we are faced at the outset with the problem that, as one scholar despaired, "the word is used to refer to an entire spectrum of attitudes," from mild discomfort to genocidal loathing.[19] At first blush, this range of adverse responses is congruent with the spectrum of anti-Israel attitudes as well. There are surely some who would wish genocide upon the Israeli people. This may include former Iranian president Mahmoud Ahmadinejad, who famously pledged to wipe Israel off the map. Ahmadinejad likely maintains a different sentiment than what French diplomat Daniel Bernard expressed when he decried Israel as a "shitty little country"—a term of contempt, to be sure, but not necessarily of violent rage.[20] These attitudes are not all passions, and they cannot all be described as forms of hate. Nevertheless, all of these variations fall within a relatively narrow band: they are all attitudes, which is to say that they are framed in terms of adverse individual mental states. Many definitions of anti-Semitism begin and end with attitudes, which may be as specific as hatred or as general as hostility or aversion. For its primary definition, the venerable *Oxford English Dictionary* defines anti-Semitism as "[h]ostility and prejudice directed against Jewish people."

Some social scientists speak of a "cognitive dimension" of anti-Semitism, by which they mean the measurable extent to which individuals endorse certain negative statements about Jews. This cognitive dimension is reflected in studies that measure anti-Semitism against a set of statements that are said to be anti-Semitic. For example, we have seen that the Anti-Defamation League uses an index to measure anti-Semitism in its surveys based on respondents' agreement or disagreement with a series of statements, such as: "Jews don't care what happens to anyone but their own kind," "Jews are more willing than others to use shady practices to get what they want," "Jews are more loyal to Israel than to this country," "Jews have too much power in the business world," and "Jews have too much power in international financial markets."[21] This kind of index has important practical uses. It is not a definition, but its indicia collectively suggest an underlying definition, which conceives anti-Semitism as a set of false, stereotypical opinions about Jews together with actions motivated by those opinions.

Attitudinal approaches, whatever their hue, have significant drawbacks, however, which have led to their wholesale rejection by many authorities. Methodologically, attitudinal definitions tend to bias the explanations that can be offered as to why people engage in anti-Semitic conduct by defining anti-Semitism in terms of the perpetrator's mental states. That is to say, they are biased toward the view that individuals engage in anti-Jewish conduct because of how they feel about Jews. This bias implicitly discounts explanations that focus instead, for example, on social conditions or economic systems.

Philosophically, attitudinal responses approaches tend to assume what critical theorist Judith Butler has called the "sovereign conceit."[22] The sovereign conceit assumes that those who engage in hate speech wield "sovereign power" over what is said.[23] That is to say, they assume that anti-Semitism is a feature of individual consciousness. This assumption in turn relies on contested theories of epistemology and linguistics. For example, they assume that anti-Semitic words begin in the mind of an anti-Semitic speaker. This assumption conflicts with those theories that posit that hate speech neither begins nor ends with individual subjectivity. We will disagree with Butler on many points in this volume, but her analysis of the "sovereign conceit" is not one of them.

Politically, attitudinal approaches tend to generate resistance by provoking arguments over whether particular people should be described as anti-Semitic. Kenneth Stern correctly observes that the goal of governmental agencies and advocacies organizations neither is nor should be to label a particular person as an "anti-Semite."[24] Stern's view is not unanimous. At least one reader, given a synopsis of this book, delightedly exclaimed that it would help him to wag his finger at a political adversary and declare, in an argument-ending way, "You, sir, are an anti-Semite!" As satisfying as that exercise may be, it is not always useful as a means of resolving disputes. By emphasizing attitudes or emotions, attitudinal definitions tend to shift the discourse on anti-Semitism into irresolvable disputes over individual states of mind. This tends to coarsen public dialogue, harden conflicting positions, undermine social consensus, and increase personal invective.

Legally, attitudinal definitions are problematic because mental states are hard to prove. The alleged perpetrator may have good reason to obscure the motivations for engaging in conduct that is harmful to a persecuted minority. Worse, the perpetrator may not even be fully aware of these motivations. The last point is especially important. The attitudinal approach cannot account for the person who insists, with evident sincerity, to harboring no ill-will toward any Jew, but who then proceeds to engage in anti-Jewish conduct. After all, it has been well demonstrated since Sigmund Freud published *The Interpretation of Dreams* that people do not have complete, undistorted access to their own psychological dispositions. More recently, the psychological study of tacit prejudice has confirmed that individuals are seldom fully aware of their own prejudices. Thus, when anti-Semites ritually deny any kind of hatred, their statements may be based more on self-deception than on cynicism. (Consider, for example, Mel Gibson's formal statement urging the public to "please know from my heart that I am not an anti-Semite."[25]) This point is particularly important with respect to the so-called new anti-Semitism. Those who disdain Israel frequently disavow any form of prejudice, either to the state itself or to its Jewish population. This denial is precisely what connects contemporary anti-Semitism with other contemporary forms of bias, such as anti-black racial hatred.

At one time, it was socially acceptable to describe oneself in polite company as an anti-Semite. But that time has passed, at least in most Western societies. Over the decades since (as one wag put it) Adolf Hitler gave anti-Semitism a bad name, it has become commonplace for people to deny their own anti-Jewish attitudes and conceptions, even becoming incensed when their biases are correctly identified. Thus, the current lament: "You can't even blow up Jews these days without being labeled an anti-Semite."[26] This is especially true of those who despise Israel but insist that they do not dislike Jews. Studies have shown, at least among Europeans, that negative attitudes toward Israel strongly correlate with negative attitudes toward Jews.[27] But statistical correlation is not sufficient to prove that any particular critic of the Jewish state bears animosity toward Jews. This problem is not unique to anti-Semitism. During roughly the same period, other forms of racism have become similarly socially unacceptable in the United States. So we now speak of *unconscious* bias, as well as *coded* racism: the idea is that people do not fully know their own minds, at least when it comes to socially unacceptable interior states, and that our words often say more than we intend. Since unconscious mental states are difficult to interpret, it is often necessary to draw inferences from conduct.

Given the disadvantages of attitudinal definitions, some scholars insist that anti-Semitism is neither exclusively nor primarily a question of attitudes or emotional states.[28] For example, one philosopher has argued that anti-Semitism "cannot be ascribed either exclusively or decisively as a function of feelings, not even as the measure of a *disposition* to act or speak in a certain way."[29] In other words, he rejects definitions that focus in any part on the perpetrator's state of mind. This has also been the trend among governmental agencies and nongovernmental organizations, although these organizations have tended to reject attitudinal definitions for more practical reasons. That is to say, regulatory and law enforcement agencies as well as nonprofit organizations often eschew definitions that require them to prove what people are thinking. They have sought instead definitions that avoid the question of intent.

Where Anti-Semitism Matters

The clearest alternative is to focus instead on conduct. "Where anti-Semitism matters," as philosopher Berel Lang has argued, "is in the acts or conduct for which the concept (and term) stand[s]."[30] That is to say, if we are principally concerned with certain forms of behavior, then our definitions should focus directly on this concern. This thinking has led some to define anti-Semitism based solely on action. One salient example is the definition that sociologists George E. Simpson and Milton Yinger made prominent in the 1970s: "Anti-Semitism may be defined as any *activity* that tends to force into or to hold Jews in an inferior position and to limit their economic, political, and social rights."[31] Similarly, *Tikkun* editor Michael Lerner's definition also focuses mainly on action: "For our purposes," he writes, "anti-Semitism is the systematic discrimination against, denigration, or oppression of Jews, Judaism, and the cultural, intellectual, and religious heritage of the Jewish people."[32] Defining anti-Semitism in this manner would in principle eliminate the disadvantages of attitudinal approaches.

The International Working Definition largely follows this *praxeological* or action-centered approach, notwithstanding the language with which it begins: "Antisemitism is a certain perception of Jews, which may be expressed as hatred toward Jews." Despite this feint toward "perception" and "hatred," the definition proceeds to enumerate the "rhetorical and physical manifestations" of anti-Semitism. As the drafters intended, the Working Definition has been used almost exclusively for these manifestations, rather than for the perception that they are said to embody. This quality of the Working Definition reflects the drafters' goal of providing a more effective way for governments and nongovernmental organizations to monitor, catalogue, quantify and compare anti-Semitic incidents within and among particular countries.[33] The EUMC's decision to focus exclusively on conduct—downplaying motivations, intentions, or perceptions—was something of a stroke of genius but it is also a limitation. Historian Dina Porat explains, "Because it is short and is presented as a practical tool, not merely a theoretical one, this document . . . does not deal with the image of the Jew, but rather with antisemitic activities. . . . What it does do is facilitate the monitoring and evaluation of manifestations of antisemitism and enable observers to gauge and compare the level of antisemitism among countries."[34]

Apart from the merits *vel non* of the Working Definition per se, praxeological definitions do have certain weaknesses. The most conspicuous is that they fail to account for people who do not act on their anti-Jewish impulses. In other words, these definitions have a Harold Nicolson problem: they exclude from the definition of anti-Semitism people who unquestionably dislike Jews but do not show it by their actions. Indeed, there are many reasons why some people do not act on their dislike of Jews.[35] For example, they may live in places with few Jewish people, so they have little opportunity. Or they may live near Jews but be restrained by moral scruples or sheer timidity from confronting them.

Analytically, praxeological definitions have a more serious flaw. Kenneth Stern, a significant contributor to the International Working Definition, inadvertently highlights this problem in his criticism of the definition that the European Union proposed prior to its development: "If a Jew on the streets of Paris is beaten up because he is the victim of a random mugging, this is not antisemitism. But if he is beaten up because he is a Jew, it need not matter whether the attacker thinks that his victim is one of the Elders of Zion, or picks on him because he is angry at Israeli Prime Minister Ariel Sharon."[36] Stern adds a compelling analogy: "If a Jew is selected for attack because he is a Jew, this is antisemitism, just as beating up a gay person because he is gay is homophobia."[37] Under this definition, Halimi's kidnapping would be "anti-Semitic" even if the Barbarians had targeted a Jew for his perceived wealth rather than because they hate Jews.

The main problem with Stern's argument is not that it is false. Rather, it is true in a manner which points to the limits of praxeological approaches. Although Stern argues that examination of mental states is not "helpful," he is forced to rely on them. "It is neither necessary nor helpful for groups that monitor or combat antisemitism to examine the head of perpetrators," he begins, "asking, do they really hate Jews?"[38] Stern's alternative however brings intentionality in through the back door. "Instead," he writes, "they should look at the act and see whether the Jew (or person or property mistaken as Jewish) was selected as a victim simply *because he was a Jew.*"[39] This approach may have some practical advantages over the alternative that Stern rejects, but it hardly avoids the examination of mental states, since determining the victim selection-criteria is unavoidably a matter of identifying intent. This is the only possible meaning of Stern's insistence that misconduct is not anti-Semitic unless the victim is chosen *as a Jew.* In the end, even supposedly conduct-focused definitions must depend on a question regarding the perpetrator's mental state, to wit: Is a particular action undertaken because the intended victim is Jewish?

To be sure, the Working Definition does not explicitly require a determination of the perpetrator's mens rea. That is indeed one of its defining features. But the definition dispenses with this requirement only because certain forms of conduct give rise to (something like) a presumption that Israel is targeted for abuse because it is a Jewish state. In other words, the mental element is not avoided; rather it is the subject of a burden-shifting presumption. This is the only way in which the Working Definition can be squared with Stern's position that the anti-Semite is one who targets a particular victim "because he was a Jew." In other words, the Working Definition provides examples of anti-Israel conduct that may be considered anti-Semitic because of a presumption that Israel is targeted for abuse as a Jewish collectivity.

If this is indeed a presumption, then it merely shifts the burden of proof or persuasion, rather than dispensing with it altogether.[40] In theory, the perpetrator could shift the burden back to the accuser by proffering a legitimate, non-discriminatory reason for the challenged conduct. For example, he may argue that he questions the legitimacy of Israel because he is an anarchist who questions the legitimacy of all nation-states. In this case, the Working Definition has not dispensed with the problems of intent; rather it has merely created an analytic mechanism for negotiating them.

Moreover, the hybrid approach has a conceptual weakness that it shares with attitudinal and praxeological definitions. Since all of these approaches focus on individual attitudes or practices, they fail to ask what social and historical conditions make anti-Semitism possible.[41] They are in this sense uncritical, lacking a means of comprehending the relationship between specific incidents and the broader forces that shape them. This limitation does not impair the Working Definition's utility for the purpose for which it was designed, that is to say, for monitoring, evaluating, and comparing anti-Semitism levels in various countries. It does, however, limit its usefulness for projects that are designed to understand, explain, or predict anti-Semitic incidents or, based upon such understandings, to develop comprehensive programs for its reduction, control, or elimination. This defect is addressed by ideological definitions, which typically situate anti-Semitism within particular sociohistorical conditions or discursive practices. Moreover, ideological definitions may elucidate the relationships between anti-Semitic conduct, especially in the case of wide-scale massacres, and the ways of thinking that are said to explain, justify, or motivate them.

Anti-Semitism as Ideology

Those who proffer ideological definitions argue, in the words of one exponent, that the "peculiar and defining feature of anti-Semitism is that it exists as an ideology."[42] Sartre wrote that anti-Semitism is "at one and the same time a passion *and a conception of the world.*"[43] Indeed, one of the peculiar features of anti-Semitism is that it has repeatedly formed the center of ideologies that purport to explain all of the world's tragedies to the sinister figure of "the *Jew.*" Before the Barbarians could torture Halimi, they had to work him up into "the *Jew*." In other words, they had to make "the *Jew*" into a representative of the group thought to be at the center of the world's evil. Only then could human beings engage in torture, mayhem, and murder. Only then do they become Barbarians.

When theorists or intellectual historians speak of anti-Semitic ideology, they typically mean a global intellectual conception, rather than just the acceptance of discrete positions.[44] That is to say, they view anti-Semitism as "a set of ideas and attributes with which non-Jews can make sense of and criticize their world," rather than just a set of attitudes about Jewish people.[45] For Sartre, this conception is not just a view of Jews but of the world as a whole: "Anti-Semitism is a . . . comprehensive attitude that one adopts not only toward Jews but toward men in general, toward history and society."[46] In this view, an anti-Semite's entire worldview turns around his distorted view of the Jewish people. For example, there is a strain of Muslim thought since Abū Muḥammad ʿAlī ibn Aḥmad ibn Saʿīd ibn Ḥazm, the eleventh-century scholar and poet, that forms a systematic view of world history in terms of Jewish deviousness.[47] Similarly, it has been argued that the Muslim uprising of 1066 in Granada, in which thousands of Jews were slaughtered, can only be understood in light of then-current strains of Muslim thought in which Jews were understood to be responsible for much of the world's problems.[48] *The Protocols of the Elders of Zion* also present a comprehensive worldview, with the Jew at the center of a global criminal conspiracy responsible for all of the world's wars and other human catastrophes. Wilhelm Marr, the German writer who coined the term "anti-Semitism," confidently wrote that "the *Jewish Question* is the axis around which the wheel of world history revolves."[49] The *Hamas Charter*, which draws heavily upon *The Protocols*, reflects a similar belief. Indeed, it is for this reason that *The Protocols* have been famously described as a "Warrant for Genocide."[50]

Hannah Arendt defined anti-Semitism as "a secular nineteenth-century ideology," distinguishing it from what she called "religious Jew-hatred."[51] This approach situates anti-Semitism in a particular social context, meaning that it is a characteristic not only of individuals but of particular societies. This shift from individual to society has both theoretical and practical ramifications, since it suggests that anti-Semitism can only be fully resolved at a macro level. At the same time, Arendt's definition situates anti-Semitism within a particular historical period. This distinction is notable and controversial, since it suggests that anti-Semitism is a temporary phenomenon, not a permanent or eternal evil. The Jewish tradition had tended to see anti-Semitism as a permanent or eternal threat to the Jewish people. Arendt's conception, by contrast, situates anti-Semitism as the product of a particular historical period and social context. Subsequent chapters will examine the tensions between these two approaches. For present purposes, it is sufficient to observe that Arendt's definition has the virtue of explaining how Jew-hatred reached the virulence seen in mid-century Europe.

The historicist approach permits a more focused analysis of anti-Semitism's ideological dimension. Those who define anti-Semitism in terms of a particular ideology implicitly make two claims about the phenomenon. First, it is not just a matter of individual taste, opinion, attitude, or emotion. Rather, it is the product of a particular time and place. Second, it is not just an isolated animus but rather the core of a broader constellation of ideas and opinions. Philosopher Theodor Adorno, a key participant in the development of critical social theory, defined anti-Semitism in these ideological terms: "This ideology [of anti-Semitism] consists . . . of stereotyped negative opinions describing the Jews as threatening, immoral, and categorically different from non-Jews, and of hostile attitudes urging various forms of restriction, exclusion, and suppression as a means of solving 'the Jewish problem.'"[52] This ideological definition is important because it illuminates the extent to which anti-Semitism has become pervasive of some cultures. This pervasiveness may in turn help to understand the ferocity of attitudes and practices that it has generated.

Sociologist Helen Fein's work further develops this ideological conception, defining anti-Semitism "as a persisting latent structure of hostile beliefs toward Jews as a collectivity manifested in individuals as attitudes, and in *culture* as myth, ideology, folklore, and imagery, and in *actions*—social or legal discrimination, political mobilization against Jews, and collective or state violence—which results in and/or is designed to distance, displace, or destroy Jews as Jews."[53] Fein's sociologically informed definition reflects the insight that the ideology of anti-Semitism is not merely a matter of personal belief-system but rather a more complex network of "myth, ideology, folklore, and imagery."

Fein's definition is also easily applicable to the new anti-Semitism. Specifically, Fein's definition facilitates consideration of how anti-Israel "myth, ideology, folklore, and imagery" mediate between anti-Jewish attitudes and anti-Israel social, legal, political, and military action. Similarly, historian David Nirenberg was motivated to write his magisterial history of *Anti-Judaism* by his conviction that we "live in an age in which millions of people are exposed daily to some variant of the argument that the challenges of the world they live in are best explained in terms of 'Israel.'"[54] That is to say, many people today make sense of the world in terms of the dangers and evils of Israel and Zionism. This is not merely an attitude, although it often manifests itself in emotional responses. Nor is it best understood in terms of the conduct to which it gives rise, although the world's treatment of Israel cannot be understood in any other way. Rather, the way in which Israel is treated discursively today forms a broader ideology that parallels the historic treatment of the figure of the Jew.

Those who reject ideological definitions of anti-Semitism tend to do so based on overly narrow notions of ideology. For example, some anti-Semitism scholars object that ideological definitions elevate "vicious and degraded sentiments" to "the status of an ideology."[55] Scholars of ideology, however, will respond that "vicious and degraded sentiments" are precisely the business of ideologies. Similarly, critics of ideological definitions argue that anti-Semitism lacks the coherence or sophistication of a genuine political philosophy. "Anti-Semitism," Anthony Julius argued, "cannot claim the equivalent of a St. Paul, a Locke, or a Marx."[56] Julius, the scholarly English barrister who gained celebrity as Princess Diana's lawyer and as the author of well-regarded academic tomes on anti-Semitism, insists that anti-Semitism "is not an ideology; it is instead a protean, unstable combination of received ideas, compounded by malice."[57] Despite Julius's claim, we cannot help but note the fact that anti-Semitism can indeed claim a "Marx." In fact, it may claim *Karl* Marx, whose essay "On the Jewish Question" is a milestone in the history of anti-Semitism.[58] Much could be written and has been written on the infection of Western philosophy with anti-Semitism, as well as the infection of Western anti-Semitism with philosophy. Even if this were not the case, however, those who define anti-Semitism in ideological terms do not imply that it has the coherence of a philosophical treatise. Rather, the notion is that anti-Semitism is a way in which people make sense of the world, even if their conceptions are often distorted or nonsensical.

Anti-Semitism as a Disease

Those commentators who deny that anti-Semitism is an ideology often prefer to equate it with a disease. This metaphor is sometimes articulated as a psychological theory of anti-Semitism, in which anti-Semitism is presented as a psychological category, ranging from mild individual prejudice to full-blow exterminationist social pathology.[59] Such theories were widespread in the postwar period in the wake of Horkheimer and Adorno's *The Authoritarian Personality*. That uniquely influential volume, which marked the evolution of its authors' work toward psychological factors, spawned hundreds of academic volumes and articles throughout the 1950s. In its various forms, the pathology theory or metaphor is ubiquitous in both academic and public discourse on anti-Semitism.

The metaphor is often described in terms of a cancer, but some have analogized it to other maladies. As Susan Sontag observed, the cancer metaphor holds a peculiar grip on the modern imagination, since "it refers to a disease so overlaid with mystification, so charged with the fantasy of inescapable fatality."[60] Historian Paul Johnson by contrast famously described anti-Semitism as a mental disease. "I would call it an intellectual disease," he wrote, "a disease of the mind, extremely infectious and massively destructive. It is a disease to which both human individuals and entire human societies are prone."[61] Alternatively, one pre–World War II definition compares anti-Semitism to a sexually transmitted disease:

> Anti-Semitism is a social disease that, like syphilis, we have always had with us. Like syphilis it spares no section, no class. The gilded youth and the feebleminded are equally exposed to the infection.... Our racial body manages, however, to get on fairly well in spite of endemic syphilis, but it is always in danger of an epidemic that may prove fatal.[62]

Whether as a cancer, a mental illness, or an STD, the disease metaphor is so popular in part because it can be carried through to a discussion of common characteristics such as toxicity, mutability, infectiousness, and contagion. Moreover, like diseases but unlike rational discourses, anti-Semitism may be investigated in terms of causes rather than reasons.[63]

Nosological conceptions however have at least five significant weaknesses, even as metaphors: they do not fully reflect the reality of anti-Semitism or the difficulty in eradicating it, they cannot explain the rise of anti-Semitic political movements, they appear to reflect anti-Semitic thinking, they undermine individual moral responsibility, and they minimize the pervasiveness of the problem. Ruth Wisse identified the first of these limitations, even as she creatively continues the metaphor. Although anti-Semitism is often compared to a cancer, Wisse observes, "there is no comparable effort to finding a cure."[64] The reason is simple: the carrier typically does not suffer from the disease. "Those infected with the disease have no strong incentive to seek a cure," she writes, "since they do not suffer the physical consequences; and contrarily, the Jewish victims, who are understandably eager to diagnose the illness and discover a cure, have no access to the carriers and cannot heal those who consider themselves healthy."[65] Wisse here provides a useful refinement of the disease metaphor, rather than dealing it a deadly blow.

Others criticize such definitions, more deeply, on the ground that they cannot explain the anti-Semitic political movements of the nineteenth and twentieth centuries. The argument is that these movements cannot be understood in terms that confine them to the realm of the pathologically irrational.[66] After all, many who subscribed to these large-scale European political movements were fully functional in all other respects. This objection however misconstrues the pathological theory or metaphor. This theory, at least in its more persuasive forms, posits that anti-Semitism is a pathology that may infect otherwise apparently healthy individuals. The full extent of the disease may not manifest for quite some time.

Still others have criticized the disease metaphor in a more fundamental respect, observing that it is the mirror image of a conception that many anti-Semites have had of Jews. Anti-Semites have compared Judaism to a disease, since at least the time of Saint John Chrysostom, who denounced "the Judaizing *disease*" in the fourth century of the Common Era.[67] The Nazis repeatedly compared Jewishness to a cancer.[68] The question therefore arises as to whether those who study anti-Semitism are merely echoing, and therefore perpetuating, anti-Semitic ways of thinking. In fact, some anti-Semites may engage in what genocide scholars call, "accusation in a mirror."[69] That is to say, they may accuse their victims of precisely the conduct or characteristics that they themselves display. If anti-Semites project onto the Jews a distorted perception based on their own disowned self-perceptions, it is understandable why the scholar's portrait of the anti-Semite would come to resemble the anti-Semite's portrait of the Jew.

The disease metaphor faces a more compelling criticism, which is that it absolves perpetrators of moral responsibility. As German diplomat Wolfgang Ischinger, then the German ambassador to the United States, responded to Paul Johnson, the disease metaphor is deterministic: "if anti-Semitism is a disease, there is no personal responsibility, no free will."[70] This debate has significant ramifications, because actions are treated very differently if they are symptoms of a disease. Psychiatrist Thomas Szasz explained, "We moderns do not believe in punishing diseases or patients for having diseases. We do not imprison, much less kill, mentally ill persons; we excuse them of their crimes and hospitalize them. John Hinckley is still being treated for his anti-Reaganism. If anti-Semitism is a disease, then the Nazi leaders were very sick indeed, and the Nuremberg trials were one of the great injustices of the 20th century."[71]

UPON DISCOVERING THAT ONE HAS ACCIDENTALLY MARRIED A NAZI

Finally the disease metaphor is problematic for the reason that makes it comforting, that is, because it implies that anti-Semitism is wholly foreign to healthy persons in the post-Holocaust West. In other words, it has been psychologically important in the post-Holocaust period to define anti-Semites as wholly foreign and other, because this sustains the myth that anti-Semitism is not intrinsic to Western culture. This, for example, explains the furious judicial postwar response to one Josef Kober, a newlywed New York German groom who concealed his wartime past from his American wife Jacqueline. In response to the piqued plea of his embarrassed betrothed, upon discovering that she had accidentally married a Nazi, New York's high court put aside its then-longstanding judicial aversion to annulment, finding that there was "no reality to the consent" of Mrs. Kober, and permitted her to go forward in her effort to dissolve their marital bonds.[72] She had, after all, assumed that he was a healthy man, rather than one who evinces what the court called "a diseased mind" of the sort assumed to have been shared by a generation of Germans.[73]

In this case, of course, the disease was anti-Semitism, which New York's high court understood as a "fanatical conviction, to be effectuated where possible through the mobilization of superior force, that a race or group of people living in the same community should be put to death as at Auschwitz, Belsen, Dachau or Buchenwald."[74] This is of course an extreme formulation, which is indeed the point. The disease metaphor has the same function as other extreme formulations: by defining the anti-Semite as an extreme, foreign, virulent other, we create a myth of our own healthy bodies as untouched by this disavowed condition. The truth may not be so simple. Empirical research has repeatedly demonstrated, as we will see later on, that anti-Semitic attitudes can be found even among people who adamantly assert that they are free of any taint of racism. In other words, there may be more reality to our accidental marriages with anti-Semitism than to our indignant disavowals.

The disease myth allows us to avoid certain uncomfortable questions. For example, how is it that Jacqueline Kober permitted herself to maintain ignorance, throughout her courtship, of her beloved's background as a Nazi party member, a German officer, and an adherent to the view that all Jews everywhere must be rounded up and exterminated? How could she not have known that he would insist that she "weed out" all of her Jewish friends, eliminating them from their social circle? It must be remembered that Mrs. Kober's 1963 wedding occurred at a time when Americans as well as Germans were studiously maintaining ignorance of the prevalence of former Nazi party members in positions of power in the new Germany.[75] Indeed, American officials have been described as full if unacknowledged partners in maintaining these arrangements. In the American collective unconscious, nothing could be more soothing than to imagine that there was no reality to

American consent to this marriage. The *Kober* case is now known as one of the influential decisions that eroded traditional judicial commitment to the institution of marriage, opening the floodgates to annulment and divorce.[76] But its deeper lesson, half a century later, is that the disease metaphor enables us to deny the extent to which we have internalized anti-Semitism within our culture and ourselves. At an individual and cultural level, this lesson is important whenever we discover that we have accidentally married a Nazi. That is to say, it is important to the extent that it reminds us of a deep tendency both to embrace anti-Semitic memes and to deny their anti-Semitic provenance.

Mel Gibson's Disease

The debate over the disease metaphor and the personal responsibility critique garnered significant public attention in the aftermath of movie star Mel Gibson's 2006 arrest for drunk driving. According to the police report, Gibson asked the arresting officer, "Are you a Jew?" and then exclaimed, "Fucking Jews. The Jews are responsible for all the wars in the world."[77] Gibson's drunken rant quickly attained worldwide notoriety. Students of anti-Semitism immediately recognized that Gibson had articulated a well-known ideology. Specifically, his charge that Jews have started all of the wars of the world is lifted from *The Protocols of the Elders of Zion*.

Afterward, in a formal statement, Gibson apologized for the incident but attributed it to a health problem from which he had "begun an ongoing program of recovery."[78] As part of that recovery program, Gibson said that he was "in the process of understanding where those vicious words came from during that drunken display."[79] He then asked the Jewish community to help him on his "journey through recovery."[80] Although some commentators ridiculed Gibson's request for rehabilitative aid, Abraham Foxman, head of the Anti-Defamation League, accepted it, publicly offering to help Gibson with his "rehabilitation" from "the disease of prejudice."[81] This Gibson-Foxman colloquy became, for a time, the most prominent expression of the disease conception of anti-Semitism in the United States.

Slovenian philosopher Slavoj Žižek, one of Europe's most influential public intellectuals, publicly intervened in this dialogue, chastising Foxman for accepting Gibson's "disease" formulation. Žižek has addressed anti-Semitism as frequently as any contemporary philosopher, and his widely read commentaries are invariably provocative. In this instance, Žižek accused Foxman of being too lenient, arguing that the ADL national director had effectively absolved Gibson of personal responsibility: "Foxman's reaction to Gibson's outburst . . . accepted Gibson's refusal to take full personal responsibility for his words (his anti-Semitic remarks): they were not really his own, it was pathology, some unknown force that took over under the influence of alcohol."[82] In other words, Žižek (tacitly) applied Szasz and Ischinger's criticism of Paul Johnson to the Gibson-Foxman kerfuffle.

The twist, however, is that Žižek does not fall back on old-fashioned notions of individual autonomy. To do so would be inconsistent with his post-Marxist philosophy, which combines elements of Hegel, psychoanalyst Jacques Lacan, and philosopher Alain Badiou. Instead, Žižek attempts to displace both the disease metaphor and the assumption of individual agency with an ideological approach. Thus, he insists that "the answer to Gibson's question 'Where did those vicious words come from?' is ridiculously simple: they are part and parcel of his ideological identity, formed (as far as one can tell) to a large extent by his father. What sustained Gibson's remarks was not madness, but a well-known ideology (anti-Semitism)."[83]

In Žižek's provocative formulation, anti-Semitism has become so deeply ingrained in the modern West as to be part of what it means to be "sane" in today's world. This critique harkens back to those early exponents of critical theory who argued that the Holocaust was not only a deviation from the progress of the Enlightenment but rather the culmination of its darker tendencies.[84] In trying to explain how a nation as culturally advanced as Germany could descend to such depravity, these theorists argued that the potentiality of committing grave evil was implicit in the thought processes that had evolved during modernity. For some thinkers, the implication of this line of thought is that anti-Semitism is less abnormal in the Enlightenment West than one might think. Žižek's argument is also consistent with the observation that those who have persecuted Jews throughout history have often claimed to be acting upon the highest values of their societies.[85]

It follows from Žižek's argument that the Mel Gibsons of the world do not need therapy. "Foxman's offer implies that a person has to be insane to be anti-Semitic. This easy way out enables us to avoid the key issue: that, precisely anti-Semitism in our Western societies was—and is—not an ideology displayed by the deranged, but an ingredient of spontaneous ideological attitudes of perfectly *sane* people, of our ideological *sanity* itself."[86] Žižek plainly employs an idiosyncratic definition of "sanity" and has insisted in interviews that he is not himself fully sane. Regardless, he has offered an intriguing critique, namely, that the disease metaphor assumes counter-factually that modern Western society has developed an ideal of "health" in which anti-Semitism is not already fundamentally involved.

Žižek's critique appears at first blush to be self-contradictory. That is to say, Žižek's argument is based on three claims that are in tension with one another. First, anti-Semitism is so deeply embedded within contemporary Western culture as to be an element of normalcy (or "sanity"). Second, individuals display this trait to differing degrees depending on environmental conditions, such as the views of their parents. Third, individuals may nevertheless be held accountable for their own anti-Semitism. To the extent that anti-Semitism is an element of normalcy, however, it would seem that one cannot justifiably hold individuals accountable for embracing it—that is to say, for maintaining cultural *sanity*. In other words, Žižek's ideological definition is vulnerable to the same critique that Žižek leveled against Foxman (and that Szasz and Ischinger directed at Paul Johnson).

This appears to place students of anti-Semitism in a bind: they must adopt either a theory of ideology (or pathology) that is inconsistent with personal responsibility or a theory of personal responsibility that is incapable of explaining the conditions for the existence of anti-Semitism. In fact, some conceptions of personal responsibility are sufficiently nuanced to reflect the elements of social transmission that are reflected in the ideological definition and the disease metaphor. In other words, the "sovereign conceit" is not indispensible to a theory of personal responsibility. As Butler explains, "The subject who speaks hate speech is clearly responsible for such speech, but that subject is rarely the originator of that speech."[87] That is to say, the anti-Semite or racist makes a personal choice and may be held responsible, even though the speaker should not be assumed to originate or control what is said. "Racist speech works through the invocation of convention," as Butler elaborates, "it circulates, and though it requires the subject for its speaking, it neither begins nor ends with the subject who speaks or with the specific name that is used."[88] In this way, anti-Semitism may be an element of cultural normalcy, and yet each individual may choose whether or not to embrace this condition.

What does it mean to say that anti-Semitism is a part of Western ideological sanity? In a weak sense, it may be nothing more than a version of Nirenberg's argument that "questions about Judaism are inculcated into the habits of thought with which people make sense of the world."[89] In a nutshell, Nirenberg argues that anti-Jewish ideas have long been deeply, even centrally embedded in the way that Western peoples understand not only Jews but also the rest of humanity and the world itself. Indeed, Nirenberg insists that anti-Semitism "should not be understood as some archaic or irrational closet in the vast edifices of Western thought" but rather as "one of the basic tools with which that edifice was constructed."[90] But Žižek seems to say more. The stronger version of Žižek's argument is that anti-Semitism is central not only to Western ways of thinking but also to *healthy* Western ways of thinking. This means, at the least, that anti-Semitism is deeply connected with elements of the Western tradition that play a significant role in maintaining social stability, even if anti-Semitism is itself despicable.[91]

In short, ideological definitions situate anti-Semitism as a way of thinking about the world and not only about Jews. Some thinkers perceive this ideology as an unfortunate byproduct of our culture, while others see it as more central to our cultural institutions or ways of thinking.[92] Those who define anti-Semitism as a social pathology variously conceive it as a byproduct of modern Western society or as a persistent malady that has crossed numerous historical periods. By contrast, those who see it as a central feature of our culture conceive it as being so deeply embedded as to be inseparable from salubrious institutions, much like the *Judensau* (depictions of Jews associating intimately with pigs) that are often incorporated into the very architecture (columns, beams) of venerable European buildings. To remove the *Judensau* would, at best, compromise the integrity of the structures, if it would not actually cause them to fall.

Summing Up

To sum up, depending on the purposes for which we deploy the term, "anti-Semitism" may be defined as attitude, conduct, ideology, or pathology. To oversimplify somewhat, attitudinal approaches best reflect common-sense understandings, while conduct-based definitions uniquely support governmental responses, and ideological definitions facilitate the deepest social explanations. At the same time, each approach is problematic in its own way. Broadly speaking, attitudinal approaches tend to overemphasize individual minds, conduct-based approaches underemphasize social conditions, and ideological definitions deemphasize personal responsibility. In terms of the most pressing contemporary questions, these three approaches provide different but mutually compatible viewpoints both on anti-Semitism per se and on its relationship with anti-Zionism.

2

Race and Religion

ANTI-SEMITIC IDEOLOGIES ARE ARTICULATED in different ways, depending on the needs they satisfy, and it is tempting to conflate the general problem with its particular manifestations. In this way, anti-Semitism is sometimes defined as a racial prejudice, even as "the purest, so to say, distilled, form of racism," and other times as a religious bigotry.[1] Some authorities add a third category, ethnic bias, although others use the overlapping concepts of race and ethnicity as interchangeable or nearly so. The distinctions between racial and religious prejudice are elided by those definitions, such as *Merriam-Webster's*, which straddle the difference, defining anti-Semitism as "[h]ostility toward or discrimination against Jews as a religious group *or* 'race.'"[2] The best definitions however make no mention of either concept, since they are varying articulations of the same underlying phenomenon.

The Strength of Racial Definitions

The tendency of many scholars to define anti-Semitism in terms of race may be an unavoidable result of the term's origins as an expression of late nineteenth-century racialist German Jew-hatred. To some scholars, the emergence of the term "anti-Semitism" at that time reflected the emergence of something qualitatively different in the attitude of non-Jews toward Jews that could not adequately be conveyed in other terms, such as Jew-hatred, Jew-baiting, or Judeophobia.[3] The racial conception of anti-Semitism is further entrenched by the dominant role that the *Shoah* has had in the study of anti-Semitism.[4] Given that many of the seminal works of anti-Semitism studies began as an attempt to understand the Nazi Holocaust, it is unsurprising that anti-Semitism scholars have tended to understand the general phenomenon in the light of its most cataclysmic manifestation. Moreover, the tendency to view social phenomena in terms of race is a natural proclivity for many American scholars, who are prone to thinking in racial terms when they speak of prejudice.[5] In the Jewish context, the tendency is reinforced by a belief that racial anti-Semitism, especially in its nineteenth- and twenty-first-century German forms, is uniquely virulent, complex and distinctive.

Racial definitions of anti-Semitism are often tied to theories of how modernity created conditions uniquely favorable to the emergence of genocidal anti-Jewish hatred. These definitions provide numerous theoretical and practical advantages, and they give clarity to certain aspects of anti-Semitism that are otherwise typically misunderstood. In some cases, these definitions have served broader programs in which scholars have attempted to draw connections between the ideas of individual anti-Semites and the purportedly pathological tendencies of capitalist development, modern industrial production, the rise and fall of the nation-state, and the unavoidable disruptions to traditional lifestyles and mores. At the same time, racial definitions invariably share the fatal flaw that they are based on an idea of "race" that is historically recent, conceptually unstable, and morally compromised.

Early Racial Definitions

Those who favor racial definitions observe that the term was specifically devised in order to advance a racial opposition to the Jewish people. A self-confessed anti-Semite, German journalist Wilhelm Marr, popularized the term (or its German cognate, *antisemitismus*) in 1879, hoping that it would facilitate greater adoption of the racial hatred of Jews and Judaism that he and his compatriots promoted.[6] It may not be true, as many historians claim, that Marr invented the term, but he gave it the meaning for which it is now known.[7] Thanks to the research of Heidelberg historian Georg Christoph Berger Waldenegg, we now know much about the early history of this slippery word.

In the term's first known usage, Moritz Steinschneider, a Bohemian scholar of Jewish history, used the term in 1860 to describe and criticize the racial thinking of classicist and orientalist Ernest Renan.[8] The term was next used five years later, when orientalist Gustaf Weil employed the term quite idiosyncratically in an article on "Semitic Peoples" for the third edition of the Rotteck-Welckerschen State Dictionary. Specifically, Weil used the term to describe the birth of the "Kingdom of Jews," reflecting his view that the monarchy was inconsistent with a republican Jewish constitutional tradition. The term then disappeared until 1879, when Marr, the first gentile known to use the word, gave it its current meaning.[9]

Marr built a movement around the term, based on his belief that Jews were destroying the German people. In doing so, he built upon the earlier work of Christian Lassen, who had fused linguistic and anthropological concepts in arguing that Semitic peoples are greedy, unproductive, and selfish, while the Indo-Germanic people are gifted and productive.[10] For this reason, many early definitions of anti-Semitism, especially in Europe, were written from the perspective of avowed anti-Semites. This can be seen, for example, in the work of nineteenth-century French anti-Semitic leader Jules Guérin, who defined anti-Semitism as "a precise and formal claim of national labour against Jewish speculation."[11]

In light of this origin, many authorities have restricted use of the term "anti-Semitism" to those forms of Jew-hatred that resemble Marr's own racial theories. As the English *Jewish Encyclopedia* explained in a classic 1901 formulation:

> The term 'Anti-Semitism' has its origin in the ethnological theory that the Jews, as Semites, are entirely different from the Aryan, or Indo-European, populations and can never be amalgamated with them. The word implies that the Jews are not opposed on account of their religion, but on account of their racial characteristics. As such are mentioned: greed, a special aptitude for money-making, aversion to hard work, clannishness and obtrusiveness, lack of social

tact, and especially of patriotism. Finally, the term is used to justify resentment for every crime or objectionable act committed by any individual Jew.¹²

The bottom line for these authorities is that "anti-Semitism" refers to a particular racial theory as opposed to a religious prejudice.

Such early definitions stressed the relationship between supposed Jewish racial distinctness and repugnant moral attributes. For example, one 1882 German dictionary defined an anti-Semite as "[a]nyone who hates Jews or opposes Judaism in general, and struggles against the character traits and the intentions of the Semites."¹³ This definition conspicuously assumes that "character traits" and "intentions" can properly be attributed to an ethnic group and may even imply that the traits that anti-Semites ascribe to "Semites" are accurately perceived. The racial dimension is similarly evident in a definition offered five years later by an architect of modern political anti-Semitism, who explained the concept as follows: "anti—to oppose, Semitism—the essence of the Jewish race; anti-Semitism is therefore the struggle against Semitism."¹⁴ Thus, anti-Semitism was classically understood, by its formative figures, as a struggle against attributes that are essential to the Jewish race.

Semitism and Anti-Semitism

It is sometimes maintained, generally for political reasons, that the term "anti-Semitism" cannot be limited to hatred of Jews, because the term "Semites" refers to speakers of a language family consisting of many historical Middle Eastern languages, including not only Hebrew but also Arabic. As we have seen, this approach is inconsistent with the history of the word "anti-Semitism," which was developed to describe a form of hatred that is specifically directed at Jews, not Semitic peoples generally. Nevertheless, those who would expand the definition of anti-Semitism to include anti-Arab discrimination argue that anti-Jewish and anti-Arab discrimination have both involved a combination of "racial" and "religious" elements. Additionally, Arabs and Jews have arguably been harmed by orientalism.¹⁵ That is to say, Jews and Arabs have both been racialized as "oriental" in some periods and places.[16] Nevertheless, the argument is incorrect historically, descriptively, and normatively.

Most English speakers understand that anti-Semitism refers to hostility toward Jews. This common-sense observation is confirmed by a rigorous 2011 University of Birmingham study that applied corpus linguistics methodology to a large body of English and American newspapers and online news sources (over 450 million words). The Birmingham researchers concluded that in common English usage, the terms the terms *anti-semite, anti-semitic,* and *anti-semitism* are used "almost exclusively in relation to Jews," even though the same cannot be said of the words "semites" or "semitic."[17] For this reason, as a descriptive matter, the term "anti-Semitism" cannot be defined to include hostility toward non-Jewish Semitic groups.

Similarly, the pan-Semitic approach has been rejected by nearly all reputable authorities on historical grounds. A decade ago, the European Union Monitoring Centre on Racism and Xenophobia correctly observed that "almost all" definitions of anti-Semitism refer to hostile attitudes or actions toward *Jews*.[18] From the beginning, anti-Semitism has meant hatred of Jews, not hatred of Arabs or Semites.[19] Bernard Lewis has debunked the canard that Arabs cannot be anti-Semitic, since they themselves are Semites. "The logic of this," he responded, "would seem to be that while an edition of Hitler's *Mein Kampf* published in Berlin or in Buenos Aires in German or Spanish is anti-Semitic, an Arab version of the same text published in Cairo or Beirut cannot be anti-Semitic, because Arabic and Hebrew are cognate languages. It is not a compelling argument."[20] Lewis's *Mein Kampf* example is not perfect, since that execrable text is susceptible to multiple interpretations. Given Hitler's contempt for Egyptians and belief in Aryan superiority, some readers infer that his hatred of Semites extended to other peoples of Middle Eastern origin. The Nazi foreign ministry took considerable pains to disabuse them of that interpretation, however, assuring Turkish, Arab, and Iranian governments that German anti-Semitic race laws applied only to Jews and not to other Semites. Nazi propagandists later abandoned the term "anti-Semitic," replacing it with "anti-Jewish," in order to assure these governments that their enmity was directed specifically at the Jews.[21]

From a normative perspective, it is preferable to adhere to the common English usage, because the figure of the "Jew" has been made to do a very different work than that which has been assigned to the "Arab." Jews and Arabs have both been racialized, that is to say, perceived as racially distinct in ways that impute (or "code") racial inferiority to traits that are perceived as simultaneously religious and genetic. Yet the figure of the "Jew" has been constructed uniquely as the "other" in opposition to which Western cultures have defined themselves. Only the "Jew" has been perceived as the basis of all evils in the modern world, from wars to natural disasters. Indeed, the Jewish "race" was historically understood in terms that borrowed heavily from a Christian theological worldview in which Jewry are understood to be racially connected with Satan. Anti-Semitism has involved the working over of a people into a world-historical danger in a way that has been absent in anti-Arab discrimination regardless of its severity.

The Hyphenation Question

In recent years, no reputable authority would embrace a definition, like some that are discussed above, which assumes that Jews actually possess the character traits that their antagonists attribute to them.[22] The term "anti-Semitism" persists as the primary term for identifying anti-Jewish animus despite its problematic origins and not because of them. This is due in part to inertia and in part to the inadequacies of all of the alternative terms. "Jew-hatred," "judeophobia," and "anti-Judaism" are all too narrow, because they are restricted, respectively, to those forms of anti-Jewish animus that manifest as a "hatred," a "phobia," or a religious animus. As we have seen, anti-Semitism may take other and broader forms. Similar problems stymie the broader range of terms that the German language offers to describe ill-feelings toward Jews, including *judenfeindschaft* (hostility toward Jews) and *judengegnerschaft* (enmity towards Jews). Here again, the alternatives are too narrow to encompass the range of phenomena properly designated by the term "anti-Semitism," which may exceed (or fall short of) the bounds of enmity and hostility.[23]

In the English-speaking world, many scholars and some formidable institutions omit the hyphen in a futile effort to conceal or diminish the racial connotations in the meaningless "Semitism." Sometimes this gesture has a political undertone. Erasing the hyphen is intended to deny the claim that non-Jewish groups assert on the term. In other cases, it is used to avoid the term's reifying tendencies or to reflect a contemporary shift from racist to cultural forms of Jew-hatred.[24] But the gesture is as flimsy as the claim that it attempts to efface. With or without the hyphen, the term contains the same awkward empty reference to a supposed "Semitic" population. In other languages, such as German, the word is routinely written without a hyphen, but this does not solve the problem. Nor does de-hyphenation ameliorate the problem in spoken English.[25]

Common usage, however, can accomplish what punctuation cannot. As one historian recently observed, anti-Semitism "has long been *the* key category in the study of anti-Jewish prejudice, and in a way, this history has freed the concept from its beginnings."[26] As a descriptive matter, common usage has established that anti-Semitism refers to Jews not Semites. That is to say, this awkward term has referred primarily or exclusively to an anti-Jewish posture since Marr first coined it. As a normative matter, linguistic clarity is best served by reserving this term for this limited usage.

The Problem of Race

Despite the embarrassment of the term's racial history, some authorities continue to define anti-Semitism as a "racial" animus. For example, Italian parliamentarians found during a recent formal inquiry on the current status of anti-Semitism "that anti-Semites are anti-Semites because they base their belief that a Jew remains a Jew, even if secularised or converted, on racist and nationalist, rather than religious, grounds."[27] Similarly, the Swiss Federal Commission Against Racism (FCR), defines anti-Semitism as "the hostility towards Jewish people, who are defined and perceived as a uniform 'race.'"[28] Like the *Merriam-Webster* definition, the FCR supplies scare quotes around the term "race." To the alert reader, the scare quotes suggest a problem at the outset. The awkwardness in the formulation reflects awareness that one can no longer speak without irony of a Jewish "race," nor even of any race of persons other than the human race as a whole.

Judge Richard Posner, one of America's most famous jurists, posits that the concept of racial anti-Semitism is based on either an anthropological error or an antiquated sense of the term "race." "Nowadays," Posner wrote for the Chicago-based, Seventh U.S. Circuit Court of Appeals in *Bachman v. St. Monica's Congregation*, "the use of the term 'race' is pretty much limited to the three major racial divisions—Caucasoid, Negroid, and Mongoloid—but historically the term was used much more broadly, to denote groups having common ancestry or even a common culture (or, as often, both). And in this sense Jews are members of a distinct race."[29] The scare quotes indicate the author's uncomfortable use of this discredited term.

Racialist definitions have been criticized on the ground that that they appear to accept, or at least to assume, the discredited idea that Jews can be meaningfully described in terms of "race."[30] "Since the best present knowledge so obviously invalidates the Aryan theory," Gavin Langmuir argued, "it follows that we cannot use 'racism,' the central and false concept of that myth, to explain the hostility toward Jews . . . displayed by the propagators of the myth."[31] Indeed, the very idea of "race" has now long since been discredited. More than half a century ago, the UN Economic and Social Council issued a widely embraced report, primarily authored by Columbia anthropologist Ashley Montagu, which announced that "[s]cientists have reached the general agreement that mankind is one: that all men belong to the same species, *Homo sapiens*."[32]

A more specific way to frame the conundrum is to observe that the terms which anti-racism uses to explain the problem of racism apply to anti-racism too. Scholars have tended to agree that the idea of race is based on a reification, naturalization, or essentialization of human difference. Racism, philosopher Pierre-André Taguieff argues, is an "absolute affirmation of difference, the naturalization or essentialization of differences, either perceived or imagined."[33] In other words, racism reduces persons to the features that are imagined to be essential to the particular group to which they belong. This essentialism is always an illusion, because it ignores the variety of groups to which any individual belongs, increases the sense of difference and distance among groups, sustains group stereotypes, and facilitates intergroup violence.[34] This is the meaning of sociologist Pierre Bordieu's dictum that "every racism is an essentialism."[35]

The problem with Taguieff and Bordieu's formulations is that they are themselves a form of essentialism.[36] That is to say, rather than taking each form of "racial" animus in its own particularities, they reduce them to a common essence, which they identify as "essentialism." This essentializes the varieties of racism and is therefore an example of the very practice they criticize. While many forms of anti-Semitism essentialize "the *Jew*," the racial definition reduces the variety of anti-Semitic phenomena to those that share this feature, which is taken to be the essence of the category. The French police failed to understand Ilan Halimi's killers because the Barbarians did not appear to essentialize the Jew, focusing instead on an attribute (wealth) that is not central to the anti-Semitic conception of the "Jew." More generally, such definitions improperly exclude forms of anti-Jewish prejudices that do not essentialize the Jew or comport with the peculiar notion of race.[37]

Anti-Semitism as a Racial Bigotry

Racialist definitions tend to rely on a narrative that goes like this: Prior to the nineteenth century, Jews faced hostility because of their religious beliefs (anti-Judaism), because of their competing needs (ethnic conflict), or because they were perceived as different or strange (xenophobia). During the late nineteenth century, Jews faced a new and more virulent animus, which was based on their perceived racial distinctness (anti-Semitism proper). In this narrative, the nineteenth-century animus is said to be particularly notable, because it is more virulent than the older hostilities. This narrative reflects important differences in the way that Jews have been perceived over time, and it has yielded valuable insights about modern Jew-hatred. At the same time, this understanding also overstates the divergence between modern and premodern hatred of Jews and understates the extent to which religious anti-Semitism has historically exhibited racial elements.

Although racial anti-Semitism is often described as a modern nineteenth- or twentieth-century phenomenon, its roots may be traced further back, further indeed than the idea of race itself. Some historians have argued that racial anti-Semitism cannot be found in the ancient world if we understand "racial anti-Semitism" to mean the hatred of Jews just for being alive. The term "anti-Judaism" is often used for religiously inspired opposition to Judaism, such as the efforts by early Christian supercessionists to delegitimize the Jewish religion. Others, notably Benjamin Isaac, have demonstrated however that racial anti-Semitism can be discerned even in the ancient world if we mean by "racial anti-Semitism" the attribution to the Jews as a collectivity of unalterable, hereditary traits.[38] This can be seen, for example, in Hellenistic Egypt, where Alexandrian texts provide an alternative version of the Jewish exodus story, describing the Jews as a diseased, misanthropic, and outcast people. Some Alexandrian authors accused Jews of ritually slaughtering non-Jews and engaging in cannibalism, a charge that would echo through history. Hellenistic authors also argued that Jews lacked the ability to make meaningful contributions to civilization, a charge that would also recur in subsequent periods.[39]

Certainly in the late Middle Ages, Spanish Catholicism developed the notion of "purity of blood" and became obsessed with lineage. Jews were depicted not only as religiously despicable but also as having *mala sagre* (bad blood). This racially inflected bigotry proved to be particularly virulent, prefiguring the Nazi era. In 1391, Spaniards massacred four thousand Jews in Seville; the killing then spread elsewhere in Spain, where nearly fifty thousand Jews were killed, while many others were forcibly converted. The wave of conversions continued into the fifteenth century, and the converts came to rise into the top echelons of Spanish universities, professions, the judiciary, and even the Church. This led to a backlash against the new converts, or *conversos*, and led to an anti-Semitism based on Jewish blood or lineage. The prevalence of crypto-Judaism, the secret practice of Judaism among the so-called *anusim* (hidden Jews) exacerbated this blood-centered hatred. The fanatical inquisitor general Torquemada was convinced that all Jews must be expelled from Spain. Ferdinand and Isabella agreed, issuing the fateful decree on January 2, 1492.[40]

In modern times, racial ideologies provided coherence to the diverse and contradictory forms of anti-Semitism that preceded the emergence of Nazism in Germany: liberal, conservative, socialist, Protestant, Catholic, anti-Christian, *völkisch*, et cetera.[41] Racial anti-Semitism provided a more comprehensive discourse on the innately malevolent, criminal, dangerous, perverse, and parasitic characteristics that were attributed to Jews, ultimately with genocidal ramifications.[42] Nevertheless, racial anti-Semitism, even in its purest articulations, never fully departs from the religious concepts that had long undergirded Jew-hatred. Implicit in racial conceptions of the "Jews" was a secularized vision of the medieval Christian perception of Jews as children of the devil, which had achieved a particular resonance in Germany.[43] Adolf Hitler, for example, saw Jewishness as a cosmic form of evil.[44] Influenced by *The Protocols*, Hitler and his inner circle viewed world history as essentially a struggle between God's chosen race (the Aryans) and Satan's chosen (the Jews).[45] For this reason, the Nazis believed that they were doing God's work in destroying the Jewish people.[46]

Contemporary Racialism

Some writers assume that if anti-Semitism is a nineteenth-century racial ideology, or a twentieth-century form of genocidal hatred, then it does not apply to contemporary hatred of Israel. The argument proceeds along four lines. The first argument is that, as we have seen above, the idea of "race" is so discredited that it cannot be applied to anti-Semitism without resurrecting and perpetuating outdated and pernicious ideas about human difference. This may be a good reason to strike the word "race" from our lexicon. It does not however prove that the underlying animus no longer exists, even if there are reasons why we should describe it in other terms.

The second argument is that it is ahistoric to mix historical periods and believe that an ideology that emerged in one century and on one continent could persist or reappear in very different centuries and continents. We will examine this historiographic question in the next chapter. For present purposes, however, it is useful to observe that racialization of the Jewish people has repeated itself continually over time, although each time in a somewhat different form. That is to say, non-Jews have repeatedly ascribed characteristics to the Jewish people that are imagined to be immutable and malevolent.

The third argument, influenced by post-colonial theory and Palestinian nationalism, is that anti-Zionism cannot be racist, either because Zionism is racist or because Semites are on both sides of the equation. Ultimately, neither of these arguments is persuasive. We have already seen that anti-Semitism, properly understood, is hostility toward *Jews* not *Semites*. The argument that Zionism is racism, even if it were true, would not disprove that some forms of anti-Zionism are also racist.[47] In the same way, the fact that white supremacy is racist does not disprove the possibility that some anti-white ideologies are similarly bigoted.

The fourth argument is that those who criticize Israel today seldom do so in racial terms. As Taguieff put it, "the new forms of anti-Jewish discourse no longer carry a racist legitimation (so no longer an 'anti-Semtic' ideology in a strict sense) except as a remnant."[48] Indeed, it is absurd to conflate Nazi racism with the anti-racist ideologies that have emerged in light of the Middle East conflict. Nevertheless, the anti-racist legitimation of contemporary left-wing anti-Semitism has a distinctly racial hue.

In some (outlier) cases this has been made explicit. For example, Columbia University Professor Hamid Dabashi reportedly wrote in 2004, "Half a century of systematic maiming and murdering of another people has left . . . its deep marks on the faces of [Israeli Jews], the way they talk, walk and the way they greet each other. . . . There is a vulgarity of character that is bone deep and structural to the skeletal vertebrae of its culture."[49] Jews, who were once stigmatized as dark strangers in Europe, are now stigmatized as white settler colonialists in Palestine and throughout the world. This is a racist anti-racism, characterized by the sort of self-contradiction that has been described as a defining feature of anti-Jewish hatred.

In a deeper sense, contemporary anti-Semitism harkens back to older forms of racism because it imposes a new, distinct, and harmful form of coercive racial identity upon Jews.[50] This new racial construction retains antiquated European stereotypes of the Jew as sinister, greedy, criminal, conspiratorial, treacherous, power-hungry, and diabolical, while joining these characteristics with newer derogations, such as racism, colonialism and imperialism.[51] This tendency has been particularly apparent since the United Nations' 1975 proclamation that "Zionism is racism," but its roots extend back several years beforehand, and it has continued to evolve over the decades since, merging with the notion that Israel is an "Apartheid state."

It has been argued that this anti-Semitism is "racialist but not racist."[52] The argument is that contemporary anti-Semitism resembles the so-called "new racism," which has been said to employ a coded language that is based more on cultural rather than racial distinctions. This argument is not entirely without merit, but it overstates the similarities between new and older forms of racism, which is precisely the error that its exponents accuse those who speak of a "new anti-Semitism" of making. The new anti-Semitism, like the new racism, is surely different in these respects from some older forms of racism, yet they largely continue the trajectory that the older forms had followed.

On some university campuses, such as the University of California at Irvine, public speeches lambasting Jewish cultural arrogance participate in this racial formation by fusing misconceptions of Jewish chosenness with accusations of white supremacism.[53] This emphasis on Jewish arrogance plays upon traditional stereotypes in recent textbook descriptions of a putative "aggressive [and] evil tendency that is rooted in the Jewish personality."[54] This tendency can be seen in the University of California at Irvine speeches of Amir Malik Ali, an Oakland Muslim religious leader who has been a frequent invited speaker on university campuses. In February 2005, Malik Ali argued, "This ideology of Zionism is so racist, so arrogant, based so much on ignorance." Invited to return the following year, he called Jews "the new Nazis . . . they're saying . . . when you see an Israeli flag next to an American flag, they're saying we're with imperialism. We are down with colonialism. We are down with white supremacy." More bluntly, he threatened that "now it's time for you to live in some fear . . . because you were so good at dispensing fear. You were so good at making people think that y'all was all that and the Islamic tide started coming up." He argued that "anti-Semitism" charges reflect Jewish arrogance and racism: "They have taken the concept of the chosen people and fused it with the concept of white supremacy." And more: "Once you take the concept of chosen people with white supremacy and fuse them together, you will get a people who are so arrogant that they will actually make a statement and imply that [they] are the only Semites. That's arrogance and it's the same arrogance they display every day and that's the same type of arrogance that's getting them into trouble today."[55]

Thus, the racializing quality of contemporary anti-Semitism can be seen in attributions of hyper-white physical or biological difference to Israelis and Jews. During earlier periods of white dominance Jews were constructed as paragons of racial color. More recently, as whiteness has become associated with racial guilt, Jews are increasingly seen as preeminently white.[56] At the same time, the new Jewish racial formation is imbued largely with precisely those forms of racial guilt that have historically marked Jewish victimization (racism, *dhimmitude*, colonialization, and genocide). This inversion is a projection onto the Jews as racialized other of all of the traits that contemporary in-groups deny or repress from within their own psyches. White supremacists continue to perceive Jews as paradigmatically unwhite and ascribe hateful characteristics to their unwhiteness. Anti-racist supremacists conversely perceive Jews as paradigmatically white, ascribing to them the loathsome attributes that they associate with racists and colonialists. In this sense, one may speak of the litmus paper (or Rorschach test) Jew, whose skin appears to turn the color most reviled by the perceiver. This is loosely analogous to the other binary opposites of which Jews have been constructed by their antagonists: as radicals by the right and arch-capitalists by the left, as cosmopolitans by provincials and ethnic chauvinists by progressives, and so on.

The Hybrid Approach

The quotation marks that *Merriam-Webster* and others place around the word "race" may create a sense of distance between the author and the concept of race, but they do not vitiate the problem created when by continuing reliance on the concept. Moreover, they signal an apparent incongruity in an approach that purports to lump together a false construction (race) with a legitimate phenomenon (religion). This suggests an odd apples-and-oranges incompatibility of the conjoined concepts, which should alert the reader to sloppy reasoning. It is as if to say that anti-Semitism can take either the form of either an irrational prejudice based on a meaningful classification (religious bigotry) or an irrational prejudice based on a meaningless classification (racism). At first blush, these appear to be different orders of delusion that should instead be named by different terms. In fact, recent research on the concept of "religion" suggests that this term may deserve its own scare quotes. At the very least, it requires historical context and caveats.

The reigning approach elides the distinction between racial and religious conceptions by positing that anti-Semitism may be either racial or religious. This idea is now so deeply ingrained in colloquial understandings of anti-Semitism as to appear to be compelled by common-sense assumptions. Judge Richard Posner typifies this common-sense dualism, under which anti-Semitism is understood as a unitary phenomenon composed of two parts. In *Bachman,* he wrote: "There is religious anti-Semitism, typified by the attitude of the medieval Roman Catholic Church, and racial anti-Semitism, typified by Hitler. The one objects to Jews because of their religion, the other objects to Jews because they are descended from Jews, even if they are converts to other faiths.[57] At first blush, this rough usage appears to avoid the work of choosing among conceptions, but it does not. As we will see, when a definition incorporates the complex, contested terms like "race" and "religion," they subsume a series of assumptions, as well as tacit theoretical commitments, which may be unexamined, incompatible, and otherwise problematic.

Religious Anti-Semitism's Hidden Racial Dimension

The Conventional Narrative

The conventional narrative of "religious anti-Semitism" provides that Jews have been persecuted primarily because of religious differences since ancient times. Indeed, religious origins appear central, even when religious faith is absent, in representations of the Jew as satanic, demonic, evil, all-powerful, and ubiquitous. Accordingly, many commentators have defined anti-Semitism as a form of religious bigotry, interpreting modern, secular, and racial forms of Jew-hatred as offshoots of an essentially religious and Christian form of hatred.[58] This *religious* anti-Semitism is sometimes described as a doctrinal rivalry between Judaism and competing religions.[59] In fact, religious anti-Semitism is seldom merely disagreement with religious tenets embraced by the Jewish religion.

To be sure, there have been times and places when Jews have been persecuted for such disagreements. For example, Jews were persecuted throughout the Hellenistic world for their refusal to acknowledge their pagan neighbors' gods, to participate in their animal sacrifices, or to send gifts to their temples.[60] Similarly, Jews have suffered from their neighbors' perception that they have claimed religious superiority over their host nations.[61] Thus, for example, Antiochus Epiphanes, the Seleucid king, forbade the practice of Judaism out of anger at Jewish refusal to bow to Greek culture.[62] Indeed, gentile antagonism toward the (misunderstood) doctrine of *chosenness* has recurred throughout the ages.[63] Moreover, some gentiles, beginning perhaps with Cicero, argued that Jewish religious practices were incompatible with secular (Roman) institutions, because the state must have the prerogative to organize such rites.[64] Later, Archbishop Agobard, whose ninth-century Carolingian teachings were influential throughout the Middle Ages, preached fiery sermons about Jewish sacrilegious views of Jesus and the apostles, rather than accusing Jews of the diabolical practices that would preoccupy other medieval Christian thinkers.[65] Notwithstanding these counter-examples, religious anti-Semitism has seldom followed from mere rivalry with a group thought to be intellectually mistaken.

Christian Religious Jew-Hatred

Whatever the reasons, early and medieval Christianity harbored considerable hatred toward the figural Jew that could not be reduced to a theological disagreement. Prominent Christians accused Jews of deicide, with desecrating communion wafers so they would bleed, with ritually murdering Christian children, with practicing witchcraft, with allying themselves with the devil, and with conspiring to undermine and destroy Christianity.[66] The emergence of demonization (as opposed to common or garden-variety hostility) at the onset of Christianity is no happenstance, as it is inextricably linked with what Bernard Lewis has called "the special role assigned to the Jews in the crucifixion of Christ as related to the Gospels."[67] That is to say, Jewry was viewed as an accursed deicidal people condemned to exile and wandering.[68] At the same time, Jews were assigned a superhuman role because this position was necessary to explain the killing of a deity. This can be traced at least as far back as the Gospel of John, which quotes Jesus telling the Pharisees, "You are from your father, the devil, and you choose to carry out your father's desires."[69] John claims that "the Jews" crucified Jesus under Jewish law, establishing the basis for the deicide charge, that is, that Jews murdered Jesus Chris, the expression of God's presence on earth.[70]

This deicide charge echoed throughout history, condemning Jews in Christian Europe as diabolically evil, spiritually blind, and carnally obsessed God-killers. As Origen, an early church father, wrote:

> We may thus assert that the Jews will not return to their earlier situation, for they have committed the most abominable of crimes, in forming the conspiracy against the Saviour of the human race.... Hence the city where Jesus suffered was necessarily destroyed, the Jewish nation was driven from its country, and another people was called by God to the blessed election.[71]

In his highly influential writings, St. Augustine depicted the Jews as a wretched, wandering, rejected people, spiritually deformed, faithless, and obsessively carnal.[72] He likens the Jewish people to Cain, the first murderer, who killed his brother and deserved death but was condemned instead to ceaseless wandering.[73] After Augustine, the Torah is seen as the mark of Cain given to the deicide people, who are condemned to wander in sin, blindness, wretchedness, and error.

During the fourth century, especially in the East with its large Jewish populations, Christian preachers developed a particularly virulent form of Jew-hatred.[74] In Antioch, St. John Chrysostom, another church founder, justified synagogue burnings on the grounds that a Jewish religious establishment is "a temple of demons devoted to idolatrous cults, a criminal assembly of Jews, a place of meetings of the assassins of Christ . . . a gulf and abyss of perdition."[75] St. John argued from this that Jews should be considered demonic: "If then, the Jews fail to know the Father, if they crucified the Son, if they thrust off the help of the Spirit, who should not make bold to declare plainly that the synagogue is the dwelling of demons?"[76]

Through the Christian Middle Ages and into the early modern period, Jews were linked to the devil and associated with black magic in sermons, painting, and sculpture.[77] Medieval Christians depicted both Satan and the Jews as the embodiment of evil and the revolt against God, with bulging eyes and horns, arrogant, lecherous, dirty, self-loving, and deviously logical.[78] This theological anti-Semitism was saliently expressed in certain anti-Semitic defamations, such as the famous blood libel. In 1144 in the English town of Norwich, a 12-year-old Christian boy named William was found stabbed to death shortly before Easter, and the local Jewish community was blamed, without evidence, for ritually murdering the boy. A Jewish convert named Theobald later claimed that the Jews of Norwich had tortured William, just as the Jews had once tortured Jesus, and that this ritual crucifixion was part of an international conspiracy in which the global Jewish community decided, each year at a meeting in Spain, to select a different ritual victim.[79] Thus, the ideas of Jewish criminality and ritual murder were fused with a claim of international conspiracy that would echo through the centuries.

From the twelfth century onward, Christian theologians increasingly opposed Jewry with arguments that had a strong racial tinge. For example, around 1147, the Benedictine abbot of Cluny, Peter the Venerable, argued that Jews must be subhuman creatures, since they reject the rational proof of Christianity: "I know not whether a Jew is a man because he does not cede to human reason, nor does he acquiesce to the divine authorities which are his own."[80] Peter concluded that Jews must be more akin to animals than to humans, comparing them to cows or donkeys.

Muslim Religious Jew-Hatred

Muslim religious Jew-hatred has also frequently been inflected with racial attitudes, if by "racial" we mean an emphasis on perceived collective hereditary characteristics. Until recently, Muslim writers did not generally demonize Jews as Christians did. Yet negative racial perceptions of Jewry can however be found in many times and places.[81] The Koran contains both positive and negative perceptions of Jewry. Muhammad's view of Jews appears to have become markedly negative after he migrated from Mecca to Medina in 622 and came into contact with a large, flourishing Jewish community.[82] In Medina, Muhammad experienced rejection and even ridicule from Jewish scholars. Thereafter, Muhammad's view of Jews turned sour, and he writes of the Jews in negative terms, charging them with mendacity, disobedience, usury and corruption, and malevolence. In such passages, Jews are described as degraded, unbelieving, ignorant, envious, dishonest, untrustworthy, usurious, hedonistic, perverse, treacherous, hateful, and murderous. Muslim exegeses interpreted Koranic passages as foretelling that Jews would remain in "abasement and poverty" forever.[83]

Classical Muslim texts, such as the canonical prophetic tradition (the *Hadith*) and the hagiographic literature (the *Sira* and the *Maghazi*), develop these negative portrayals of Jewry. Although they do not use demonic terms comparable to those of traditional Christianity, they do view Jewry as a morally and physically inferior population. This perception is articulated, for example, by thirteenth century writer Al-Jaubari:

> Know that these people are the most cunning creatures, the vilest, most unbelieving and hypocritical. While ostensibly the most humble and miserable, they are in fact the most vicious of men. This is the very essence of rascality and accursedness. . . . So beware of their company.[84]

Throughout the Middle Ages and into modern times, Muslims typically had more condescending attitudes toward Jews than Christians did during similar periods. Jews were tolerated in the inferior legal category of *dhimmitude*. The fact that this category was shared with Christians and Zoroastrians suggests limitations on the specifically anti-Jewish attitudes that were commonplace during this period, although some commentators have argued that Muslims generally viewed Jews as being more treacherous and iniquitous than members of these groups.[85]

Contemporary Religious Jew-Hatred

Although religious anti-Semitism is generally associated with premodern periods, it has in fact repeated, in myriad manifestations, into the present. In recent years, Christian theological images have been used to support Arab anti-Jewish causes, as when crucifixions of Jesus Christ and Yasser Arafat were merged into a timeless image of global suffering at Jewish hands.[86] A de-Judaized image of Jesus is routinely transmuted into the first Palestinian martyr, while contemporary Palestinians are portrayed as new victims of recurrent Jewish criminality.[87] Contemporary religiously inflected anti-Semitism is reflected in the statement of Portuguese Nobel laureate José Saramago that Israel's relations with its neighbors pose "a unique and even metaphysical quality of general evil."[88] Similarly, it can be found in the infamous words of renowned Greek composer Mikis Theodorakis, who just a few years ago called Jews "the root of evil."[89]

At the same time, Islamist refinements of traditional Christian religious Jew-hatred have become influential throughout Muslim countries in recent years, even as they have been marginalized throughout the Christian world. Beginning in the late nineteenth century, European-style anti-Semitic literature appeared in Arab-language publications throughout the Arab world, especially in Beirut, and became popular first among Middle Eastern Christians before taking hold among Arab Muslims. For example, the Christian blood libel appeared in the Muslim world among Christians in Aleppo, Syria, first in the seventeenth century and then again in the mid-nineteenth century. During the Damascus Affair of 1840, Syrian Christians accused the Jews of killing two men to obtain blood for their Passover *matzhot*.[90]

During the twentieth century, European anti-Semitism spread throughout the Arab world. This was to some extent orchestrated by the Nazi propaganda machinery, but the Germans also had notable Arab collaborators. The conflict over Zionism and control of Palestine also inflamed pre-existing tensions, leading to a new preoccupation with the Jew and evolving stereotypes of the Jew as the Muslims' eternal other.[91] In particular, the birth of Israel in 1948 and the Zionists' military defeat of Arab countries in the war launched to defeat Israeli independence contradicted the long-held Muslim view that Jewry would always remain subordinate to Islam. Just as the economic rise of Jewry in late nineteenth-century Germany reversed the historic Christian assumption of Jewish inferiority, so also did the military rise of Israel in twentieth-century Palestine topple ancient Muslim assumptions of Jewish subordination. In the wake of Israel's initial, dramatic, and unexpected military success, Arab commentators began to describe the Jews—in terms drawn more from the Christian anti-Semitic tradition than from Islam's indigenous history of Jew-hatred—as an all-powerful sinister regime that manipulates international institutions and foreign nations. From this point forward, classical Christian anti-Semitic motifs, such as the blood libel and accusations of global

Jewish conspiracies, became increasingly common throughout the Muslim world. This can be seen, for example, in the extraordinary popularity of the *Protocols of the Elders of Zion*, which first appeared in Arabic only in the 1920s, but which appeared in nine editions in the Middle East by 1970 and over sixty by 2007.[92]

In short, religious anti-Semitism has seldom been driven primarily by disagreements over the tenets of religious belief. Rather, it has emerged with perceptions of an ethno-religious group associated with various negative social attributes and, in extreme forms, with descent from the Christian devil. This anti-Semitism may be "religious" in the sense that it has been informed by the religious beliefs of those who have persecuted the Jewish people. It is not however religious in the sense that of being directed at Jews as an exclusively religious group. The religious animus described above is not directed at the tenets of Jewish theology. Rather, this animus has been directed at Jewry as an ethno-religious population group that is perceived to hold inherited, ineradicable traits.

The Problem of Religion

Another problem with viewing anti-Semitism as a religious animus is that the concept of "religion" has baggage of its own, just does the concept of "race." Princeton religion scholar Leora Batnitzky has shown that the concept of religion, as it is commonly used, reflects a distinctly modern and Protestant understanding of the relationship between the individual, faith, and community. Jews did not historically perceive themselves to members of a "religion," at least in the narrow, individualistic sense of that term. Rather, the idea that Jewishness is a religion emerged as Judaism assimilated into Protestant European norms. "Religion," Batnitzky explains, "is a modern German Protestant category that Judaism does not quite fit into."[93] Previously, Judaism was understood as combining what we now know as religion, community, ethnicity, and even race, in an undifferentiated whole. The process of reducing Jews and Jewishness to a "religion" has not had the devastating consequences that followed from the parallel process by which Jews were reduced to a distinct "race."[94] Nevertheless, the process has created different kinds of harm, which has not been insignificant.

As Jews have attempted to integrate into the modern world, especially in the mid-twentieth century, the Jewish community increasingly saw itself and was seen as a "religion." This process was likely hastened by the Holocaust, when the racial conception of Judaism came into disrepute and Jews, especially in the United States, increasingly insisted on being seen as members of a religious denomination, like Presbyterianism or Methodism, without racial overtones. During the 1950s and 1960s, the high water mark of the idea that Judaism is just a religion, the major surveys of American Jewish life did not even ask whether Americans were Jewish in any sense other than their religion. Today, 6,600,000 American adults view themselves as Jewish, while 4,200,000 view themselves as Jews by religion.[95]

In constructing Judaism as a religion, Jews have paid a price. First, in embracing a distinctively Protestant individualist conception of faith, Jews have denied or diminished the richness of Jewish tradition's communal elements. In this way, Jewish Americans have faced at least the same loss of social capital as other groups.[96] Indeed, their losses are arguably higher since they started with a greater vault. Second, there is an inevitable sense of alienation when a community attempts to robe itself in intellectual garments fashioned to fit the form of another people. Third, in portraying themselves as exclusively a religious group—and therefore racially indistinguishable from white ethnic groups—Jews distanced themselves from people of color, losing a historical sense of kinship, and perhaps also fueling resentment among some African Americans.[97] Fourth, by denying racial or ethnic distinctness, Jews lost the benefit of those civil rights laws that protect racial (but not religious) minorities from discrimination for many. Only in very recent years has this been reversed, as for example in the Office for Civil Rights' 2004 policy asserting jurisdiction over Jews, Sikhs, and other groups that share ethnic or ancestral as well as religious characteristics.[98]

In many respects, the process by which American Jews "became a religion" parallels the process by which Jews "became white."[99] In both cases, Jewry adapted to a dominant paradigm in order to achieve socio-economic privilege and avoid social stigma. This has generally involved covering, in sociologist Erving Goffman's sense of the term, or muting Jewry's distinctive social characteristics.[100] In both cases, the process has remained largely incomplete. In the case of religion,

Jewry has never fully fit within this rubric for various reasons. Many Jews reject Judaism but still maintain a strong sense of Jewish identity. Judaism itself has never fully fit within the Protestant conception of an individualist faith, given Judaism's privileging of practice over belief, as well as the central roles played by family and community in Jewish ritual observance.

Jews are hardly the only group that has negotiated assimilation into a modern, individualist, Protestant conception of religion. To varying degrees this can be seen in other non-Protestant religious denominations as well. Batnitzky has shown this, at least preliminarily, with respect to Islam and other religions.[101] In the United States, the ramifications of burgeoning religious diversity have only begun to play out, as mainline Protestant denominations decline in influence, minority religions proliferate, and religious identification liquefies in an increasingly pluralistic and fluid environment. The day may come when the concept of "religion" is understood to be as problematic as that of race. If that day has not yet arrived, it is because the concept of "religion" has not led to the devastating results that the racial delusion has yielded.

Does this mean that anti-Semitism is not discrimination on the basis of "race" or "religion"? To the extent that legal authorities continue to parse human difference in such terms, it will be necessary to stress the sense in which anti-Semitism fits into these awkward categories. To begin with, bigots may perceive Jews to be members of a (despised) religion and attack Jewry based on this perception. Then, if it comes down to a legal dispute, American courts following *St. Francis College vs. Al Khazraji* would apply the original intent of Congress in using these terms, even if the courts should come to develop the same skepticism toward "religion" that they showed toward "race" in that case.[102] Nevertheless, defining anti-Semitism in terms of "religion" or "race" is hardly clarifying in view of the analytical and political problems both concepts entail. To do so would be to reinforce historically anachronistic, conceptually unstable, and politically discredited understandings of human difference. Moreover, as we have seen, the articulations of anti-Jewish sentiment as "racial" or "religious" are not as distinct as some accounts would have us believe.

While it is not helpful to define anti-Semitism in terms of "race" or "religion," we may yet gain some insight from the themes that emerge from the study of both. As we have seen, the figure of the "Jew" has been constructed in part from perceived inherited group traits, often associated with bestial characteristics, even during periods when anti-Jewish animus is presumed to have been largely "religious." Conversely, this figure has been constructed, again in part, from a notion of Jewry's cosmically evil status, even by Jew-haters who are driven by a more modern, racial conception of the "Jews." The co-existence of these seemingly irreconcilable conceptions (the *demonic* and the *bestial*) points to a distinctive quality of the anti-Jewish mindset. We have already observed the tendency of anti-Semitic ideology to subsume irrationally paired opposite views of the figural Jew. The conjunction of this particular pair of opposite perspectives, which mirror the "religious" and "racial" strands within anti-Semitism, has been peculiarly important to the development of the figural Jew, as the next section will explain.

Demonization, Bestialization, and the Demon-Beast

In widely different periods and cultures, anti-Semitic ideology has tended toward *dehumanization*. More specifically, anti-Semitism historically tended to construct Jews as less than fully human by defining them in a manner that simultaneously excludes and includes them within a political context that gives them both protection and vulnerability. This has involved processes of both *demonization* and *bestialization*. *Demonization* is the ancient convention of attributing malevolent diabolical powers to the Jewish people, imagining the Jew as diabolical horned practitioners of black magic and children of Satan. As we have seen, this practice began with the onset of Christianity, evolved throughout the ancient and medieval world, and has repeated itself into the present. *Bestialization* by contrast refers to the equally ancient anti-Semitic tradition of comparing Jews to animals. In some cases, especially in Christian polemics, anti-Semites take their abusive terms from the self-critical terms which Jewish prophets directed at their own people. By way of illustration, Saint John Chrysostom borrowed language from Jewish scripture when he wrote that "Israel is as obstinate as a stubborn heifer," and an "untamed calf."[103] But these polemics often go further their Jewish sources.

In the Muslim world, Jews have traditionally been described as the "sons of apes and pig," a depiction which remains ubiquitous today in the Arab and Muslim worlds.[104] This can be seen for example, in a 2009 poem published in the Saudi *Al-Jazirah* newspaper:

> You were merciful, oh Hitler.
> [That is my conclusion] when I see around me
> The cruel acts "Of the descendants of apes."
> You were wise, oh Hitler "To rid the world
> Of some of these wild pigs."[105]

Some Islamic scholars insist that references to Jews as apes and pigs in the Koran should not be read to refer to all Jews, but this point seems to be lost on other Islamist writers.[106] Throughout the Arab and Muslim world, Jews are now also often portrayed as snakes, wolves, and scorpions.[107]

Demonization and dehumanization are quite different processes, and it is unusual to find them employed either by the same perpetrators or against the same out-groups. The tendency to demonize out-groups has been characterized as an "obsessional prejudice," like certain forms of anti-Communism or anti-Asian prejudice.[108] Obsessional prejudices are typically associated with psychologically rigid, super-ego dominated personalities and societies. Obsessional personalities tend to be estranged from their feelings and psychological states. They have aversions to ubiquitous pollutants, dirty people, and filth, which they feel compelled to wash away, eliminate, or demolish. They attribute to their victims special extraordinary cleverness, ubiquitous influence, and conspiratorial power. By contrast, the tendency to bestialize has been described as a "hysterical prejudice."[109] Hysterical prejudices are associated with the unconscious tendency to appoint an out-group to perform forbidden sexual, and especially sexually aggressive, desires that the perpetrator has repressed or disowned.[110] Obsessional prejudice is expressed in the view that certain out-groups have not fully progressed, remain spiritually retarded, and are both sexually lascivious or powerful and intellectually uncivilized.

The two conceptions seem antithetical, yet they are combined with surprising fluidity. Consider for example the representative case of

Sheikh Haitham al-Haddad, a Saudi-born scholar who stirred controversy when a Dutch university invited him to attend an academic conference and then canceled the conference when certain of his views were revealed. Al-Haddad had stated both that "Jews are the enemies of God" and that "Jews are descended from apes and pigs."[111] These views, though now commonplace in the Middle East, remain sufficiently offensive to stir alarm. For present purposes, though, what is interesting is the frequency with which they are uttered at the same time, combining to what can be identified as the figure of the *demon-beast*. Intuitively, they are mutually contradictory. No entity as mundane and powerless as an ape or pig could rationally be as seen as supernaturally powerful. Al-Haddad's theozoomorphism (to borrow Jacques Derrida's term) which permits the representation of persons in terms of "divinanimality" (another Derridaism) requires some elucidation.[112] What is interesting here is the discernment of a shared ahumanity of the excluded superhumanity and subhumanity.

Aristotle's conception of man as political animal (*zōōn politikon*) provides a means of understanding the duality of anti-Semitic stereotype, in which the Jew is conceived as both demon and beast.[113] The key is that Aristotle locates the polity as a middle space between the realm of the gods and the domain of mere animals. This provides a double figuration of both the political (a domain which Christians would later occupy in Western politics) and the apolitical (a domain to which the Jew would be assigned by a process of elimination). The political being is figured as both inferior to the gods (and thus bestial to their eyes) and also as superior to the animals (and thus supernatural by their comparison).[114] In defining the polity in opposition to these two traits, Aristotle thus implicitly discloses an anxious self-conception of the political in-group as bearing reflected forms of both. More explicitly, the apolitical being is figured as either *above* the polity, in some otherworldly sense, or else *beneath* it in some beastly condition. This accords with the two primary eliminationist strategies by which in-groups have historically sought to exclude or exterminate despised others: either demonization, the ascription of sinister otherworldly attributes, or bestialization, the ascription of subhuman zoological characteristics.[115] At the same time, it prefigures the most salient rhetorical method by which these strategies are effectuated in genocidal regimes, for example, accusation-in-the-mirror, or the in-group method of falsely accusing out-groups of precisely the characteristics, intentions or actions that characterize the in-group.[116]

The excluded Jew is a distorted mirror image of the gentile's self-conception, just as any out-group reflects the in-group's disowned self-perception. Following Aristotle's *Politics*, the political in-group's anxious self-conception reflects distorted forms of *non*-godliness and *non*-animality. The primal opposition to divinity and bestiality arise from anxieties, respectively, about mortality and weakness. The fear of mortality informs the political animal's self-conception as a non-god, while physical frailty informs his self-conception as a non-beast.

In a deeper sense, this struggle reflects the Freudian conflict between *Thanatos* and *Eros*, the drive toward death and the principle of pleasure.[117] In the polity, the mortal's sense of ungodliness is fed by the need to curb tendencies toward aggressive behavior.[118] Similarly, the sense of inanimality is increased by need to curb sexual activity.[119] As Horkheimer and Adorno explain, "The sexual impulses suppressed by humanity survived in both individuals and peoples and asserted themselves in the imaginary transformations of the surrounding world into a diabolic system."[120] The in-group, despising these internal traits, draws a circle around the polity and projects the disowned characteristics upon those positioned as outsiders. Thus, the Jewish political outsider is imagined as demon-beast.

This process prefigures the two methods of political exclusion, as godliness and bestiality share the singular characteristic of outlawry, the one being above and the other below the law. The gods, like sovereigns, can suspend the law or place themselves outside of it, while beasts are below its reach. The political animal is, as Foucault has taught us to read Aristotle, a "living animal with the additional capacity for political existence."[121] This "additional capacity," however, implies that man has the potential either to live the good life in the city or to live a more animal existence outside its walls. In this conception, politics is the process through which mere life (*zoē*) transforms itself into good life (*eu zēn*). Implicit in this schema is the observation that in Western politics, mere life ("bare life," in Agamben's lexicon) is "that whose exclusion founds the city of men."[122] In this way, we see that Western politics is predicated upon the exclusion of mere life, defined in terms of either otherworldly or subhuman characteristics, from the *polis*. By excluding mere life in this way, however, Western politics assures that mere life remains always present in the form of an exclusion. That is to say, it remains as something that is included exclusively through its exclusion.[123]

This corresponds with the historical treatment of Jewry from Vespasian's time throughout ancient and medieval Europe, in which the ruling authorities (emperors, popes, magnates, etc.) held themselves as guarantors of the safety of the Jews while also frequently exterminating them.[124] Throughout the Christian world, Jews lived as "protected exile," in St. Augustine's formulation. Like Cain, they were to endure extraordinary suffering but also to enjoy unique protections. The function of the Jew, according to St. Augustine and his medieval followers, was to survive as living testimony to the revelation of God's law until their conversion at the end of time. Until then, Jews should not be harmed or forcibly converted because their dispersion and degradation confirm Christianity's superiority and the promise of the establishment of a heavenly City of God at the end of days.[125]

Similarly, under the English "Laws of Edward the Confessor," medieval jurists considered the king to be "defender" of the Jews, who were simultaneously understood to be the king's property.[126] This distinguished the Jew from all other people, since other subjects participated to varying degrees in *res publica*, but the Jew did not. The Jew's peculiar status provided both special protections but also peculiar disabilities, as the Jew was considered to be the property of the king. For centuries, Jews were given a monopoly over money-lending but faced onerous laws over ownership of land, employment of Christian servants, and payment of taxes.[127] Since Jews were the king's chattels, Jewish property belonged to the king.[128]

The echoes of this approach can be seen in the present day international treatment of Israel, which is often considered to be less a full member of the community of nations than a special protectorate of the United States or the United Nations. This follows from the chimerical representation of the "Jew" as demon-beast. Moreover, international treatment of Israel uniquely reflects Agamben's concept of bare life. There is no other country about which it is constantly said that it has a right to exist and to enjoy secure and recognized borders. As Pascal

Bruckner has observed, this statement "is stupefying because it immediately suggests the converse: that this right is in itself an exorbitant privilege."[129] The point here is not merely that the legitimacy of the Jewish state is constantly thrown into question, nor that the prospect of a second extermination lies behind this very discourse. More saliently, the constant focus on Israel's right to mere existence reduces the rights of the Jewish state to the base-minimum features of human existence.

Race, Religion, Ideology, and Anti-Semitism

It is not ultimately significant whether anti-Semitism is defined as racial, as religious, or as alternatingly racial or religious. Both conceptions bespeak the projection of distorted characteristics on constructed notions of the "Jew," whether as "race," "religion," or otherwise. That is to say, anti-Semitism has involved a working up of the "Jew" into a particular figure, on whom is projected distorted forms of disowned desire, in an amalgam of traits that have variously been perceived as "racial" or "religious." The figure may be articulated at one moment in its bestial figuration, at other times as demon, but these articulations are all variations on the same figure of the demon-beast. Other designations miss the point of anti-Semitism, which is not to denigrate Jews "because" of race or religion but rather to construct a false image of the "Jew" that may be expressed in various terms. The difference between religious and racial anti-Semitism reflects a shift in what Sander Gilman astutely deemed "the articulation of perception" rather than in the perception itself.[130]

3

Time and Eternity

THE SIMILAR MISPERCEPTIONS OF Jews in different cultures and periods have led to a debate among commentators. Those whom we call *eternalists* emphasize continuities over time while those whom we call *historicists* stress discontinuities. The former define the term "anti-Semitism" narrowly to describe a modern movement, while the latter apply the term broadly to hatred that Jews have faced for many centuries. This distinction was articulated as early as 1901 by *The Jewish Encyclopedia*, which maintained (in historicist fashion) that "the term 'Anti-Semitism' should be restricted in its use to the modern movements against the Jews." Then, in a nod to eternalists, the *Encyclopedia* concedes, "in its wider sense it may be said to include the persecution of the Jews at all times and among all nations."[1] In fact however neither view is quite right.

Esau Hates Jacob

Eternalism recapitulates the old-fashioned Jewish view of history that perceives, in essayist Leon Wieseltier's formulation, that "every enemy of the Jews is the same enemy, and there is only one war, and it is a war against extinction, and it is a timeless war."[2] In this way, the rabbinic tradition conceives anti-Semitism as a basic, eternal fact of Jewish existence, as reflected in the ancient saying of the Jewish sages: "It is a known fact that Esau hates Jacob."[3] The name "Esau" is intended here to stand for all of those gentiles who hate the Jewish people, not only the biblical figure who spurned his spiritual birthright and forever resented his brother Jacob for embracing it. This saying not only equates all anti-Jewish animus to a perceived original source in Jewish scriptures but also suggests that the persistence of this animus is a "given fact" impervious to reason or resistance.

The rabbis trace Esau's eternal hatred through other biblical figures of differing periods and cultures, such as Amalek and Haman, and then down to the present. Amalek, a descendant of Esau's and progenitor of the nation that bore his name, rejected God's revelation and repeatedly sought to destroy the Jewish people.[4] For this reason, the Amalekites are identified as the leading threats to God's sovereignty on earth.[5] Haman, a descendant of Amalek in the court of Persian King Ahasuerus (or Xerxes), sought to exterminate all of the Jews under Persian dominion. Like Esau, Haman is thought to have acted from contempt for the righteous. The Midrash connects the two by describing Haman as "a contemptible person, the son of a contemptible person" (Esau).[6] All other anti-Semites, from Pharaoh to Hitler, are seen as links in this never-ending chain. "And so," as Wieseltier summarizes, "Amalek became Haman (who actually was an Amalekite), who became the Romans, who became the Crusaders, who became Chmielnicki, who became Petlura, who became Hitler, who became Arafat."[7]

This eternalism may be taken to great lengths, as in the midrashic interpretation of the Canaanite King Arad's war on the Israelites. According to the Book of Numbers, "The Canaanite king of Arad, who dwelt in the South, heard that Israel had come by the route of the spies, he engaged Israel in battle and took some of them captive."[8] Despite the Torah's explicit statement that the attacker was the king of Arad, the midrash nevertheless insists that it was Amalek, who also lived to the South.[9] This is interpretation demonstrates a remarkable disregard for the words of the Torah, but it is consistent with the rabbinic insistence on recognizing close continuities among seemingly disparate forms of hostility to the Jewish people. The medieval commentator Rashi explains, in his still-authoritative exegesis, that the attackers merely pretended to be Canaanites by speaking the language of Canaan but that their true identity could be discerned from the Amalekite attire.[10] Since there is no textual support for this interpretation, it can only be understood as a prominent example of a powerful need within Jewish culture to find a larger meaning behind seemingly unrelated and obscure forms of Jewish suffering. By connecting Esau, Amalek, Haman, and Arad through a chain of descent and shared aversions, the rabbinic tradition counter-intuitively denies the discontinuity and historical specificity of the various forms of Jew-hatred, discerning unity in the diverse misfortunes that Jews have faced in far-flung locations, among different cultures, and at different historical periods. In this tradition, Haman hated Mordecai for the same reason that Esau hated Jacob and Amalek hated the Israelites, namely, because the Jews pursued lives of sanctity under the sovereignty of God.

Modern eternalists tend to advance their position in secular terms, emphasizing persistence and continuity among manifestations of anti-Semitism in widely different periods and cultures and arguing that it is both ancient and "impervious to change."[11] "The *permanence* (as well as depth) of antisemitism is attested to by the obsessive attention given to the "Jewish problem by anti-Semites throughout history," according to one popular articulation of this argument:

> At one time or another nearly every major country that has had a large Jewish population has regarded this group . . . as an enemy. To the Roman Empire in the first century, the European Christian world for over fifteen centuries, the Nazi Reich, the Soviet Union, and to the Arabs and much of the Muslim world, the Jews have been or are regarded as an insufferable threat.[12]

Some degree of eternalism can be discerned in any analysis of anti-Semitism that assumes, as do many histories of the subject, a multi-millennial sweep. Those who speak of ancient, medieval, and modern anti-Semitism, describing a vast stretch of history, are engaged in some form of this practice, even if they abandon theological overtones and speak of the "persistence" as opposed to "permanence" of what is sometimes called the "longest" or "oldest" hatred. These modern eternalists may concede that anti-Semitism "is *not* a natural, metahistorical or a metaphysical phenomenon whose essence has remained unchanged throughout all its manifestations over the centuries."[13] They may even mock the notion of eternal hatred, arguing that anti-Semitism is not "an intrinsic part of the psychic structure of Gentiles, a kind of microbe or virus which invariably attacks non-Jews, provoking the 'eternal hatred' for the 'eternal people.'"[14] Yet they nevertheless write of anti-Semitism as a hatred that stretches across eras, continents, and cultures.

This approach has served multiple functions, beginning with the religious function that has sustained normative Judaism over the centuries. Theologically, it sustains rabbinic beliefs in the unchanging character of God, Torah, and the Jewish people, while bolstering the notion of Jewish exceptionalism. "What makes that fallacy attractive to many people," Gavin Langmuir explains, "is their prior assumption that, whether by divine choice or otherwise, there has always been something uniquely valuable in Jewishness, because Jews have always incorporated and preserved uniquely superior values. They then assume that the resolute and enduring expression of those unique values by Jews has aroused a correspondingly unique type of hostility against them as bearers of that unique quality throughout their existence."[15]

The more modern formulations have also served secular functions. Sociologically, eternalism sustains the collective Jewish self-conception as an eternally suffering people, defined in large part by the persecution faced since ancient times.[16] Philosopher Emmanuel Levinas has given theoretical voice to this self-conception, arguing that "the ultimate essence of Israel derives from its innate predisposition to involuntary sacrifice, its exposure to persecution."[17] Analytically, it explains (or at least rephrases) common intuitions about anti-Semitism's strange durability. In its moderate form, it provides a sufficiently broad view of history to illuminate continuity, evolution, and mutation in the perceptions and treatment of Jewry. Psychologically, it satisfies the need to find reason, meaning, and comfort in the seemingly irrational and yet achingly repetitive hatred that Jews have faced in diverse lands and epochs. Hannah Arendt, a critic of eternalism, argues that it has an advantage over some alternatives approaches in that "it answers the uncomfortable question—Why the Jews of all people?—if only with the question begging reply: Eternal hostility."[18] These functions explain eternalism's continued popularity, even in its more implausible versions, in the face of withering critiques.

The Critique of Eternalism

Historicists have criticized eternalism as unhistorical, essentializing, unphilosophical, self-deceptive, self-defeating, and paradoxically absolving. These criticisms, which we will review in turn, are partly successful, even devastating, at least with respect to the strong, traditional form of eternalism. As we will see, however, the criticisms are not fully successful, leaving some aspects of eternalism untouched. In other words, the historicist critique ultimately falls short in ways that point to historicism's own conceptual incompleteness.

Eternalism as Ahistoric

The primary criticism is that eternalism is unhistorical and unscientific thinking, which ignores differences among periods and cultures in favor of a "gross, immutable, edifying similarity."[19] David Nirenberg (although not exactly an eternalist) smartly observes that multi-millennial histories, including his own important volume, "will perhaps offend most against the current conviction that, as Michel Foucault famously put it in the late 1960s, 'history is for cutting.'"[20] The latter conviction is now entrenched among many historians of ideas, who guard so much against false continuities as to reject any analysis that illuminates the connections among incidents that occur during different periods. Such critics rebuke eternalists for forgetting that Jews have often been warmly received by surrounding gentile societies; that their equal rights and status were accepted in many countries during modernity; and that Jews have enjoyed remarkable economic, social, cultural, and political success since the Enlightenment.[21] Moreover, they argue that profound, irrational hatred of Jews has not existed during all periods; for existence, some insist that hostilities toward Jews in the ancient world did not rise to this level.[22]

There is something to this critique, but it also has its limitations. To argue that eternalists eschew historical context in favor of perceived underlying historical continuities is merely to beg the question, since that is indeed what eternalism means. Eternalists may cop to this accusation, since it is little more than a reframing of their position, insisting that other approaches fail to address anti-Semitism's puzzling historical ubiquity. Alternatively, others argue that the strong critique of eternalism can be a straw man, at least insofar as few scholars or activists argue along the extreme lines that historicists tend to criticize.[23] Some eternalists acknowledge that anti-Semitism waxes and wanes, becoming sometimes dormant, while still insisting that Jew-hatred invariably reappears in varying strengths and strains.

Eternalism as Essentializing

The second criticism is that eternalism tends to essentialize and reify anti-Semitism in a manner ironically similar to the way in which anti-Semitism performs those same functions on Jewish identity. That is to say, the eternalist tends to eradicate difference, reducing varying phenomena to a false eternal core, and confusing the particular phenomenon with its abstraction. Walter Benjamin nicely illustrates this critique in his description of the perspective provided by the "angel of history": "Where we perceive a chain of events, he sees one single catastrophe which keeps piling wreckage upon wreckage and hurls it in front of his feet."[24]

Hannah Arendt argues that this vision is an inversion of the anti-Semite perception of an eternal, ahistoric, unchanging, all-powerful "Jew":

> The notion of an unbroken continuity of persecutions, expulsions, and massacres from the end of the Roman Empire to the Middle Ages, the modern era, and down to our time, frequently embellished by the idea that modern anti-Semitism is no more than a secularized version of popular medieval superstitions, is no less fallacious (though of course less mischievous) than the corresponding anti-Semitic notion of a Jewish secret society that has ruled, or aspired to rule, the world since antiquity.[25]

This view instantiates the fallacy of misplaced concreteness, as Gavin Langmuir explains: "Like the Aryan myth, this conception of 'anti-semitism' depends . . . on the fallacy of misplaced concreteness or illicit reification, in this case on the unproven assumption that for centuries, and despite innumerable changes on both sides, there has been a distinctive kind of reaction of non-Jews directed only at Jews that corresponds to the concept presently evoked by the word 'antisemitism.'"[26]

This critique has its limitations. While some views of anti-Semitism's persistence are vulnerable to the charge of reification, others are not, and to assume that they are may itself reflect misplaced concreteness. Historians Léon Poliakov and Robert Wistrich, for example, have written extensively of anti-Semitism's long history while meticulously detailing the differences among its permutations. Additionally, eternalism and the traditional anti-Semitic view of Jewry's immutable characteristics are not perfectly parallel. Even in its most naïve, or romantic, or mythologizing formulations, the eternalist conception does not, for example, posit a conspiracy or a secret cabal, nor do all eternalists reduce the anti-Semite to the sort of figure to which anti-Semites reduce the Jew. Moreover, as we have explained above, there is no intuitive reason why a theory of anti-Semitism must not resemble the anti-Semite's perception of the Jew, at least in this one respect, especially if the theory of projection has any validity.

Eternalism as Philosophically or Politically Incorrect

Third, eternalism has been criticized as sloppy, self-deceptive thinking that undermines Jewish resolve and displaces the sort of critical thinking that could be the basis for more effective action on behalf of others. Walter Benjamin, who gives this critique its most effective formulation, argued that the timeless view of history tends to perceive each historical period through the perspective of the victors, whom Benjamin equates with rulers and oppressors. "The current amazement that the things we are experiencing are 'still' possible in the twentieth century," Benjamin wrote, "is *not* philosophical."[27] To view history in this way, Benjamin argued, is to privilege oppressive perspectives over the viewpoint of the oppressed. It is not clear that this critique is applicable to the rabbinic tradition, which after all views anti-Jewish oppression from the point of view of the persecuted people themselves. But it nevertheless arguable that mainstream historical approaches that view multi-millennial anti-Semitism from a contemporary Western vantage point privilege a non-neutral subject position.

Eternalism as Self-Defeating

Fourth, this unworldliness can be understood as objectionable for its inaccuracy, for its tendency to advance anti-Semitic stereotypes, and for its tendency to undermine strategies for Jewish collective self-assertion. The stereotype problem is that it tends to perpetuate one of the ancient sources of anti-Semitism, namely the belief that Jews are "outside of history."[28] Wieseltier has called eternalism's mythologizing tendency "the Amalekization of the present enemy," arguing that such thinking is not only imprecise and inaccurate, but also self-deceptive and unworldly.[29] Even those who do not explicitly embrace an eternal conception of anti-Semitism often appear take is as a hidden assumption. Ruth Wisse shrewdly discerns this unspoken premise in their assumption that anti-Semitism may be managed or controlled but never fully extinguished: "All across the civilized world, people track anti-Semitism, expose it, oppose it, decry it. And yet no one seriously considers the possibility of bringing about its end. Is this because of some lack of capacity or courage? Or do we face in anti-Semitism a challenge, to use the phrase of Yiddish writer L. Shapiro, as eternal as the eternal God?"[30] One of the great dangers of eternalism may be the temptation to this fatalism, which capitulates perhaps too quickly to an evil that it believes to be immutable.

Eternalism as Absolving

Finally, Arendt argues that eternalism absolves anti-Semites of responsibility by suggesting that anti-Semitism will always recur and implying that it must arise from some fault in the Jews.[31] Arendt reasoned that if humanity has murdered Jews for more than two thousand years, then some may rightly conclude that Jew-killing is a normal, appropriate activity and anti-Semitism is fully justified.[32] This would, as Arendt emphasizes, be a deeply perverse conclusion in light of the Nazi experience: "In view of the final catastrophe . . . the thesis of eternal anti-Semitism has become more dangerous than ever. Today it would absolve Jew-haters of crimes greater than anybody had ever believed possible."³³ This criticism is at best over-stated. It is entirely plausible for a theory to maintain that a phenomenon is both unchanging and blame-worthy; indeed, these two characteristics are often conjoined in theories of evil, as in many forms of Manichaeism.

What Is Left of Eternalism?

What survives of eternalism after facing these withering critiques? The historicist critique succeeds in refuting some forms of eternalism, but it falls short of its goals. Ironically, the historicist critique of eternalism frequently relies on the assumptions that it abhors. That is to say, those historicists who discern the same *eternalist* faults in ancient and modern sources are themselves viewing eternalism from an eternalist prism. They view the ancient rabbis and modern writers as articulating the same viewpoint. Even when historicists avoid this trap, they nevertheless fail to land the deadly blows that they think they have scored against the methodology that they tend to mock. Some forms of eternalism are indeed sufficiently naïve to commit the sins attributed to them. They reduce the varieties of anti-Jewish sentiment to an implausible artificial "essence"; overstate the virulence of anti-Jewish hatred during some periods; ignore the warm reception that Jews in some gentile societies; and fail to account for the vicissitudes and gaps in anti-Jewish animus. They also frequently fail to appreciate the ways that the perception and treatment of Jews in differing cultures reflect the history and politics of those cultures. Nevertheless, there are more sophisticated approaches, which stress long continuities among anti-Jewish hostilities while nevertheless avoiding these pitfalls. While these approaches are seldom as sensitive to culturally specific developments, they nevertheless provide valuable insights into the evolution of anti-Jewish perceptions over time.

Historicism

In contrast to eternalism, historicists define anti-Semitism as a modern historical phenomenon, viewing its historical episodes as discrete, socially embedded, and contingent. Anthony Julius articulates this view in broad, historiographical terms, "I regard anti-Semitism as a discontinuous, contingent aspect of a number of distinct *mentalités* and milieus."[34] Julius reasons that Jew-hatred's diversity belies any attempt to sweep them under the same rubric:

> It is a heterogenous phenomenon, the site of collective hatreds, and of cultural anxieties and resentments. The search for a single, unified theory of anti-Semitism is an idle one. There is no essence of anti-Semitism. It is instead in the irreducible plurality of its forms of existence that "anti-Semitism" is to be understood and studied.[35]

This postmodern conception of anti-Semitism's "irreducible plurality" belies any attempt to frame a sweeping historical narrative. The historicist school emphasizes instead the role of time in history, arguing that the hardships that Jews have faced in each historical period must be understood contingently within social context.[36]

Many who share this view of "irreducible plurality" reserve the term "anti-Semitism" for the particular manifestations that most concern them, sometimes distinguishing this phenomenon from earlier forms of religious bias, which they define as "anti-Judaism." Gavin Langmuir perspicuously observed that scholars have defined (and dated) the emergence of "anti-Semitism" according to their respective intellectual or political motivations. Religious motives, for example, have led some commentators to conceive anti-Semitism as a millennial reaction to Judaism. Others, who are focused on the responsibility of Christianity for the Holocaust, locate its emergence in the early centuries of the Christian Church. Still another group, to whom we will next turn, have defined anti-Semitism as a secular phenomenon that emerged as recently as the nineteenth century, either because they wish to absolve Christianity completely, or because they are less concerned about religion.[37] This group argues that *anti-Semitism* was uniquely shaped by the failures of the Enlightenment, the disruptions of the Industrial Revolution, the rise of secularization, the emergence of democratization, or the conflicts arising from Jewish emancipation.

Historicism and Wilhelm Marr's Movement

These historicists reserve the term "anti-Semitism" for the particular form that was taken by hostility toward Jews from roughly the 1870s, when the word itself was coined, until the end of the Second World War.[38] Implicit in this usage is the view that the term emerged concurrently with a form of Jew-hatred that was categorically different than its antecedents and descendants. The subtext is their shared assumption that the horrors of the Nazi Holocaust are better understood in the context of their particular era rather than in the context of the history of anti-Semitism. In general, this assumption is consistent with those schools of thought, rooted in historical materialism, which stress the social conditions that make changing human developments possible.

The strongest forms of historicization may be found in encyclopedia entries published immediately the Holocaust. For example, the *Everyman's Encyclopedia* published in England and the United States, in 1949 and 1951 respectively, defines "antisemites" as: "those who were opposed to the Jews in the second half of the 19th century. This hatred of the Jews, or antisemitism as it was called, was not the outcome of antipathy to their religion, but arose on account of their wealth and power which they were accumulating."[39] As historian Dina Porat observes, this definition reflects not only a belief that anti-Semitism is a historically specific phenomenon, but also the early post-war hope that it had been eliminated.[40] Porat has speculated that this early Cold War document focused on perceived Jewish acquisitiveness rather than racial distinctiveness because public attention was increasingly turning from Nazi racial theory toward the emerging threat of the Soviet Union.[41]

Some writers focus on history because they believe that a focus on individual attitudes and practices is insufficient to understand the conditions under which the catastrophes of modern anti-Semitism can be possible.[42] These writers typically see anti-Semitism as a European reaction to an emancipated and assimilated Jewry that emerged in the nineteenth century after years in which Jews and gentiles had viewed one another as fundamentally different.[43] Arendt, for example, defines anti-Semitism as a secular nineteenth-century ideology, and she argues that it became possible only because Jews first and then non-Jews had begun in the fifteenth and sixteenth centuries to think that Jews and gentiles had a fundamentally different inner nature.[44] The difference in the modern period is that Jews were conflated with the state, so that a turn against the one became a turn against the other, since Jews were seen as invisible manipulators of the political order. Arendt argues that modern anti-Semitism arose as the nation-state fell into decline and resentment developed against the Jews for their perceived role in supporting, financing, and controlling it.[45]

Historicism, the Enlightenment, Emancipation, and the Holocaust

Some thinkers argue that anti-Semitism, and modern racism generally, was made possible by modern science, technology, and state power—and made necessary by modern boundary-guarding and boundary-drawing concerns.[46] Given the unique horrors of the Holocaust, they tend to treat anti-Semitism as a function of modernity, the Enlightenment, and emancipation, rather than a vestige of premodern religious discrimination or an eternal, unchanging phenomenon.[47] There is irony to this charge, since modernity and the Enlightenment are usually associated with a diminution of ancient prejudices and the rollback of legal disabilities on Jews and other minorities. Some historians and social theorists characterize modern anti-Semitism with limits or failures of the Enlightenment. Others, going further, argue that anti-Semitism is not an exception to the Enlightenment but rather the realization of its darker tendencies.

Historicists may stress then-prevailing characteristics of the Jewish community, or of relationships between Jews and gentiles. For example, Arendt argued that the decline of the nation-state divested Jewry of their historical function as court financiers, leaving them peculiarly vulnerable.[48] Alternatively, they may relate to features of modernity that fueled the rise of totalitarianism, or of "mythical" thinking, or of conspiracy theory, or of "racial" science. Michel Foucault theorized that modern anti-Semitism emerged during the nineteenth century because it was at that point that the state assumed in some places the role of ensuring racial purity:

> The old religious-type anti-Semitism was reutilized by State racism only in the nineteenth century, or at the point when the State had to look like, function, and present itself as the guarantor of the integrity and purity of the race, and had to defend it against the race or races that were infiltrating it, introducing harmful elements into its

body, and which therefore had to be driven out for both political and biological reasons.[49]

Those who focus on the changing position of the Jewish community during the nineteenth century may observe that the recent emancipation of Jews from restrictions on occupation, habitation, and citizenship fueled unprecedented Jewish social and economic success. This led to a rapid reversal in the economic relations between Jews and non-Jews, as Jews became empowered thanks to liberal reforms, leaving non-Jewish natives feeling the anxieties of a suddenly displaced people.

In explaining the uniqueness of this milieu, some historicists point to the relatively large number of Jews who lived in Germany during this period and their increasing wealth and prominence to describe the growing threat that their gentile neighbors perceived them to pose.[50] For example, they may observe that 80% of German Jews had lived in poverty as the eighteenth century came to a close but that, a century later, their skyrocketing incomes were reflected in the fact that Jews in Frankfurt am Main were paying four times as much taxes as Protestants and eight times what Catholics were paying.[51] By the late nineteenth century, when German racial anti-Semitism emerged, Jews formed 9% of the Prussian university population, which represented nearly ten times their proportion of the local population. By any analysis, Jews were heavily over-represented among the era's prominent figures in the arts, science, and philosophy.

The Critique of Historicism

Historicism has been criticized for several weaknesses: it lacks a sufficiently broad historical sense to appreciate anti-Semitism's enduring character and its continuities over time; fails to appreciate evolutions and transformations; and lacks sufficient perspective to allow for comparison or to recognize commonalities. These criticisms are compelling. Ultimately, though, they are no more dispositive than historicism's critique of eternalism. That is to say, each approach has both significant strengths and formidable weaknesses.

Historicism's Failure to Grasp Continuity

It can hardly be coincidental that, as one medievalist has observed, virtually every contemporary stereotype of the "Jew" can also be found in medieval Europe.[52] In focusing on how people are embedded within their present conditions, historicists lose appreciation for continuities over time.[53] In this way, their disdain for false nostalgia dooms them to historical amnesia. Along these lines, historicists may tend to believe, inaccurately, that there are unique qualities to the anti-Semitism that existed during that period. For example, Gavin Langmuir argued that anti-Jewish attitudes changed fundamentally in the twelfth century. During this period, according to Langmuir, some Christians developed a "chimerical" hatred of Jews. That is to say, they hated Jews based on a heavily distorted misperception of "the Jew" that developed at this point. For this reason, Langmuir argued that the term "anti-Semitism" should not be used to describe earlier hostility toward Jews. Other scholars, however, have responded that this is historically inaccurate, because chimerical representations of Jews can be found even during ancient times. One historian argues that such *chimerica* can be found at least as far back as the first century of the Common Era in the writings of Greek rhetorician Apollonius Molon.[54] He also points to other examples, such as ninth century beliefs that Jewish men menstruate and pray to Satan.[55]

Historicism's Failure to Grasp Evolution

Historicism has also been criticized for failing to register transformations over time. Here Nirenberg quotes Montaigne, who was in turn quoting Seneca: "Cut anything into tiny pieces and it becomes a mass of confusion."[56] Historicists may be right to insist that premodern anti-Jewish religious fervor was different in many respects from modern anti-Semitic racial hatred, but there are unquestionably similarities and continuities among the two, and there is value in tracing the course of evolution from one to the other. Similarly, there is value in tracing the path from twentieth-century racial anti-Semitism in Central Europe to twenty-first-century political anti-Semitism in the Middle East. To the extent that historicism lacks sufficient analytical tools to trace such paths, it cannot fully explain some of the most important historical questions about anti-Semitism.

Historicism's Loss of Perspective

Moreover, the tendency of other historicists to equate anti-Semitism with the Nazi period has had an unfortunate social consequence. By equating anti-Semitism with Nazi exterminationism, this practice has tended to obscure the existence of real, tangible anti-Jewish hostilities that do not rise to this high bar. Indeed, anti-Semitism can be defined out of existence when commentators decline to use the term except in narrow historical contexts or where present genocidal results are achieved.[57] This tendency has made it much more difficult to identify and address anti-Jewish hostilities when they arise in the present time.

What Is Right in Historicism

Historicism's strength is its focus on the specific, historical, and contingent sources of anti-Semitism within particular cultures. This allows for very valuable insights about the operation of Jew-hatred in specific contexts. Historicism's weakness is its failure to grasp continuity, evolution, or nuance. This precludes the insights that only a broad historical vista can afford. Although historicism and eternalism are mutually antagonistic, they are also mutually complementary. That is to say, the strength of each is the weakness of the other. One might be tempted to suggest a marriage between the two, involving compromise and cooperation. It is not clear however that this star-crossed marriage would be a happy one, insofar as the two schools are fundamentally opposed. As it happens, a third approach exists that combines the strengths of each, while avoiding their weaknesses, and avoiding the need for unhappy compromises.

Anti-Semitism as Repetition

The third way conceives anti-Jewish hostility as a repetitive pattern rather than a continuous or discontinuous chain of events. In this view, the repetitiveness of anti-Semitism can be gleaned from a survey of anti-Jewish behavior. This can be seen, for example, in the eerily similar patterns that Jew-hatred has taken in different periods and cultures. This repetition can be theorized in various ways. Ahistoric theories explain it as the unavoidable product of an underlying trauma that humanity experiences in all periods and cultures. For such theories, the underlying mechanism is continuous even if the series of events is not. Historic theories by contrast explain repetition in terms of the similar approaches that different cultures take to similar problems over time. Either way, anti-Semitism-as-repetition acknowledges that the recurrence of anti-Semitism involves continuities and discontinuities, evolutions and transformations, increases and diminutions, latencies and eruptions.

The Repetitiveness of Anti-Semitism

The theory of repetition offers a different perspective on such incidents as the 2002 distribution of a flyer at the San Francisco State University campus bearing the image of a dead Palestinian baby purportedly slaughtered by "Jewish rite." The obvious import of this incident is that it provides a contemporary recurrence of the infamous blood libel in a long chain of such defamations stretching back to twelfth-century England.[58] Those who object to this formulation may point to the wide cultural differences that separate medieval England from contemporary San Francisco; the historical discontinuities, including the relative dearth of blood libel in the United States during the twentieth century; and the disappearance of the medieval theological views that supported this defamation during its formative period. This argument only bolsters, however, the notion that these incidents should be seen as repetitions, as opposed to continuations, along a long historical chain.

As Wistrich observes, the myth of Jewish ritual murder "would repeat [itself] with stunning regularity into the modern era."[59] In this scenario, a baby or young child is supposedly killed by Jews, often torn to pieces, and eaten, with its blood drunk during ceremonial occasions, usually Passover, or baked into the unleavened Passover bread or *matzah*.[60] Strikingly similar accusations of ritual murder have been repeated against Jews around the world since twelfth-century England, beginning at Norwich (1144), Gloucester (1168), Bury St. Edmonds (1181),

Bristol (1183), and Winchester, England (1192, 1225, 1235).[61] Spreading to the continent, such defamations were repeated in Bois (1171), Fulda (1235), Valréas (1247); Weissenburg and Pforzheim (1270), Oberwesel am Rhein (1286), Thuringia (1303), Prague (1305), Baden (1332), and Rinn (1462).[62] Seventeenth- and eighteenth-century Poland and Lithuania became the center of blood libel cases, with similar cases, for example, in Lublin (1598) and Zaslav (1747).[63] During the nineteenth century, these cases recurred in Russia, notably in Velizh (1823), Saratov (1853), the Caucasus (1878), Vilna (1902), and Dubossary (1903).[64] During this period, in Austria-Hungary, there were not less than twelve ritual murder cases.[65] In the Eastern Mediterranean, such allegations arose in Aleppo (1810), Beirut (1824), Antioch (1826), Tripoli (1834), Jerusalem (1838), Damascus (1840), and Corfu (1894).[66] Numerous blood libel allegations circulated throughout Egypt (1870–1892), including especially in Damanhur near Alexandria (1873–1877).[67] During the late nineteenth and early twentieth century, the ritual murder accusation was still circulated in Europe. For example, the Jesuit periodical *La Civiltà Cattolica* published a number of articles attempting to prove this myth.[68] In Shiraz, Iran, Jews were accused of ritual murder in 1945.[69] Even after the Holocaust, similar defamations were made in Kielce (1946), leading Poles to massacre 42 Jews, including children, with axes, clubs and guns.[70] As recently as 1996, a Romanian periodical accused Israelis of smuggling babies out of Romania for illicit organ transplantation, commenting, "As is well known, Jewish unleavened bread requires fresh, kosher Christian blood."[71]

In some cases, the repetition is all too familiar. During the Nazi period, German researchers and propagandists developed a body of work in which anti-Semitism and anti-Zionism fully converged.[72] In these writings and broadcasts, Nazi spokesmen built an ideological system in which insatiable Zionist greed manipulated British and American policy in the Middle East and around the world. This laid the ideological groundwork on which Soviet, Arab, and later Western progressives would build an anti-Zionist edifice that continually repeated tropes historically directed at Jews. This is not to suggest, in a teleological or deterministic fashion, that later developments were dictated by work done between 1938 and 1945. Too many contingencies stood between war-time activities and post-war outcomes, and history could have taken many other directions. Nor is it to suggest that contemporary anti-Zionism has evolved in a steady, continuous fashion from Nazi propaganda. Those contemporary figures who espouse Nazi-like perspectives do so for their own reasons, as a result of very different forces that their cultures are working out. Rather, the repetition of anti-Jewish discourses, often in anti-Zionist garb, reflects the instinct of successive generations to assume anti-Jewish tropes that had been made readily available for what may be very different social purposes.

The repetitiveness of anti-Semitism can be seen even more clearly in anti-Semitic motifs that have gone dormant only to recur again after a period of time. This is evident, for example, in the twenty-first century-resurgence of popularity that *The Protocols of the Elders of Zion* has experienced after roughly two generations of post-war dormancy.[73] Like most modern anti-Semitica, *The Protocols* draws on the ancient and medieval store of anti-Jewish stereotypes and defamations, such as the ideas of Jewish criminality, malevolence, and conspiracy, as well as the medieval association of Jews with the devil and the anti-christ.[74] *The Protocols*, a notorious hoax and forgery, had played a prominent role in inspiring and rationalizing Adolf Hitler's attempt to exterminate the Jewish people during its first wave of influence (1905–1945).[75] After the devastation wrought by Nazi Germany's response to the fictitious Jewish conspiracy concocted in the *Protocols*, the book became as taboo in the West as the old hatred with which it was associated.[76]

The Theory of Repetition

The idea of repetition has been theorized in ways that resolve the impasse between eternalism and historicism. In so doing, repetition theory compensates for the former's failure to grasp our embeddedness in time and the latter's failure to appreciate historical continuity. The theory of repetition provides that, in certain circumstances, the past is open to us in its possibility, not because we have assumed an external, neutral gaze, but because we are caught in a comparable deadlock or abyss.[77] In this view, anti-Jewish episodes in widely different epochs and cultures should be understood neither as a single continuous phenomenon, nor as a discontinuous series of discrete incidents, but as a repeating sequence of phenomena arising from the same (or similar) underlying social antagonism.

The theory of repetition equally eschews both the idea of anti-Semitism as an unchanging, continuous phenomenon and also the idea of Jew-hatred as an unconnected series of calamities. Rather, it is a phenomenon that must be identified by the abyss or antagonism from which it arises. In other words, the way to save anti-Semitism's *historicity* from the discredited notion of a linear succession of history is to rethink its historical periods as a series of engagements with the same underlying trauma.[78] In classical Marxism, this trauma is analogous to the class struggle, while for certain messianic theologies it is the effort to heal a world torn by primordial fissures in the figure of God. The implication here is that far-flung episodes of anti-Jewish behavior are united by their repetition of the same traumatic unfolding, rather than by their manifestation in superficially similar guise.

The challenge then is to identify the fundamental trauma that repeatedly yields this tragic result. The theories of *projection* and *displacement* can help with this task. According to the projection theory, aversions arise as a means for people to resolve or at least ameliorate their internal conflicts.[79] The theory is that people often repress or disown desires, which then return as projections onto other people or groups. For example, a person who is internally conflicted about greedy or sexual impulses might project those impulses on members of another group, whom he or she will then see as possessing those attributes. Those who have aggressive desires that are suppressed by the demands of their own superegos may project those desires onto Jewish people. "Anti-Semitism," wrote Max Horkheimer and Theodor Adorno, "is based on false projection."[80] The "displacement" theory is also sometimes known as the "ventilation" theory or the "aggression-resentment" theory. According to this theory, prejudice results from the externalization or displacement of aggression.[81] Simply put, people who are frustrated with personal disappointment take their frustration out on other persons or groups, who are often seen as scapegoats for their misfortunes. The greater the frustration, the greater the aggression that is vented on others. Empirical studies have shown, for example, that non-Jewish Americans who are distrustful of politicians and perceive themselves to be victims of economic forces are more likely to exhibit anti-Semitic attitudes than others.[82]

Socio-economic trauma may also trigger a repetition of extreme prejudice. For example, some theorists have associated racial prejudice with the prejudiced person's economic failure. Bettelheim and Janowitz, for example, argued that there is a strong correlation between racial and religious intolerance and anxiety about unemployment and other forms of downward economic mobility.[83] Ackerman and Jahoda, similarly, argued that "a strongly competitive society gives permanent cause for social anxiety to everyone, even to those who have achieved material success." They shrewdly theorized that the key role of these tensions could be discerned in the acquisitive traits that prejudiced persons projected onto Jews, e.g., stinginess, greed, social ambitions.[84] More generally, some Marxist thinkers argue that anti-Semitism arises when the class struggle is displaced or mystified and its cause is projected onto "the *Jews*."[85]

The salient point here is not the persuasiveness of any particular social or economic theory but rather the general insight that anti-Semitism recurs when structurally similar individual or social traumas arise, despised traits are projected onto the Jew, and deep frustrations are vented onto this persecuted group. There will likely be both continuities and discontinuities with earlier forms of Jew-hatred. The primary underlying connection between different hostilities toward Jews does not lie so much in the continuities as in the repetition of a similar traumatic response. The key to understanding prior forms of anti-Semitism then is not so much to perceive them as part of a steady historical flow. Rather, older forms of anti-Semitism are present to contemporary thinkers when, to borrow from Walter Benjamin, they stand at the same brink to which the Jewish people were previously brought.[86] It is precisely because anti-Semitism achieves the *unthinkable*, to borrow this time from Kierkegaard, that it permits privileged glances into prior incarnations of the same horrors.

Repetition and the Double-Bind

The theory of repetition frees us from the double-bind in which Jew-hatred is either eternal and immutable or else culturally specific and disconnected. The latter view prevents us from understanding anti-Semitism in its broad historical cycles while the former prevents us from combating it. If anti-Semitism is not eternal, then it may be curable, and we can focus on addressing the specific cultural elements that support its recurrence in particular times and places. If it is not entirely culturally specific, then we can apply lessons from each of the times and places in which it has been fought.

Historical repetitions are often obscured by the nostalgic images we often develop about the past.[87] Thus, for example, in Marxist dogma, a nostalgic image of idyllic precapitalist society is said to distort the class struggle that recurs before and after the transition from feudalism to capitalism.[88] In the same way, as Žižek observes, nostalgic representations conceal the reiteration of socio-psychological traumas through the resurgence of anti-Semitism in divergent historical periods. Ironically, contemporary students of anti-Semitism now tend to create a false nostalgic image of the present, against which the historical narrative of anti-Semitism is told. The English sociologist Robert Fine explains that commentators from several different intellectual perspectives tend to create the same implausible narrative of anti-Semitism's development in order to present the phenomenon as the creature of a period which is now safely past: "Modernists treat it as a symptom of pre-modernity. Postmodernists treat it as a symptom of modernity. Postnationalists treat it as a symptom of the age of nationalism. Theorists of the second modernity treat it as a symptom of the first modernity that is no longer with us. And so it goes on."[89] In each case, Fine observes an insistence that the present moment is uniquely free of the malaise. Commentators argue, variously, that anti-Semitism has been marginalized in the wake of the Holocaust, that it has been banished by the rise of human rights culture, or that it has been displaced by the emergence of Islamophobia and anti-Roma racism. "Either way," Fine concludes, "it would appear that the long history of European antisemitism was strangely resolved shortly after the unprecedented killing spree against Jews."[90] This nostalgic image of the present conceals the same trauma that instigated anti-Jewish hostility in prior periods.

4

Universality and Particularity

The Homogenists

Many modern formulations have defined anti-Semitism as a discrete but largely generic form of a more general phenomenon, such as xenophobia or "heterophobia." That is to say, they have defined anti-Semitism as an aversion toward all difference, implying a preference (explicit or implicit) for homogeneity, rather than a specific form of hatred.[1] This accords with a more general trend to lump together all forms of intergroup antagonism and to extend the category so broadly as to encompass all forms of collective resentment.[2] Indeed, this approach sees heterophobia as a manifestation of a still wider category of anxieties arising from the feeling that one has no control over one's situation, that one can neither steer one's course nor foresee its outcome.

Early Zionists, from Chaim Weizmann to David Ben-Gurion to Vladimir Jabotinsky, regarded anti-Semitism as an extreme version of general xenophobia that emerged from the de-territorialization of the Jewish people throughout the diaspora.[3] The theory was that anti-Jewish sentiments had been closely connected to perceptions of Jewish difference or otherness since at least the Book of Esther, which is retold each year in Jewish communities during the festival of Purim. The Zionist solution to this problem was to normalize or de-"other" the Jewish people by resettling them in their own homeland. Then Jews would no longer suffer discrimination because they ceased to live at the sufferance of other people. History has not been kind to this theory, inasmuch as anti-Jewish animosity has recurred globally since the establishment of the Jewish state.[4]

A similar view rose in influence within the Jewish communal world immediately after World War II as Jewish Americans sought to assimilate into the broader American culture. Indeed, the adoption by major of Jewish organizations of this idea of "the unitary character of prejudice" has been described as one of the hallmarks of the evolution of Jewish communal organizations from Jewish advocacy to intergroup relations.[5] Under this theory, the prejudiced attitude divides the world into in-groups and out-groups, directing a generally negative mindset toward out-groups. This theory is based on the observation that people who are prejudiced against members of one group tend to be prejudiced against other groups as well.

By 1947 or 1948, this "unitary theory" or homogenism was hardening into an orthodoxy. For example, Stephen S. Wise, as president of the American Jewish Congress, told Congress in 1947 that, "We regard ethnic discrimination, whether directed against Jews, Negroes, Chinese, Mexicans, or any other group, as a single and indivisible problem and as one of the most urgent problems of democratic society."[6] In the same year, the American Jewish Committee adopted a resolution resolving "that there is the closest relation between the protection of the civil rights of all citizens and the protection of the civil rights of the members of particular groups."[7] The following year, the American Jewish Congress's then–executive director, David W. Petegorsky, announced that "the campaign against anti-Semitism had to be viewed as part of the much broader struggle against racism in America generally."[8]

Homogenism became similarly dominant in academia during this period. This is not entirely coincidental, as the Jewish communal world, and especially the American Jewish Committee, funded influential research that articulated this Jewish communal orthodoxy. In particular this took the form of the American Jewish Committee's five-volume series of *Studies in Prejudice*. These *Studies* were anchored by Horkheimer and Adorno's landmark treatise on *The Authoritarian Personality*, which was predicated on the notion that anti-Semitism "probably is not a specific or isolated phenomenon but a part of a broader ideological framework."[9] Horkheimer and Adorno associated extreme prejudice with a new anthropological type, the "authoritarian personality." According to this theory, the "authoritiarian" or "pre-fascist" personality could be identified by a number of personality traits, such as cynicism, conformism, psychological rigidity, a weak grasp on reality, aversion to introspection, and difficulty forming close personal relationships. Conveniently, Horkheimer and Adorno associated this anthropological type with the political views of their adversaries, to wit: illiberalism or "pseudo-conservatism." Other major works, such as Gordon Allport's *The Nature of Prejudice*, also supported the unitary theory of prejudice. "If a person is anti-Jewish," Gordon Allport wrote, "he is likely to be anti-Catholic, anti-Negro, anti any out-group."[10] Under Horkheimer, Adorno, and Allport's influence, many scholars tended to view these various antipathies as manifestations of a single "generalized attitude."

In a strong version of this approach, anti-Semitism is defined as being merely "the dislike of the unlike."[11] Thus, for example, the Italian parliament, in concluding its recent formal inquiry into anti-Semitism, announced that "while it could also be said that all anti-Semites are racists while not all racists are anti-Semites, it is beyond doubt that a racist mentality is what it is because *it is based on categories of thought centering around the idea of a 'different' form of humanity, qualitatively superior or inferior*, which therefore accept anti-Semitic theories as possible and justifiable."[12]

Such definitions treat anti-Semitism as distinguishable only in its objects from other forms of discrimination such as anti-black racism or anti-Hispanic ethnocentricity, rather than identifying a peculiar characteristic of the hatred of Jews. Conceptually, they reveal the common underlying anxieties that arise from the stranger, in the sense that any other being of human life is foreign and dangerous. This often stirs antipathy, which may provoke aggressiveness or defensiveness. If Jews have been more frequently persecuted than other groups, under this theory the reason is merely that they have been more vulnerable, as a small, discrete, insular, and physically powerless group scattered throughout the Christian and Muslim worlds. By focusing on anti-Semitism's heterophobic aspects, homogenizing definitions are able to perceive not only its continuities with other animus but also the ways in which distrust of otherness can engender negative attitudes toward Jews. This theory also explains why anti-Jewish attitudes sometimes correlate with aversions to other out-groups. For example, prejudices against Jews, Muslims, and gays have all recently risen in the Netherlands.[13] It is difficult not to see some degree of xenophobia under these conditions.

Some homogenist approaches also square well with grand theories or ideologies. Such theories are typically founded upon the conviction that one cannot resolve any particular social conflict without resolving all of them; that is to say, without resolving the fundamental antagonisms that lie at the roots of them all. Thus, for example, Marxists argue that the rights of women, the condition of the environment, the health of democracy, and the establishment of peace all ultimately require a global resolution without which their underlying conflicts cannot be resolved.[14] Analogous arguments could be found within radical feminism, radical environmentalism, or even some forms of psychoanalysis. In any of these grand theories, anti-Semitism is merely a generic manifestation of a broader phenomenon.

The tendency to blur the lines among forms of prejudice has had practical advantages and uses. Analytically, it facilitated research, particularly in the period immediately following World War II, which demonstrated similarities among the divergent forms of hatred directed at different groups.[15] Politically, it provides a basis for coalition-building activities by various minority groups. The Anti-Defamation League's then–national chairman, Judge Meier Steinbrink, articulated this political argument in 1946, exhorting ADL members that "[t]here must be no cleavage in the ranks of America's millions; as we worked together—all races, religions, creeds, side by side—toward victory, so we must continue to work to cement that victory, to make meaningful the enormous investment in life, limb and labor."[16] This strategy is facilitated by an approach which sees all forms of "racism"—indeed all forms of prejudice, including sexism, agism, and heterosexism—as minor variations on a common social pathology.[17] Legally, it supports the development of parallel regulatory regimes to protect persons who face discrimination under different suspect classifications. In Europe, where Jews are the paradigmatic case of a persecuted minority, other historical out-groups may seek legal protections by comparing their lot to the Jewish condition. In the United States, however, where African Americans are the paradigmatic case, other groups tend to achieve protection by comparing their status to that of American blacks.

Understandably, homogenist definitions have proliferated because they serve a number of practical objectives and functions. This is particularly true at times and in places where opposition to the persecution of Jews is perceived to be weaker, standing on its own, than if combined with other forms of anti-racism, multiculturalism, or human rights activity. During the 1950s, when such definitions gained strength, they served an additional function. That is, they allowed Jews to be seen as victims no different than other groups, such as African Americans, and therefore fit with mid-century American hopes for assimilation.[18]

The problem with such theories is that they offer no basis for explaining why Jews, rather than some other group, have so often been the victim of scapegoating and projection. One is reminded of the old joke World War I joke about Jews and bicyclists.

POLICE CHIEF: The Jews are responsible for the world's suffering.
DEPUTY: And also the bicyclists.
CHIEF: Why the bicyclists?

It has been said that how quickly you get this joke depends on how comfortable you are with the idea of rounding up the Jews.[19] Anti-Jewish aggression has been so commonplace in so many places and historical periods that may seem to require no explanation.[20] Yet a proper understanding of anti-Semitism must indeed supply an explanation.

Shortcomings of the Homogenizing Approach

In the end, these definitions served not so much to broaden academic focus on anti-Semitism, as to eliminate it altogether. When anti-Semitism is reduced to the features which it shares in common with all other prejudices (e.g., the exclusion of a persecuted group from full membership in society or the stigmatization of that group as socially inferior), the frequent result is to minimize the extent of anti-Semitism, since contemporary anti-Semitism does not exhibit to a great extent those aspects of racism that it shares in common with other groups.[21] For example, when the focus of attention shifted to the generalized plight of "disadvantaged peoples" or "people of color," anti-Semitism fell out of view, since Jews are typically considered to be socio-economically privileged and are now mainly perceived as "white."

One impact of this thinking was the virtual disappearance of anti-Semitism studies after the golden age of research in the 1940s and 1950s and until the renewed attention that the field has found in the wake of a global resurgence of Jew-hatred since the turn of the twenty-first century. In the interim, anti-Semitism studies were largely replaced first by studies of "generalized prejudice" and then by studies of other groups. Commenting on the impact of homogenizing approaches, one legal scholar penned an academic article entitled, "Whatever Happened to Anti-Semitism?"[22] That article observes that "anti-Semitism has faded from our consciousness, in part because theorists began to view anti-Semitism as part of a larger phenomenon of prejudice."[23] Interestingly, the study of other forms of prejudice did not disappear during this entire period: whole literatures emerged to study discrimination against women, blacks, and other groups. In these literatures, the distinctive forms of each prejudice emerge.

One problem with defining anti-Semitism as a heterophobia, however, is that it fails to reflect the significant differences in complexity between anti-Semitism and other forms of antipathy.[24] Taguieff provides a means of accommodating this distinction, observing that simple heterophobia is transformed when a theory is developed that supports resentment directed at another group. He uses the term "xenophobia" to distinguish this "secondary" animus from simple heterophobia. When the respective groups are defined in ethnic terms, he uses the term "ethnocentrism" to describe the secondary animus. By this definition, anti-Semitism can be understood as heterophobia when it is based on an undifferentiated fear of the Jew as the gentile's "other," but it becomes xenophobic or ethnocentric when it arises from a belief that Jews are, for example, economically unscrupulous or morally defective.

The most obvious deficiency of such approaches is that they suggest that anti-Semitism may be different from other forms of ethnocentrism or xenophobia only in the choice of persecuted out-group, rather than in the nature or intensity of hatred. To this extent, they fail to account for anti-Semitism's distinctive features, including its exceptional virulence. Historian Ben-Zion Netanyahu recognized the difference in intensity when he defined anti-Semitism as an animus that combines "hatred of the other, hatred of the alien and hatred of the weak" but "in a more forceful and consistent form than in any other form of hatred of minorities."[25] This recognition of intensity levels is important. Nevertheless, if anti-Semitism differed only in degree from other forms of heterophobia, then one would be justified in lumping them all in together.

Exceptionality

Beyond the question of intensity, anti-Semitism differs from other animus in ubiquity, depth, complexity, and persistence. For this reason, some scholars insist that anti-Semitism is "much more than mere prejudice about or discrimination against Jews."[26] Léon Poliakov in his magisterial multivolume history stresses this uniqueness in his definition of "anti-Semitism" as "an effective *sui generis* attitude of the gentiles toward the Jews, an endemic hatred pregnant with explosive outbursts, reducing the children of Israel to pariah status and exposing them, as traditional scapegoats, to numberless and endless massacres."[27] Gavin Langmuir expresses a similar insight when he admonishes that the hatred symbolized by Auschwitz must be distinguished in more than intensity from the hostility represented by a swastika on the Eiffel Tower.[28] One response to Langmuir's argument has been the observation that many self-styled anti-Semites were horrified by the genocidal excesses of the Holocaust, just as in the period immediately preceding World War I there were many politicians who urged mundane discrimination against the Jews while rejecting more extreme recommendations.[29] But this response misses the gist of Langmuir's argument, which is that genocidal anti-Semitism differs from other hatreds because of its potentiality to trigger mass slaughter, even though anti-Semitism does not always manifest with that severity.

Langmuir's comment reflects a recurring theme among those who have struggled to craft a proper definition of this elusive term. To wit: there is an intuition, shared by many engaged in this effort, that any proper definition of anti-Semitism—and certainly any workable explanatory theory—must account for its exceptionality. That is to say, many scholars recognize that a basic characteristic of anti-Semitism is the extent to which it is fundamentally different in character than other forms of hate or bigotry. Langmuir's notion is that we cannot properly understand anti-Semitism—indeed we cannot properly name it—without conveying something of what has made it capable of such extraordinary evil.

While some will find resonance in this notion of exceptionality, others will reject it as unduly parochial or ethnocentric. In fact, the exceptionality doctrine is not logically necessary to a conclusion that anti-Semitism is a specific phenomenon. The other alternative is to conclude that all forms of hate stand on their own two feet. In this sense, it is precisely as a specific phenomenon that anti-Semitism finds connection with other biases, because they too are incomparably separate. This anti-essentialist position identifies an irreducible plurality in the various struggles that different peoples face, insisting that their articulation in a string of equivalences ignores historical contingencies.[30]

The Critique of Exceptionalism

Like any doctrine of exceptionality, this approach is controversial. Sociologists debate whether the intensity and endurance of anti-Jewish hostility means that it is different in its basic nature and etiology from animus directed at other groups.[31] Theories of exceptionalism, such the view the United States has achieved a unique national greatness, are highly controversial in academic circles, just as they are hotly topical in contemporary politics. Exceptionality theories carry particular baggage when applied to any facet of Jewish experience. Like the doctrine of chosenness, to which it runs parallel, the notion of anti-Semitism's exceptionalism has stirred resentment. Moreover, some argue that preoccupation with historical suffering has come to define Jewish identity and Jewish life to an unhealthy extent, squandering resources that would be better invested on other projects.

The critique of exceptionality is sometimes infused, at its extreme points, with anti-Semitism denial or minimization. That is to say, those who insist that anti-Semitism is not exceptional often deny the existence or severity of anti-Semitism. Such arguments are sometimes combined with arguments that anti-Semitism research and advocacy are detrimental to the interests of other groups, especially Palestinian Arabs. For example, the English University and College Union (UCU) once responded to the United Kingdom's Parliamentary Inquiry into Anti-Semitism by assailing the singular inquiry into that subject:

> It could be argued that, at a time when racial and religious intolerance generally is on the rise on campus, to inquire into antisemitism alone was misconceived and unhelpful . . . it seems inappropriate to have taken as a topic in isolation at a time when Islamophobia is also on the increase and when the two issues surely need a balanced approach.[32]

The UCU provides no explanation for why anti-Semitism and Islamophobia "surely" need a "balanced" approach. The idea has intuitive resonance with some people, and it supports some political projects, but it does not stand up to scrutiny. Anti-Semitism can no more be balanced against Islamophobia than discrimination against lesbians can be balanced against harassment of Puerto Ricans. Those who accept the principle of non-discrimination are compelled to oppose invidious discrimination against all groups, rather than to balance one against the other. Those who resist efforts to fight anti-Semitism ultimately do so for reasons other than balance. Nevertheless, efforts to address anti-Semitism's peculiar virulence are unavoidably met by opposition.

Controversy has increasingly attached even—perhaps especially—to the view that the Holocaust represents a unique evil in human experience.[33] Critics charge that Holocaust obsession has overstated the extent of Jewish suffering, downplayed the suffering of other peoples, distracted attention from current evils, justified Israeli aggression, or aggrandized the Jewish people. The Muslim Council of Britain, for example, has boycotted England's Holocaust Memorial Day for the last decade. The MCB's representatives have protested that Holocaust commemoration ignores other human rights abuses around the world including especially those that they insist are occurring in Palestine.[34] The implication, they claim, is that Jewish lives are more valuable than Muslim lives. This argument in turn feeds into a narrative of Jewish racial supremacy.

Some cultural critics uses the term "Holocaust envy" to describe the resentment, the "morbid passion," which members of such groups express over the amount of attention paid to Jewish victimhood.[35] Writing in the tradition of psychoanalyst Jacques Lacan, cultural critic Gabriel Noah Brahm, Jr., theorizes that anti-Zionists not only resent the "enjoyment" that they perceive Jews draw from the memory of their victimhood, but also believe that Jews have stolen from the world at large the similar enjoyment that others would otherwise enjoy from their suffering.[36]

The alternative has been to globalize and generalize the concept of the "Holocaust," using the term to denote crimes against humanity throughout the world.[37] In this way, the "Holocaust" is transformed from a specific historical event to a universal symbol of human suffering. Thus, some people speak of a "black Holocaust," an "Indian Holocaust," a "Ukrainian Holocaust," and even a "Homocaust," to name just a few. Most of all, activists speak of a "Palestinian Holocaust," aiming to undermine support for the Jewish state by accusing Jews of committing precisely the crimes that were committed against them. This generalization is unnecessary, since another term was coined to do the work that Holocaust minimizers want the word "Holocaust" to do. Specifically, the term "genocide" was coined as a generic term to describe the elimination of any population group, while the term "Holocaust" emerged for the extermination of European Jews between 1938 and 1945.

The "Jew" as "Exceptional Signifier"

Sadly enough, serious thought about anti-Semitism's exceptionality, as it transpires in French philosophical circles and in American academia, can also be invested with deeper antipathies. This is unfortunate because, as we shall see, this problem occurs conspicuously in some works that are, in other respects, promising for an elucidation of this phenomenon. In the philosophy of Alain Badiou, the ongoing debate over the very word "Jew" boils down to a question of "whether or not, in the general field of public intellectual discussion, the word 'Jew' constitutes an exceptional signifier, such that it would be legitimate to make it play the role of a final, or even sacred, signifier."[38] That is to say, this leading French philosopher argues that much public debate about the nature of anti-Semitism turns on whether the term "Jew" should play an exceptional, ultimate, or "sacred" role in Western languages. This proposition, so stated, cannot be reasonably maintained, and Badiou has no difficulty dispatching it, because it makes an extreme caricature out of the homogenist position. What is troubling about this analysis is the direction in which Badiou and his protégés take it.

Badiou's "exceptional signifier" argument provides that the radical evil of the Nazi genocide not only establishes the "Jew" as the archetypal Other, but also insulates the Jewish people from criticism.[39] Thus, Badiou argues that this "exceptional-signifier" argument has been deployed to protect Israel against fallout for its alleged colonialism, militarism, invasion, massacres, and even genocide.[40] The position that Badiou attributes to certain Jewish writers is as easy to reject, even to mock, as any straw man, not only as the symptom of an errant victimology, but also as an inherently anti-egalitarian ideology. Conceptually, it also presents various philosophical problems concerning, for example, the possibility, comprehensibility and speakability of radical evil.[41]

Unfortunately, this characterization of the "exceptional signifier" updates, amplifies, and extends certain traditional anti-Semitic stereotypes. In a nutshell, Badiou's argument boils down to this: since the Holocaust, Jews have monopolized the global supply of moral capital and used this power to exploit the vulnerable Arab minority living among them. This argument relies on stereotypes of the Jew as greedy, conspiratorial, power-hungry, and corrupt. Indeed, it is little more than a dressed-up version of every anti-Semitic diatribe that has distorted the doctrine of chosennness as a petard on which to hoist the Jewish people. There is however also something new at play in the way that Badiou splices these old defamations with newer canards about Jewish colonialism, militarism, and racism.

This is seen even more clearly in the work of Badiou's protégé, Cécile Winter, who contributes an illuminatingly entitled essay to Badiou's *Polemics*: "The Master-Signifier of the New Aryans: What Made the Word 'Jew' into an Arm Brandished Against the Multitude of 'Unpronounceable Names?'"[42] As the title suggests, Winter extends Badiou's analysis to argue that Israeli Jews have exploited the moral power which Nazi criminality imparted to the very name of "Jew," wielding it as a weapon against a disempowered, vulnerable population whose lives (and names) lack meaning in the "Jewish" understanding. Thus Winter argues that the sacralized post-Holocaust name of "Jew" has been used to defend a "colonial situation, a terrible situation, with racist laws, apartheid, colonizers with free rein," et cetera.[43]

In identifying contemporary "Jews" as "new Aryans," Winter (and Badiou) take yet another step, justifying the tendency of among some progressives to castigate Jews for their putative "hyper-whiteness." Winter argues that Holocaust memorialization in works such as Claude Lanzmann's *Shoah* documentary functions as a "transcendental overqualifier," which shapes the way in which the name of "Jews" is understood, marking Jews as either more or less than human. The function of this argument is to fuse traditional anti-Jewish stereotypes with qualities associated with the iniquities of white supremacy and colonialism. In this way, Badiou and Winter's treatment of the name of the "Jew" symbolically connects historical anti-Jewish canards with the symbolic equivalents of the same despised qualities that we observed in our consideration of the anti-Semitic imaginary. This is the logical end-point of certain critiques of homogenism.

Anti-Semitism as a Nodal Point

There is a third possibility, which is that anti-Semitism is neither a discrete phenomenon nor a mere generic manifestation. Rather, anti-Semitism may be the paradigmatic case of a broader ideological structure that it makes possible. In this argument, anti-Semitism is the nodal point that quilts together a multitude of proto-ideological elements or floating signifiers and fixes their meaning.[44] Slavoj Žižek, Ernesto Laclau, and Chantal Mouffe have developed this idea of ideological nodal points, drawing on the psychoanalytic work of Jacques Lacan and the linguistics of Ferdinand Saussure, to explain how meaning is established within the free flow of signification by certain privileged signifiers that fix meaning within a signifying chain.[45] Žižek explains that ideology consists of a multitude of elements that may be defined in various ways. He has cogently described the central role that anti-Semitism has traditionally played in uniting these elements, even if he has failed to grasp the similar role that anti-Zionism has played.

The "nodal points" in an ideological field fix their meaning and tie them together in a manner that appears coherent. Žižek provides the clearest explanation of how this is done:

> Ideological space is made of non-bound, non-tied elements, 'floating signifiers', whose very identity is 'open', overdetermined by their articulation in a chain with other elements—that is, their 'literal' signification depends on their metaphorical surplus-signification. *Ecologism*, for example: its connection with other ideological elements is not determined in advance; one can be a state-oriented ecologist (if one believes that only the intervention of a strong state can save us from catastrophe), a socialist ecologist (if one locates the source of merciless exploitation of nature in the capitalist system), a conservative ecologist (if one preaches that man must again become deeply rooted in his native soil), and so on; *feminism* can be socialist, apolitical; even *racism* could be elitist or populist . . . The quilting performs the totalization by means of which this free floating of ideological elements is halted, fixed—that is to say, by means of which they become parts of the structured network of meaning.[46]

To recognize that anti-Semitism is a "nodal point" is to observe that it gives specificity to related ideological elements while giving unity to an assemblage of otherwise unrelated political stances.

This observation helps us to understand how anti-Semitism has functioned, at various times and places, as a cultural code for resistance to a broader range of social developments. For example, nineteenth-century European anti-Semitism functioned as a code for the political identity of those who opposed modernity, while twenty-first-century right-wing Hungarian anti-Semitism serves as a code for opposition to parliamentary democracy.[47] In the same way, contemporary left-wing anti-Israelism serves as a code for opposition to globalism, Americanism, or Western liberalism.[48] In each case, anti-Semitism has sutured a broad range of hostilities.

Anti-Semitism serves as a "nodal point" in the sense that it provides a central inexplicable figure by means of which everything else can be explained. "All comes from the Jew," as Édouard Drumont wrote in a bestselling nineteenth-century tract, and "all returns to the Jew."[49]

Similarly, in Nazi ideology, the "Jew" was seen as the central evil figure who "pulls the strings" behind the scenes to create all of the world's great problems, from social disintegration to economic crisis to moral decadence.[50] In the same way, the ideology of contemporary Muslim anti-Semitism sees the Jews as the source of all supposed catastrophes, even those that appear to be entirely unrelated, such as Marxism, psycholanalysis, materialism, pornography, sociology, sexual permissiveness, and the degradation of morals.[51] "There is no disaster in the world that was not caused by the Jews," wrote journalist Safaa Saleh in 2011 in the Egyptian government newspaper *Al-Gumhouriyya*.[52]

In the same manner, the ideology of anti-Israelism has fixed otherwise free-floating elements of the contemporary global left. Anti-Zionism has been closely related to elements within a diverse set of intellectual currents, ranging from Third Worldism and Islamism to Marxism, post-Marxism, post-colonialism, postmodernism, multi-culturalism, and even certain strains of feminism.[53] Such intellectual trends have helped to form the intellectual and political identities of at least the last two generations of Western academics, especially in the humanities and social sciences.[54] Ernest Sternberg explains the phenomenon in his classic article on "Purifying the World." Echoing the old joke about Jews and bicyclists, Sternberg asks, "Why Israel?" The clue, Sternberg suggests, is in the astonishing variety of groups held together in the new anti-Western coalition: post-Christian humanitarians, third-worldists, Islamists, Arab Nationalists, and anti-globalizers of various sorts. "This," Sternberg explains, "is the movement's ticklish problem: how to keep so much diversity in check. If Empire is too abstract as a nemesis, and the United States seems too formidable, Israel represents a scapegoat manageable enough in size, and devilish enough in the popular imagination."[55]

5

Jewish Identity and the Figural Jew

Jewish Identity and Anti-Semitism

Jews form a diverse group, and they may face disadvantages because they are also gay, communist, old or disabled, et cetera. For this reason, it is generally said that anti-Semitism must be directed against "Jews *as Jews*," rather than as individuals or as members of the various other groups to which individual Jews may belong. Accordingly, anti-Semitism is frequently defined as hostility toward Jews *as* Jews, that is to say, *because* they are *Jews*, or because of their (actual or perceived) *Jewish* race or religion.[1] In one influential formulation, for example, Charles Glock and Rodney Stark define anti-Semitism as "the hatred and persecution of Jews as a group; not the hatred of persons who happen to be Jews, but rather the hatred of persons *because* they are Jews."[2] This formulation has been widely influential, because it serves the important conceptual function of screening out certain hostilities that are not anti-Semitic. At the same time, as we will see, it has important drawbacks. In particular, it raises complicated questions of causation and Jewish identity, and it is in tension with the notion that anti-Semitism is based on misperceptions. These challenges have led some to argue that anti-Semitism must be directed not at actual Jews but rather at a distorted image of Jewish identity. This turns out to be a helpful idea, but it too has conceptual limitations. As we will see, the best understandings of anti-Semitism focus instead less on the actual or perceived character of Jewish identity and more on the process by which Jews are worked up into the distorted figure of "the Jew."

Jews as Jews

The 1990s debate over multiculturalism illustrates how the Jews-as-Jews formulation can be used to screen actual examples of anti-Semitism from their simulacra. During that period, especially in legal academia, multiculturalist supporters of affirmative action argued that traditional, seemingly race-neutral ideas about merit were tacitly based on pernicious racial stereotypes or assumptions. Constitutional law scholars Daniel Farber and Suzanna Sherry counter-argued however that multiculturalism is itself implicitly based on invidious stereotypes. Specifically, they argued that those who insist that "merit" is an illusory concept or a racist construction can ultimately offer no explanation for disproportionate Jewish success other than to fall back on anti-Semitic stereotypes about, for example, Jewish power and conspiracy.[3]

For present purposes, what is most interesting about Farber and Sherry's argument is the definition of anti-Semitism on which they tacitly rely, rather than whether they are right or wrong about multiculturalism. Specifically, they argue that radical multiculturalism is anti-Semitic because it has a hidden adverse impact on Jews. "Although anti-Semitism was traditionally based on religious aversion," they write, "modern anti-Semitism more often takes the form of rejection of Jewish success, and radical multiculturalism falls into this latter category."[4] In other words, radical multiculturalism is anti-Semitic because it is committed to propositions that are inimical to the interests of most Jews. This notion is loosely analogous to the concept of "disparate impact," which provides that it is discriminatory to adopt a policy that appears neutral on its face but that adversely impacts a particular minority group.

Farber and Sherry's definition of anti-Semitism is unsatisfactory, because it does not provide an adequate basis for the normative sting that we expect the term "anti-Semitism" to carry. Some groups invariably fare better than others under virtually any public policy, and the term "anti-Semitism" is inappropriate for a policy that impacts Jews only incidentally. "Progressive taxation is bad for WASPs," as Edward Rubin responded to Farber and Sherry, while "health care funding is bad for Christian Scientists, cuts in public education are bad for African-Americans, closing a military base in Minnesota is bad for Norwegians."[5] An action or policy cannot be characterized as anti-Semitic merely because it is bad for the Jews. Similarly, as Helen Fein has argued, it is unhelpful to classify as anti-Semitic actions that affect the interest of Jewish people as students, consumers, tenants, or residents of particular neighborhoods merely because those groups include many Jews.[6] Thus, Fein rightly concluded that controversies over affirmative action programs, the price of kosher meat, licensing criteria, housing policies, et cetera, might impair the interests of individual Jews as students, consumers, professionals, or tenants without being instances of anti-Semitism. In other words, they do not harm Jews *as Jews*.

In some cases, the causal relationship may be harder to ascertain. Indeed, it is often concealed or denied even when it is unquestionably present. This can be seen, for example, among those writers who have distinguished between the Jewish religion, which they claim to find unobjectionable, and the practices of Jewish exploiters whom they abhor. Since anti-Semites routinely distinguish between "good Jews," whom they purport to support, and "bad Jews," whom they oppose, this pattern arises repeatedly in anti-Jewish discourse. For example, Wilhelm Hasselman, a nineteenth-century follower of German Social Democratic Party founder Ferdinand Lasalle, exemplified the practice when he insisted that "we shall never object to the paring of the flesh in the Judaic rite of circumcision, while strenuously opposing the Jewish habit of paring of the ducats."[7] In the Soviet Union, especially during the late Stalinist period, "anti-Zionist" campaigns maintained the official illusion that the communist regime was opposed only to Zionism and not to Jews *as Jews*.[8] Similarly, many writers today insist that their opposition to Israeli practices should not be confused with hostility to the Jewish people. Like the Soviet propagandists and German Social Democrats discussed above, they insist that they abhor only Jews as *exploiters*, not Jews *as Jews*.

This issue frequently arises for the State of Israel. For example, does the United Nations condemn Israel *as a Jewish state* or merely as an alleged violator of international human rights norms that happens to be Jewish? For the most part, the U.N. phrases its resolutions in the language of human rights, rather than the language of racial or religious bias. Nevertheless, the nature and frequency of its actions has led many observers, including the United States Department of State, to conclude that anti-Semitism lies beneath the surface. Between 2001 and September 2006, the U.N. General Assembly's plenary and main committees adopted over 120 human rights–related resolutions focused on the State of Israel while adopting only ten resolutions about North Korea, Burma, and Sudan put together.[9] For many years, the U.N. Human Rights Council and its predecessor agency have instituted a separate permanent agenda item that permits Israel's enemies to charge numerous violations against it. No other country can face more than one such resolution each year. Many nations adopt a practice of voting on principle against any resolution that criticizes any specific country unless that country is Israel, in which case they generally vote in favor. Moreover, the U.N. General Assembly established several whole bureaucracies that have the sole mandate of singling out Israel for human rights violations.[10] At the same time, the General Assembly adopted several resolutions condemning traditional forms of anti-Semitism, such as Holocaust denial. Nevertheless, no other United Nations member state is as consistently singled out for disparagement as Israel is.[11] The volume and intensity of ill-treatment suggests that the United Nations is motivated by something other than Israel's actual conduct. Indeed, the facts presented above are drawn from a U.S. State Department report on *Contemporary Global Anti-Semitism*.[12] Moreover, even some United Nations officials have acknowledged that their record on anti-Semitism has at times "fallen short" of its ideals."[13]

Jews as a Normative Category

A harder challenge is to say what is meant by facing hostility "as a *Jew*." There is no fixed, stable, and generally agreed upon notion of what it means to be Jewish. For this reason, it is famously difficult to say exactly what it means to be targeted as a *Jew*. Imre Kertész once wrote that "the name or label 'Jew' is an unambiguous designation only in the eyes of anti-Semites."[14] The Jews-as-Jews approach runs into trouble when it is applied to attributes that may or may not be centrally identified with what it means to be a Jew. This is true because of the famous difficulties involved in defining what it means to be Jewish.

To begin with, is Jewish identity a religion, race, or ethnicity?[15] This problem is analogous to our earlier discussion of whether anti-Semitism is racial or religious in character, but it is not the same. Let us assume, for example, that Jewishness is defined strictly in terms of religion. What then would we then make of the racist who abuses Jewish people based on their supposed membership in a Jewish "race"? Based on this assumption, a purely racial bias would not be directed against the Jew as Jew, since Jewishness *ex hypothesi* is strictly religious. Alternatively, we can assume, for purposes of discussion, that a Jew is defined in racial terms, as members of a perceived racial group. In this case, how would we view someone who despises Jews for their rejection of Jesus? Does she despise the Jew as a Jew or as something other than what it means to be Jewish? Must anti-Semitism, to be identified as such, be directed at Jews *as Jews* understood along whichever axis is considered determinative?

There is no Jew who counts as fully Jewish under all putative criteria for Jewishness. Consider, for example, the opposed arguments of Alain Badiou and novelist A. B. Yehoshua, who have maintained respectively that virtually no Israeli can be counted as a Jew and that no non-Israeli can be so counted. Badiou maintains that one should not be counted as Jewish if one does not meet certain moral and political standards of Jewishness, and he argues that Israelis fail to meet them.[16] As an anti-Zionist, Badiou insists that Israelis cannot be considered "Jews" because they do not meet his external standards for Jewishness. Badiou, it would seem, has divided the world into "good" and "bad" Jews, and slotted virtually all "Israelis" into the "bad" category, insinuating that they are so bad as not to be Jews at all. This is a common strategy among progressive European intellectuals, who frequently sort the Jewish community into "good Jews" who are willing to castigate Israel for its putative sins and "bad Jews" who defend the Jewish state.[17] The "bad Jews" are the majority who identify with their people, defend the Jewish state's right to self-defense, criticize Israel's enemies, and fear the global resurgence of anti-Semitism.[18] Thus, Badiou argues that Israel is, in the title of one of his polemical articles, "the Country in the World where there are the Fewest Jews."[19]

Yehoshua conversely has argued that there are no true Jews *outside* of Israel, since participation in Israeli collectivity is, in his conception, an essential component of Jewish identity.[20] Like Badiou, Yehoshua has divided the Jewish community into *good* and *bad* Jews, the latter not counting as Jews at all. In Yehoshua's argument, one can discern echoes of the Jewish self-hatred that had entered early secular Zionism, generating claims that *Galut* Jews were morally reprehensible, that *diasporic* life is immoral, and that assimilation to non-Jewish cultures reflects spiritual weakness.[21] Curiously, both authors draw the line at roughly the same place, although they affix the true "Jew" label to the opposite side of the line. Yehoshua's conception is as Zionist as Badiou's is anti-Zionist, dismissing Jewish Americans for example as "partial Jews." Under Badiou and Yehoshua's logic, those who hate Israeli or diasporic Jews (respectively) would not be labeled "anti-Semitic," because these "Jews" are not normatively Jewish by their standards. In other words, one can hate them as Israelis or Americans but not as Jews.

Badiou and Yehoshua are both wrong because they have developed implausible exclusionary conceptions of Jewishness. Yehoshua is wrong because Jewish identity has developed too variously throughout the diaspora to be limited to his narrowly Zionist conception. In this respect, Judith Butler (of all people) is partly right to admonish us to "remember that the identification of Jewishness with Israel, implied by the formulation that maintains that to criticize Israel is effectively to engage in anti-Semitism, elides the reality of a small but dynamic peace movement in Israel itself."[22] To be sure, Butler's argument employs a straw man argument about all criticisms of Israel, and one can quibble with her about the size or dynamism of Israel's "peace movement." The kernel of truth in her argument however is that there are too many authentic ways of being Jewish for Jewish identity to be strait-jacketed into one Zionist or anti-Zionist perspective.[23]

Badiou is wrong because he insists that the only true Jews are those who engage in self-criticism. This argument has a lengthy pedigree but not a distinguished one. The basic argument is reflected in Camillo

Berneri's 1935 volume on *Le juif antisemite,* which sarcastically explains how the Catholic Church has used Jewish self-critics to establish the fallacy of Jewish faith:

> The Jewish convert and supporter of the Inquisition should not be considered fundamentally antisemitic. To the contrary, if one accepts that the Inquisition was, in the most profound spiritual manifestation, an act of love (eternal punishment being avoided thanks to the temporary suffering of a painful death) then the converted Jew is, in a certain sense, showing a sense of attachment to his old coreligionists by causing their persecution.[24]

There are many exclusionist forms of Zionism, and they draw lines in different places. For Yehoshua, the key question is whether one lives in Israel. For other exclusionary Zionists, what is decisive is that one defend Israel against criticism, or at least that one not engage in certain kinds of criticism of Israel, such as those that they consider to be anti-Semitic. In response to such claims, Judith Butler asks, reasonably enough, "What do we make of Jews, including myself, who are emotionally invested in the state of Israel, critical of its current form, and call for a radical restructuring of its economic and juridical basis precisely because they are so invested?"[25] At a minimum, we must concede that they are Jews, no less than those who oppose them, and that they are equally vulnerable to the sting of anti-Semitism, even when they allow themselves to be its unwitting facilitators.

Pathological Jealousy and the Cheating Spouse

Butler errs again, albeit in a way that usefully illuminates an important aspect of anti-Semitic ideology, when she takes her argument a step further, as an argument about the meaning or scope of anti-Semitism. Butler argues, with obvious exaggeration, that it has become nearly or completely impossible to criticize Israel without being labeled anti-Semitic.[26] In fact, as Butler's own experience demonstrates, what is increasingly difficult is to criticize Israel without being afforded a large lecture hall, publication in the *London Review of Books,* and a choice of publishing contracts. Butler's extreme formulation is over-simplistic, existing primarily as a straw man argument for Israel's critics to beat, rather than an actual position advanced by serious commentators. Indeed, the equation that every criticism of Israel is anti-Semitic is not only a straw man argument, but also a rhetorical gambit by anti-Zionists that gains its resonance from historical stereotypes of Jewish conspiratorial power.

Although the notion that all criticisms of Israel are anti-Semitic exists primarily as a straw man, it has gained extraordinarily widespread currency. Anthony Julius dispatched the argument nicely in the recent case of *Fraser v. University and College Union*, although the tribunal ultimately ruled against his client.[27] In his closing argument, Julius described his cross-examination of Alan Whitaker, president of the UCU: "I asked: Do you know of any member of the union who actually takes that view—that any criticism of Israel is anti-Semitic? And he paused, and then said: "No.""[28] In this way, it is common for those who minimize contemporary anti-Semitism to repeat the any-criticism-of-Israel canard as if by reflex. When subject to the penalty of perjury, some who take Butler's position will concede that they are rebutting an argument that no one actually advances.

Nevertheless, Butler fails, rather astonishingly, to defeat this straw man, insisting implausibly that it is impossible to do so. Specifically, she insists that there is only one way to beat the argument that all criticism of Israel is anti-Semitic, and it is surprisingly indirect: "The *only way* to fight against the equation of criticism of Israel with anti-Semitism is to clearly and repeatedly, and with strong collective support, show both that the criticism of Israel is just and that all forms of anti-Semitism, along with any other racism, are absolutely unacceptable."[29] This claim is patently false. There are many ways to "fight" this equation, which is so simplistic and implausible that no serious commentator actually endorses it, although a small army of commentators has risen up to defeat it.

It is also false in the sense that Butler's argument does not disprove the equation (if any disproof were necessary). Butler instead makes the mistake of assuming that a statement cannot be anti-Semitic if it is true. In fairness to Butler, her mistake is quite common. Indeed, some definitions provide that anti-Semitism consists, at least in part, of "beliefs about Jews . . . that are both false and hostile."[30] Indeed, this has been promulgated by distinguished experts as a self-evident axiom, *to wit*: "[W]hat is true cannot be anti-Semitic."[31] In fact, the truth of a proposition (whether about Israel, Jews, or anything at all) does not determine whether it is anti-Semitic, since a factually correct statement may be uttered for hateful reasons, advanced together with untrue statements, or evaluated by double standards. One who claims that members of a particular racial group are malodorous cannot defeat the charge of racism on the grounds that group members really do smell foul; nor should those who wish to combat this racist perception join issue on the scent of the target group. The question, instead, is whether the claim is motivated by prejudice, whether it advances prejudicial stereotypes or memes, and whether it foreseeably harms the target group.

The anti-Semite's claims about Jews may occasionally be true, just as every broken clock is right twice per day. This does not render the anti-Semite less anti-Semitic any more than it makes the clock less broken. Jacques Lacan once observed that a jealous husband may suspect that his wife is engaged in adultery. If his fears turn out to be true, his jealousy may nevertheless still be pathological. Lacan is right for the same reason that a person may be paranoid even if others truly are out to get him. Given the frailty of human nature, every shrewd bigot will occasionally identify an actual weakness in his despised group, but this does not disprove the fact of his bigotry. This is not to suggest that any of Butler's statements about Israel are true but only that it does not matter either way.

A factually true claim may, for several reasons, emerge from a false ideological construct. A form of consciousness may be false in that it proceeds from a perverse ulterior motive, incorporates false beliefs, functions in a reprehensible way, or has a morally blame-worthy origin.[32] In this way, the Nazis' factually accurate claims would be anti-Semitic because they sustain the Nazis' ideological position.[33] For example, Adolf Hitler's claim that Jews were disproportionately represented in mid-century Viennese sex industries was unquestionably anti-Semitic, regardless of the representation of Jews in those trades, because his claim emerges organically from his ideology of Jewish iniquity.[34] If one could prove that Jews actually were overrepresented in this area, it would not absolve Hitler of anti-Semitism. American anti-Semites frequently insist that Jews controlled most Hollywood studios, and their pronouncements are no less anti-Semitic for being true. Even truthful claims may be invidious, especially when they employ double standards, ignore contextual information, or are intended to inflict harm. "Every tool is a weapon," as Ani DiFranco teaches us, "if you hold it right."[35]

Indeed, Hitler's assertion would be anti-Semitic even if it did not emerge from his particular ideology of anti-Semitism. When hatred of Jews arises from unrealistic perceptions, and it sustains an ideology of Jew-hatred, it should not matter whether that hatred arises from any particular perception of the "Jew." If a factually accurate Nazi claim about Jews were based on prejudice, then we should call it anti-Semitic even if it were at odds with Nazi ideology. Thus, for example, if a Nazi said that Jews had historically become usurers because of their religion, then this statement would have some truth to it (since Christians were forbidden from lending in medieval Europe, while lending was one of the few occupations that Jews were permitted), but it would also be anti-Semitic (to the extent that it is based on factually unrealistic religious stereotypes about unethical business practices), even though it conflicts with Nazi ideology (since it explains purported Jewish transgressions in religious rather than racial terms).[36] In other words, it is not based on particular Nazi perceptions of the "Jew," although it emerges from other erroneous perceptions about Jews. In a broader sense, we could say that it sustains an anti-Semitic ideology even if it does not support the particular ideology of Nazism.

In order to address the theoretical possibility that some anti-Jewish attitudes may be deserved, the definition of anti-Semitism must exclude realistic assumptions but not insist on falsehood. False assumptions may be understood roughly as assertions that are based on the same assumptions as those used to describe the in-group and its members.[37] For example, long-standing survey measures of American anti-Semitism may falsely indicate anti-Semitism among people who respond affirmatively to questions like: "Do Jews control or play an important part in the movie industry?" The problem with using an affirmative answer to this question as an indicium of anti-Semitism is that happens to be correct.[38] One would have to be overcome by political correctness not to notice the disproportionate representation that Jewish Americans enjoy in Hollywood. At the same time, a particular speaker's need to express these views, especially if obsessive, may be anti-Semitic.[39] To qualify as "anti-Semitic," negative statements about Jews as Jews must be based upon erroneous assumptions that flow from the application of false assumptions and double standards. It is only with this qualification that anti-Semitism may be considered to be a prejudice, that is to say, a distorting view of a group maintained without regard to actual experience of the group or its members.

Jews as *Not* Jews

At this point, we may be tempted to define anti-Semitism as a set of negative attitudes, ideologies and practices directed at Jews *as Jews*, individually or collectively, and based on unrealistic assumptions. The problem with this developing definition however is that its elements are in tension with one another. On the one hand, this definition asserts that anti-Semitism must be directed at "Jews as Jews." On the other, it insists that this animus is based on unrealistic assumptions concerning Jews. The question, then, is whether anti-Semitism is directed at *Jews* or whether it is directed at *erroneous assumptions, beliefs, and images about Jews*.

While anti-Semitism is certainly directed at Jews as Jews, it occurs in a context in which Jews are perceived as being something other than what they actually are. In this sense, it may be maintained that anti-Semitism is directed not at Jews as Jews, but rather at Jews as *not* Jews. In other words, anti-Semitism is focused on what Arendt called "the phantom of *the* Jew."[40] In Brian Klug's formulation, anti-Semitism could be defined as "a form of hostility towards Jews as Jews, in which Jews are perceived as something other than what they are. Or more succinctly: hostility towards Jews as not Jews. For the 'Jew' towards whom the antisemite feels hostile is not a real Jew at all. Thinking that Jews are really 'Jews' is precisely the core of antisemitism."[41] The original insight here is Jean-Paul Sartre's: it "is . . . the *idea* of the Jew that one forms for himself which would seem to determine history, not the 'historical fact' that produces the idea."[42] This idea is reflected in Israel Gutman's "anti-Semitism" entry for the *Encyclopedia of the Holocaust*: "Throughout the generations, concepts, fantasies and accusations have stuck to the term [anti-Semitism] that portrayed a negative cognitive and emotional web, at times independent of Jewish society as it was fashioned and existed in realty."[43]

The larger problem with the Jews-as-Jews formulation is that it does not account for the irrational quality of anti-Semitism. In his classic exposition, Gordon Allport defined "prejudice" not just as thinking ill of others but as "thinking ill of others *without sufficient warrant.*" In other words, it is "a feeling, favorable or unfavorable, toward a person or thing, prior to, or not based on actual experience."[44] This insight underlies the quip, variously attributed to H. L. Mencken, George Orwell, and Hungarian nobleman Joseph Eötvösz, that "an anti-Semite is someone who dislikes Jews more than is absolutely necessary." This witticism draws some of its sting from the fact that anti-Semites invariably insist that their enmity is entirely rational.[45]

In order to accommodate Allport's insight, not to say Mencken, Orwell, or Eötvösz, the definition of anti-Semitism must be restricted to *unwarranted* animus or animus which is not based on *actual experience*. As Gavin Langmuir explained, "the quality of hostility against Jews cannot be determined by premises about Jews, for it is a characteristic of the mentality of non-Jews, not of Jews, and it is determined, not by the objective reality of Jews, but by what the symbol 'Jews' has signified for non-Jews."[46] In this way, some definitions have stressed the misperceptions upon which anti-Jewish animus is based. Thus, for example, historian David Berger defines anti-Semitism as: "(1) Hostility toward Jews as a group which results from no legitimate cause or greatly exceeds any reasonable, ethical response to genuine provocation; or (2) a pejorative perception of Jewish physical or moral traits which is either utterly groundless or a result of irrational generalization and exaggeration."[47] One may think of anti-Semitism as the practice of confusing Jews with their false images. "Thinking that Jews are really 'Jews'," in this formulation, "is precisely the core of anti-Semitism."[48] In a similar formulation, it has been argued that anti-Semitism consists of the difference between the real Jew and the imagined "Jew."[49] Dina Porat has illustrates this position by contrasting the pitiful state of European Jews at the outset of World War II with the Nazis' perception of omnipotent Jewish power.[50]

This emendation excludes some attitudes and conduct that is directed at Jews as Jews but which is nevertheless based on actual experience. For example, some Christians harbor negative attitudes toward Judaism on the grounds that Jews rejected Jesus as their savior. These Christians may urge Jews to convert to Christianity and even, in extreme cases, view Judaism as an enemy of the Church. Such attitudes are not necessarily anti-Semitic, because they are based on the actual experience, rather than *chimerica*.[51] In the same way, some Palestinian Arabs may despise Zionist Jews because they view Zionism as directly opposed to the interests of Arab nationalism.[52] To the extent that resistance to Israel is based on actual conflict over land, resources, or treatment of populations, it does not properly fall within the ambit of anti-Semitism per se (although it may come to incorporate anti-Semitic stereotypes and defamations over time). Intuitively, it seems awkward to conflate anti-Semitism with hostility that is based either on interpersonal conflict or accurate assessments. Hostility against Jews that is based on intergroup conflict can be distinguished from animus that is based on prejudice, stereotypy, and the like.[53]

This distinction is important because many forms of conflict may be resolvable through negotiation and mediation, but those that are based on deeper animus tend to resist this kind of resolution. This observation is implicit in sociologist Melvin Tumin's definition: "We mean by anti-Semitism . . . that sentiment or action which maligns or discriminates against persons called Jewish on the ground that, being Jewish, they possess certain undesirable features."[54] A Palestinian activist who has grown to despise Jews for reasons relating only to the Arab-Israel conflict should not, on this basis alone, be considered an anti-Semite, unless we conclude that the conflict is based primarily on his animus toward the Jewish character of the state.[55] This is implicit in the notion that anti-Semitism is directed at Jews as *not*-Jews.

Anti-Semitism and Ethnic Conflict

Based on this rationale, some people insist that Arab anti-Semitism is not a cause of the Middle East conflict, maintaining instead that the Middle East conflict is the cause of Arab and Muslim anti-Semitism.[56] This viewpoint is widely shared in some parts of Europe. For example, according to a 2007 Anti-Defamation League survey, 42% of Dutch respondents believe that the violence directed against Jews in the Netherlands results from anti-Israel sentiment as opposed to anti-Jewish feelings.[57] Those who take this position sometimes observe that reported incidents of anti-Semitism tend to increase in frequency and intensity during times of strife in the Middle East. Some commentators go further, arguing that this anti-Israel sentiment is due to blameworthy Israeli conduct.

In recent years, French authorities have portrayed violent anti-Jewish assaults by Muslims in France as inter-ethnic conflicts, even during periods when no Jewish violence against Muslims has been reported in that country, and even when individual French Jews have been violently attacked.[58] Badiou has tried to justify this position, arguing that what young French Muslims feel is not anti-Semitism, but rather an understandable hostility toward "the position of the Jews in France" based on the support of Jewish communal organizations for Israel.[59] Similarly, some German scholars have refused to participate in academic studies of Arab anti-Semitism unless the studies assume that Arab perceptions of Jews are the "mirror image" of Jewish perceptions of Arabs.[60] There are various reasons for this, especially in the European context. Many commentators are reluctant to attribute prejudice to Muslim immigrants who have themselves experienced persecution. This reluctance may be due to fear of stigmatizing a persecuted group, fear of being accused of prejudice, and fear of favoring (or being perceived as favoring) one side (and worse, the politically incorrect side) of the Israeli-Palestinian conflict.

Jewish Collective Responsibility

Even if some French Muslims hold French Jews collectively responsible for the actions of the Israeli government, rather than simply hating them as "Jews," their actions nevertheless have an ugly historical pedigree. Diasporic Jews are often seemingly held collectively responsible for Israel, as for example in the Toulouse massacre. The attribution of collective responsibility has deep historical roots that can be traced, most significantly, to the deicide myth in Christianity. It can also be seen in the tendency of medieval and early modern Europeans to associate Jews with the monarchs who both protected and exploited them. If gentiles came to resent the monarchy, they often expressed their wrath through attacks on Jews.[61] In more recent years, the collective responsibility problem can be seen in the attitudes of some of Israel's antagonists toward individual Jews who may have little or no personal connection to that state other than the fact of their Jewishness.

This can be seen, for example, in Raymond Barre's famous reaction to the terrorist bombing of a synagogue in the Rue Copernic in Paris on October 3, 1980. The bomb was intended to explode as Jewish worshipers exited the building but in fact detonated prematurely, killing four people, of whom two were non-Jewish passers-by, and injuring ten. Barre, then the prime minister of France, appeared on television to express his outrage at this "odious act." "They aimed at the Jews," Barre exclaimed, "and they hit innocent Frenchmen."[62] The prime minister's intended meaning was clear: Arab perpetrators had selected a Jewish target in furtherance of their participation in the Arab-Israeli conflict. But his unstated implication was equally transparent: Parisian Jews are neither French nor innocent.[63] As one journalist interpreted Barre's remarks in *Libération*, "Those passing in the streets were French and innocent, those praying in the synagogue were strangers and guilty."[64] Barre may not have intended to convey this impression, but this meaning nonetheless was clearly and widely discerned.[65] No matter how French Jews may feel after generations of Parisian citizenship, their Jewishness renders them ineradicably foreign and worse—inscribes them with culpability for whatever actual or imagined transgressions other Jews may commit.

Some have argued that Jews may be held responsible for Israel's actions for reasons having nothing to do with anti-Semitism. Under one argument, Jews may be held collectively responsible because they have a *right of return* to Israel. This argument takes for granted that it is acceptable to hold all Israelis collectively responsible for the actions of their government. To the extent that this extraordinary proposition is not applied to all other governments, or at least to all other representative democracies, it is an example of *double standards*. Few serious scholars would argue that it is appropriate to hold all Americans responsible for the actions of, for example, the George W. Bush or Barack Obama administrations. Under this argument, it might be appropriate to punish Americans, regardless of their personal views or individual culpability, for arguable human rights violations at Abu Ghraib or with respect to the National Security Administration's data-gathering program.

The Empirical Evidence

As an empirical matter, recent research indicates that those young French Muslims who hold negative attitudes toward Jews generally do not in fact see French Jews as proxies for Israel. They hate Jews for being Jews regardless of any connection they may have to Israel. Günther Jikeli, who has conducted the most systematic sociological interviews with young Muslim men in France, Germany, and England, identifies the following dialogue with a 25-year-old Berliner of Turkish origin as representative of the attitudes that young European Muslim men express toward Israelis and Jews in formal studies:

INTERVIEWER: And then you'd rather say that because of the [Middle East] conflict you have a problem with Israelis?
ÜMIT: No, not because of them. As a Muslim you have problems, not with Israelis, [but] with Jews. . . . Because they have been condemned by God.[66]

Participants in Jikeli's studies are often unable to explain their enmity toward Jews, but they portray their community as being unified in these views, which are rooted in chimerical perceptions of Jewish history and identity.[67] Egyptian cleric Muhammad Hussein Yaqub articulated this perspective during a 2009 sermon on Al-Rahma TV:

If the Jews left Palestine to us, would we start loving them? Of course not. We will never love them. Absolutely not. . . . They are enemies not because they occupied Palestine. They would have been enemies even if they had not occupied a thing. . . . You must believe that we will fight, defeat, and annihilate them, until not a single Jew remains on the face of the earth. It is not me who says so. The Prophet said: "Judgment Day will not come until you fight the Jews and kill them."[68]

Given the irrationality of chimerical hatred, the truest explanation of this hatred may be the simplest. Ganesh, a 16-year-old Londoner, explained it this way during his interview: "Jewish people are Jewish, that's why we don't like them."[69]

As this research shows, the appearance of ethnic conflict often masks a deeper anti-Semitic animus. In either of the two cases described above, a European Christian or Arab Muslim would be anti-Semitic to hold individual Jews collectively responsible for the religious or political activities of global or Israeli Jewry. This would almost certainly apply, for example, to the nearly 250 anti-Semitic incidents recorded during a single month in 2009 coinciding with Israel's military operation in Gaza.[70] Moreover, either antagonist may enter the realm of anti-Semitism, regardless of the rationality of their original grievance, if they come to adopt anti-Semitic ideology, perceiving Jews as the figural *Jew*. This can be seen, for example, in the 2004 publication by the Palestinian Ministry of Education of a public school textbook that teaches students that *The Protocols of the Elders of Zion* reveals an actual Jewish plot for world domination.[71]

More generally, there is no plausibility to the argument that hostility toward Israel is primarily a function of political conflict.[72] The ethnic-conflict thesis has always had a geography problem. Some of the most truculent criticisms of Israel in the contemporary Middle East come from countries like Iran that have no border with Israel and no apparent geo-political conflicts with that country. While countries that have real interests opposed to Israel may foster the widespread condemnation of Israel throughout the world, including at the United Nations, this hostility would not have reached current levels if it did not spring from deeper sources. In other words, the use of traditional anti-Semitic stereotypes and defamations is not simply an available choice of epithets to direct at an enemy loathed for unrelated reasons. Rather, it is the sign of a deeper animus. Recent empirical research confirms this suspicion, demonstrating that young European Muslims despise Jewish people because they are Jewish, based on irrational perceptions, rather than because of any association with Israel.

Indeed, the ethnic-conflict thesis, which holds that these incidents lack the hallmarks of ideological hatred, has largely been discredited by empirical research. This can be seen, for example, in French studies that demonstrate the extent to which these incidents are intertwined with classic anti-Semitic discourse and the use of the French term *Juif* as an insult.[73] This can be seen in German studies as well: contemporary Muslim anti-Semitism in that country also bears the hallmarks of racial hatred, rather than ethnic conflict.[74] According to this research, when young European Muslim men justify their hostility toward Jews, whether in France, Germany or England, they tend to fall back on classical stereotypes (e.g., about the wealth and power of the Jews) that cannot be reduced to their perceptions of the Middle East conflict.[75]

Given the pervasiveness of anti-Jewish discourse in the contemporary Middle East, the Palestinian anti-Israel protester regardless of motivation may find it difficult to resist Israel in ways that do not at some point traffic in anti-Semitism. Consider, for example, this representative Gazan music video that was broadcast during Operation Pillar of Defense.[76] "[O] lovers of the trigger," the song goes, "Killing the occupiers is worship that Allah made into law." Under one interpretation, taking the broadcast's timing into account, this line seems to express the Palestinian's deep anger over Israeli mistreatment. The text, however, provides, "Killing Jews is worship that draws us closer." The explicit statement of a religious obligation to kill Jews (not just Israelis or Zionists) suggests something other than just an ordinary regional ethnic or regional conflict. The song continues, "The color of [the Martyr's] blood protects the land. O masked one wearing a *keffiyeh*, terrifying the Jews . . . call out in Zionism's face: 'Muhammad's army has begun to return.'" On its face, this line refers to Zionism, rather than to Jews per se, but it references an ancient incident in which Muhammad's army killed many Jews. In other words, the song reflects an ancient Muslim hatred toward the Jewish people. That ancient hatred surely provides a source for the current conflicts. To the extent that treatment of Jews is based on such chimerical thinking, it is anti-Semitic even if it originates in ethnic conflict.[77]

Kinds of Misperception

Some authorities have argued that it is not sufficient to define anti-Semitism as chimerical hostility toward Jews (i.e., hostility toward Jews-as-not-Jews) unless the hostility is based on a *particular misperception* of Jewish people. Under this logic, some definitions restrict the term "anti-Semitism" to anti-Jewish hostilities that are based on particular misperceptions or distortions inherent in the figural Jew. For these definitions, it is the appearance of the figural "Jew" that alerts us that we are in the presence of anti-Semitism.[78] The figural Jew is often identified in terms of a discrete set of characteristics or stereotypes. For example, the EUMC once defined the figural Jew by seven widely acknowledged characteristics of classical anti-Semitic distortions. The first six are deceptiveness, strangeness, hostility, greed, corruption, and conspiratorial power.[79] To this list, the EUMC adds "Christ-killer," a deicide myth that arguably encompasses all of the others and adds to them a demonic element. Such definitions have significant deficiencies, which will be explored below. Nevertheless, the *particular perception* approach merits detailed consideration because it sheds additional light on the meaning of anti-Semitism. In addition, it yields important insights into peripheral issues such as the anti-Semitic character of Holocaust denial.

As we have seen, critics of the Jewish community frequently charge that Jewish "obsession" with the Holocaust has been self-absorbed, self-righteous, aggressive, and uncharitable. In a pointed rejoinder, Holocaust scholar Alvin Rosenfeld observed if they also add "venal," they have reiterated "the profile of the Ugly Jew in classic anti-Semitic" discourse.[80] As Rosenfeld's cutting reply suggests, the chimerical conception of the figurative Jew can been seen frequently in political contestations surrounding the use and abuse of Holocaust memory. Nowhere is this truer than in Holocaust denial. This appearance of the figural "Jew" is the key to understanding the extraordinary body of work that denies existence of facts that are so patently correct. The point here is not merely that Holocaust deniers tend to be extreme anti-Semites who camouflage their hateful ideology behind a patina of scholarship.[81] Nor is it merely that Holocaust denial tends to correlate with neo-fascist political agendas, although it does.[82] Rather, it is that Holocaust denial is itself a manifestation of Jew-hatred, an ideology that perpetuates the hatred of Jews-as-not-Jews. The literature of hard-core Holocaust denial participates actively in the creation of the chimerical Jew.[83] Familiar anti-Semitic tropes provide the building blocks of Holocaust denial: the myths of Jewish conspiracy, greed, power, control, deceptiveness, and criminality. Holocaust denial adds several new goals: to eliminate the Jewish people's martyr status, to abolish the Holocaust's uniqueness, to disavow the Jewish claim for the return of confiscated property, and to discredit Jewish acts of commemoration.[84]

In traditional fashion, Holocaust deniers argue that Jews would not be able to perpetrate such a hoax if they did not enjoy influence in the media, higher education, and government.[85]

If there was no Nazi extermination and no death chambers then Jews and Zionists, with the help of Western Allies or communists, undoubtedly perpetrated the hoax of the century.[86] Holocaust denial not only whitewashes Nazi crimes but also maligns Jewry for the hoax itself. In this way, deniers insist that Jews were not victims but victimizers.[87] In particular, the victims of this Jewish "hoax" are those persecuted peoples who are unable to garner public sympathy because Holocaust-preoccupation has left too little space for other people's suffering to be addressed.[88] As we have seen, some academics have accused Jews of over-playing the Holocaust in order to justify supposed Israeli crimes. In addition, American university student newspapers have sometimes published Holocaust denial.[89] To accuse Jews of this deception is not merely to destroy Holocaust memory or deny history but more profoundly to reinforce, in contemporary form, the stereotype of Jews as the perpetrators of vast deceptions, conspiracies, and crimes.

Beyond "Jews as Not Jews"

Philosophical Naïveté

As helpful as it can be as an analytical device, the Jews-as-not-Jews formulation has several flaws, some of which are more obvious than others. To begin with, this formulation *essentializes* the "true" Jew. To suggest that the "Jew" misrepresents the (true or authentic) *Jew* is to assume that one can speak meaningfully about what Jews truly are. In its more simplistic formulations, this approach assumes a Jewish essence that precedes the plurality of actual Jewish existences. This is inevitable whenever one defines anti-Semitism as the delta between the stereotypical Jew and the "actual" Jew. Such formulations founder upon the problem that, as we have seen, Jewish identity is irreducibly plural.

Second, the Jews-as-not-Jews formulation assumes, at least in its most common articulations, a naïve empiricism. That is to say, it assumes that one can speak meaningfully of how individual Jews would be absent misrepresentation. If the anti-Semite's conception of the Jew is conceptual, fictional, fantastic, chimerical, and excrescent, then what is the actual Jew? Substantial, actual, authentic, truthful, and normal?[90] The problem is that we can know no Jew other than a conceptual Jew, imagine no Jew other than an imaginary Jew, and speak of no Jew other than a symbolic Jew. The problem is that we have no concepts that can take us beyond conceptualization, no images to take us beyond the imaginary, no words to take us beyond language. The desire to exceed these bounds is based on a wish that one can find a deeper, truer identity that is untainted by language, fables, and chimera. The problem is that such wishes can be expressed only in language, which is always ultimately self-referential, turning us deeper in toward itself and away from the object of our pursuit.

Overstated Stability

Third, to the extent that the Jews-as-not-Jews formulation anchors the definition of anti-Semitism to particular perceptions of the "Jew," it overstates the strength and stability of the figural Jew over time. It is surely not the case that ancient, medieval, and modern perceptions of the Jew have been identical; nor is it the case that anti-Jewish stereotypes have been entirely alike in different parts of the world. For example, the chimerical fantasies of Jewish cannibalism, while prominent in Hellenized Alexandria, are not found in Greek and Roman sources from the same period.[91] Similarly, the medieval image of the wandering Jew was absent in antiquity.[92] Indeed, some commentators have concluded that stereotypes relating to "the Jews" are "mutually contradictory and shift radically from era to era and from location to location."[93] As we have seen, the figural Jew may be seen as capitalist exploiter or as Bolshevik rabble-rouser, as licentious materialist or as effete intellectual, as rootless cosmopolitan or as narrow parochialist, as inconsequential weakling or as global threat. What endures throughout the history of anti-Semitism is not a particular stereotype or figure of the Jew but rather the use of the Jew as a screen on which individuals and societies project their anxieties, especially at times of conflict or turmoil, whether at the time of the

Crusades, the Black Plague, Germany after the first world war, or the Middle East today.

The Trap

The Jews-as-non-Jews formulation creates a particular hazard for those who seek a deep understanding of anti-Semitism. Inevitably, when the Jew is distinguished from the "Jew," the analytical focus of attention is directed in either of two places: either at the false image of the "Jew" or at the "true" or invisible Jew. This conceit confuses the symptom with the disease, operating like legerdemain to misdirect attention from the real action in anti-Semitism, which takes place elsewhere. Specifically, the salient issue in anti-Semitism is the process or performance by which a Jew is rendered as "the *Jew.*" This point is equally obscured by those who focus on Jewry's false images as it is by those who seek to discern the *authentic* Jew behind Jewry's *chimera*.[94]

This point is well illustrated by the Freudian method in the interpretation of dreams. Freud explained, in a later edition to *The Interpretation of Dreams*, that readers tend to fall into two traps.[95] Initially, they focus inordinately on the manifest content of dreams (analogous to the figural Jew), without fully understanding the latent thoughts behind them:

> I used at one time to find it extraordinarily difficult to accustom readers to the distinction between the manifest content of dreams and the latent dream-thoughts. Again and again arguments and objections would be brought up based upon some uninterpreted dream in the form in which it had been retained in the memory, and the need to interpret it would be ignored.[96]

This error consists of mistaking the dream for mere physiological disorder without deeper significance. This is analogous to the scholar who focuses exclusively on the *chimera*, the figural Jew, without grasping the latent thought that lies behind it. "In other words," as Slavoj Žižek explains, "we must accomplish a crucial step towards a hermeneutical approach and conceive the dream as a meaningful phenomenon, as something transmitting a repressed message which has to be discovered by an interpretive procedure."⁹⁷ In the study of anti-Semitism, this means that we must move beyond the *chimera*.

The second trap is to focus on the latent thought (analogous to the actual Jew) without grasping that the real action is the process by which repressed desires work themselves into dreams:

> But now that analysts at least have become reconciled to replacing the manifest dream by the meaning revealed by its interpretation, many of them have become guilty of falling into another confusion which they cling to with an equal obstinacy. They seek to find the essence of dreams in their latent content and in so doing they overlook the distinction between the latent dream-thoughts and the dream-work.⁹⁸

In other words, it is too easy to get caught up in the hidden meaning of the dream. For psychoanalysts, that means being so preoccupied with the content concealed by the dream's manifest content that one misses the process by which this content is turned into the stuff of dreams. By analogy, it is a mistake to focus exclusively on the difference between the actual Jew and the figural Jew.⁹⁹ This will tend to distract us from the more important question, which is the dream-work itself or, analogously, the process by which anti-Semitism works Jews up into the distorted perceptions by which they are misrecognized.

Irrationality of the Figural Jew

Indeed, the Jews-as-Jews formulation is "not yet anti-Semitism proper," as Žižek has cannily observed.¹⁰⁰ To properly reflect the meaning of anti-Semitism, the Slovenian philosopher writes, "we must *invert* the relation and say: they are like that (greedy, intriguing . . .) *because they are Jews*."¹⁰¹ In other words, anti-Semites' perceptions are based neither on actual experience nor on a fixed set of stereotypes, but on a term that yields a fluid range of attributes. That is to say, the signifier "Jew" always means more than the set of properties with which it is associated at any particular time. This finally is why the figural Jew cannot be reduced to the seven properties that the EUMC identified, nor to any other finite list of traits.

What then is the defining feature of the anti-Semitic conception of the Jew, if it is not any of the traits that the EUMC (or anyone else) has identified? The answer is that there is no single defining trait, nor even a finite number of defining traits. Nevertheless, there is an underlying commonality, *to wit:* the surplus meaning, the overdetermination, that continually appears. This surplus meaning of the "Jew" cannot be reduced to a fixed definition but continually attracts mutually incompatible properties. In an awkward attempt to identify the defining element in the anti-Semite's conception of the Jew, Žižek points to what he calls "that unattainable X, . . . what is 'in a Jew more than Jew'."[102]

The explanation for this "X" property is not, as Žižek argues, that "Jew" is a *rigid designator*, at least in any recognizable sense of that term. In philosophy of language, a *rigid designator* is a term that designates the same thing in all possible worlds and never designates anything else. Nothing could be less true of the term "Jew." As we have seen, the word "Jew" can mean many different things: Jewishness may refer to a race, a religion, an ethnicity, et cetera. Moreover, the term is sometimes restricted normatively, as we have seen in the arguments of Badiou and Yehoshua. The defining qualities of Jewishness are sometimes perceived as obstinately fixed but elsewhere as maddeningly transient. But it may be that the true kernel in Žižek's argument is that rigidity adheres in the surplus meaning of the signifier "Jew," rather than in the term itself, the fluctuating properties with which it is associated, or the diverse ranges of persons whom it may be said to designate. Indeed, it is sometimes argued that *irrationality*, whether in the sense of meaninglessness, absurdity, internal consistency, or incongruence with empirical data, is a defining feature of anti-Semitism.[103]

This *irrationality* is such that the name of the "Jew" brings together elements that contradict one another and could never be joined in any real being. Consider, for example, Paul Johnson's observation about the general sense of anti-Semitism's irrationality:

> What strikes the historian surveying anti-Semitism worldwide over more than two millennia is its fundamental irrationality. It seems to make no sense, any more than malaria or meningitis makes sense. In the whole of history, it is hard to point to a single occasion when a wave of anti-Semitism was provoked by a real Jewish threat (as

opposed to an imaginary one). In Japan, anti-Semitism was and remains common even though there has never been a Jewish community there of any size.[104]

The irrational quality of anti-Semitism is conspicuous not only in the sense that the attributes ascribed to Jews are implausible, lacking foundation in fact or experience, but also in the more fundamental sense that they are mutually incompatible. The "Jews" are not only radical insurgents but also capitalist exploiters, religious extremists but also atheistic materialists, rigid nationalists but also rootless cosmopolitans, economic parasites but also financial manipulators, stingy misers but also ostentatious overspenders.[105] In Jonathan Sacks's astute definition, anti-Semitism "exists whenever two contradictory factors appear in combination: the belief that Jews are so powerful that they are responsible for the evils of the world, and the knowledge that they are so powerless that they can be attacked with impunity."[106] The same may be said of the figure of "Israel" as the collective Jew: Israel lacks the essential characteristics of a state, but it also has the power of a strong nation; Israel could not survive without the United States, but at the same time, it can manipulate the United States for its own purposes; Israel is a cowardly, ephemeral entity but it also displays a Nazi arrogance and cruelty.[107]

Zygmunt Bauman argues that the figural Jew has been historically constructed as a "universal viscosity," creating serious problems in a modern era that has been intensely preoccupied with boundary-drawing and boundary-maintenance.[108] He observes that the conceptual Jew is a "semantically overloaded entity," meaning that it conjoins elements that are meant to remain apart, and this unruliness has itself affronted those for whom order and boundary-maintenance are a source of anxiety.[109] Indeed, the conceptual Jew "visualized the horrifying consequences of boundary-transgression, of not remaining fully in the fold, of any conduct short of unconditional loyalty and unambiguous choice; he was the prototype and arch-pattern of all nonconformity, heterodoxy, anomaly and aberration."[110] That is to say, the "Jew" exists as a signifier that is overdetermined by a host of mutually contradictory meanings. Indeed, the very impossibility of these contradictions is itself, for Bauman, a source of the Jewish problem.

Bauman's observation is acute, but it too is subject to what we might call the "irrationality dictum": any vice that can be ascribed to Jews will be so ascribed, but the opposite trait will be attributed to them as well, and it too will be shown to be a vice when pursued by Jews. Thus, if Jews are condemned for transgressing boundaries, they will also be derogated for maintaining impermeable walls. Internationally, this is most prominently seen in the international furor over the Israeli West Bank barrier, but it can be observed more locally too, in petty disputes over Orthodox attempts to install symbolic fences or *eruvim* around "Jewish" neighborhoods. The role that these barriers play in the global unconscious parallels the way in which Jewish insularity is generally perceived. Jews are equally condemned for maintaining walls around their community and for transgressing them. Neither boundary-maintenance (clannishness) nor transgression (Bauman's "universal viscosity") is the source of the antipathy. Rather, either attribute can be invested with the always already extant antipathies that the anti-Semite projects upon the Jew.

Notwithstanding his questionable use of the term *rigid denominator*, Žižek grasps that the irrationality of the signifier "Jew" suggests that, symbolically, the conceptual Jew is something other than the sum of the distorted traits that the anti-Semite associates with that term. Indeed, if this signifier is the quilting point of an ideological signifying chain, then it cannot be reduced to a fixed set of properties. Rather, its role is purely formal or structural. Žižek defines the Jew as "one who is stigmatized with the signifier 'Jew.'"[111] This is overly simplistic, considering the positive connotations that the signifier "Jew" also enjoys. Nevertheless, Žižek is correct to observe that the function of the "Jew" in anti-Semitic discourse should be understood, not as the shifting set of significations that the term has acquired over time, but rather as the structural function that gathers antipathetic meanings to a term that is necessary to the stability of the chain as a whole. While the anchoring point has no essential meaning, it is an element that assigns meaning to many others.[112]

6

Anti-Zionism and Anti-Semitism

IN 1966, THE UNABRIDGED version of *Webster's Third New International Dictionary* provided an eye-catching secondary definition for anti-Semitism. According to *Webster's Third*, anti-Semitism can mean "opposition to Zionism: sympathy with opponents of the state of Israel."[1] This sweeping definition seems to equate virtually any opposition to Zionism, or sympathy with Israel's opponents, with a form of anti-Semitism. It provides the purest or most extreme formulation of the notion that any opposition to Israel, or its policies, may be described as anti-Semitic, since Israel is the Jewish State. In other words, it provides an actual example of the extreme categorical position that we have argued exists primarily as a straw man, embraced by no one.

In defense of *Webster's Third*, many commentators have observed that much post-War anti-Zionism is, as German journalist Henryk Broder famously maintained, "nothing more than a left-wing version of anti-Semitism." This thinly veiled form of anti-Jewish animus enables progressives (even in Germany) to use the same logic, vocabulary, symbolism, and methodology that their parents and grandparents had used to denounce international Jewry while maintaining a good conscience.[2] In this sense, Broder observed over thirty years ago that Israel had become the "Super-Jew," judged less by the standards currently used for other nations than by stereotypes historically used against Jews.

Nevertheless, to contemporary eyes, the *Webster's Third* definition is an astonishing proposition, which equates anti-Zionism more closely with anti-Semitism than even Zionism's most ardent partisans would now support. All other authorities agree that there are some forms of anti-Zionism, and certainly many criticisms of Israel, which are not anti-Semitic. Prior to the establishment of the State of Israel, indeed there were many schools of anti-Zionist thought that competed for the allegiance of world Jewry. These included, for example, classical Reform Judaism, Agudat Yisrael, the Bund, Eastern European Haredim, and liberal assimilationism.[3] Even today, there are some Jewish anti-Zionist traditions that persist, such as the ultra-Orthodox *Neterei Karta*, that are not anti-Semitic.

Spokespersons for Merriam-Webster assert that their definition reflects common usage in the aftermath of World War II. This emphasis on "common usage" is consistent with *Webster's Third*'s general methodology, which was enormously controversial when it first appeared for its rejection of normative lexicography.[4] This was after all the edition that horrified English teachers for including the colloquial *ain't*.[5] In keeping with its purely descriptive approach, the editors' judgment was not that the term is proper but rather that it is widely used. In this sense, it may be fair to conclude that *Webster's Third*'s definition of anti-Semitism ain't any more normative than its similarly nonstandard definitions of other terms. To be sure, the problems with its anti-Semitism definition were less conspicuous when *Webster's Third*'s first appeared, shortly before Israel's military victory in the 1967 war, when the Jewish state was still positively perceived in the Western world as a liberal democratic country whose enemies could reasonably be accused of anti-Semitism.[6] Nevertheless, it is not surprising that the definition is not included in subsequent Merriam-Webster publications.

Nearly four decades after *Webster's Third* appeared, the American Arab Anti-Discrimination Commission launched a petition campaign urging Merriam-Webster to delete its secondary anti-Semitism definition. By 2004, the relationship between anti-Semitism and anti-Zionism had become much more intensely argued, as anti-Semitic incidents and anti-Israel agitation were both spiking in the wake of the Second Intifada. In France, for example, there had only been one recorded incident of anti-Semitic violence in 1998, but there were nine in 1999, accelerating to 116 in 2000 and 725 in 2002 (when 80% of all racist violence in France was directed at Jews).[7] In its public messages, the ADC argued (not unreasonably) that the *Webster's Third* definition is inaccurate and that it impugns the motives of pro-Palestinian activists, undermines efforts toward Middle East peace, and stigmatizes legitimate political activities.[8] Stung by the ADC's criticism, Merriam-Webster declined to defend the *Webster's Third* definition. A Merriam-Webster spokesperson described the definition as "a relic" based on a small number of citations from around 1950 in which anti-Semitism was "linked more or less strongly with opposition to Israel or to Zionism."[9] The spokesman stated that this definition was not consistent with current usage (in 2004) and that it would likely be omitted when a new unabridged version is published.[10]

Aside from *Webster's Third*, nearly all commentators, from the most careful scholars to the most ardent activists, disassociate themselves from the position that all criticism of Israel is anti-Semitic.[11] "In every public forum," Abraham Foxman writes, "I'm always careful to say that criticism of the state of Israel is not necessarily anti-Semitic."[12] Such caveats are ubiquitous in academic, governmental, and political discussions of this topic. Indeed, the issue is now widely considered to be *beyond debate*. "No fair minded person," Robert Wistrich disclaims, "would contest the right of critics to argue that the long-term Israeli occupation of the West Bank and Gaza after 1967 may have been mistaken, counterproductive, or even corrupting in some of its aspects; nor is it anti-Zionist, let alone anti-Semitic, to criticize the building of settlements in the territories or to protest the treatment of Palestinians under military occupation."[13]

Categorical Denial

If the *Webster's Third* categorical approach garners little to no support today, the same cannot be said of the opposite categorical approach, which holds that *no opposition* to Israel is anti-Semitic. The National Association of Teachers in Further and Higher Education (NATFHE), the British trade union for teachers working with adult learners, adopted this categorical position at its June 2005 conference. At that time, NATFHE adopted a resolution stating, without caveats or limitations, that "[t]o criticize Israeli policy or institutions is not anti-semitic."[14] This is an extraordinary proposition, insofar as it suggests that no criticism of Israel is *or could be* anti-Semitic, regardless of its nature or motivations. Nevertheless, NATFHE was not alone in maintaining this extreme position. Two years earlier, the Association of University Teachers (AUT) Council had adopted a motion resolving that "anti-Zionism is not anti-Semitism" and deploring criticism of anti-Israel boycotts as "witchcraft." As David Hirsh rightly observes, the accusation of witchcraft implies not only a false accusation but moreover an accusation of something that could not possibly be true.[15]

That is to say, these unions announced not only that criticism of Israel, including boycotts of the Jewish state, is not anti-Semitic. Moreover, they implied that such activities could not be anti-Semitic under any possible circumstances. The unions' political agenda was plain: their membership openly supported the kinds of action that critics contended crossed the line into anti-Semitism. On April 22, 2005, the AUT's Executive Council voted to boycott two Israeli universities (Bar Ilan and Haifa), despite accusations that their decision was motivated by hatred of Jews. Shortly afterward, when NATFHE merged with AUT, the first Congress of the newly merged entity, the University and College Union (UCU), adopted a motion resolving that "criticism of Israel cannot be construed as anti-Semitic." Moreover, when read in context, the NATFHE resolution appears to include any support for a boycott of Israel.[16] The UCU also resolved to define Israel as a country with an "entrenched system of racial discrimination" and curbed exchanges with the Jewish state.[17]

This categorical approach is in its own way every bit as implausible as the *Webster's Third* approach and is moreover flatly refuted by empirical research.[18] For example, a well-known Yale University study found a strong correlation between anti-Semitism and hostility toward Israel among 5,000 people in 10 European countries, a relatively large group of respondents.[19] The Yale researchers' conclusion is not merely that those with anti-Semitic attitudes are be more likely to espouse negative views of Israel than those who are not anti-Semitic, which may be obvious to some readers. The researchers' more interesting conclusion is that the proportion of those holding anti-Semitic views strongly and independently increases with respondents' degree of anti-Israel sentiment (on a scale of 0 to 4).[20] That is to say, the more strongly one dislikes Israel, the more likely one is to think ill of Jews.

A smaller study, which examined the attitudes of Arab Muslims, Arab Christians, and non-Arab Muslims in the United States and Canada, similarly found a high statistical correlation between anti-Semitism and anti-Israeli sentiment.[21] Respondents, culled from a large Midwest American city and nearby mid-size Canadian city, were interviewed in English with Arabic interpreters. It should not be surprising that Arab Muslim participants scored highest for anti-Semitism, followed closely by non-Arab Muslims and Arab Christians, nor that these mean scores were double those of their non-Arab, Christian counterparts. This is evident even to casual observers. The more interesting finding, which should also be unsurprising except to those who maintain the UCU's categorical view on anti-Israelism, is that there exists a high statistical correlation between anti-Israeli sentiment and anti-Semitism among Arab and Muslim populations. As the lead researcher summarized, those respondents "who hated Israel tended to be anti-Semitic as well."[22]

In sum, there is now a surprising asymmetry among categorical views on the relationship between anti-Semitism and anti-Israeli sentiment. Despite repeated public proclamations to the contrary, there are no reputable authorities that maintain that criticism of Israel is *always* anti-Semitic. On the other hand, there is some institutional support for the view that criticism of Israel is *never* anti-Semitic. Both categorical views are demonstrably false. In fact, negative attitudes toward Israel positively correlate with negative attitudes toward Jews, although the correlation is not perfect. Some people dislike Israel without disliking Jews, but there is a high likelihood that those who dislike one also dislike the other. For this reason, the more interesting project has been to identify the boundaries between negative attitudes toward Israel that are anti-Semitic and those that are not.

Multi-National Responses

The project to find a middle ground between *Webster's Third* and the UCU was given urgency by the stunning resurgence of anti-Semitism in Europe during the early years of the twenty-first century. The near concurrence of the ADC's 2004 protest against Merriam-Webster and the British trade unions' 2005 pronouncement was not coincidental. In those years, a movement was well under way to refine the definition of anti-Semitism to reflect developing conditions in the Middle East and Europe. By 2000, the Oslo Process had played itself out and had left participants bitterly disappointed. The Second Intifada began late in that year, leading to thousands of Palestinian and Israeli deaths. The following September, the United Nations' 2001 World Conference against Racism (WCAR), also known as Durban I, generated an enormous amount of anti-Zionist agitation, in both the conference venues and throughout the streets of Durban. Some of it was clearly anti-Semitic. Durban I, which coincided almost exactly with the September 11 attacks on the United States, marked the beginning of a resurgence of global anti-Semitism unseen since the end of the Holocaust.[23]

In response to that resurgence, European agencies, parliamentarians, and Jewish organizations refocused significant energy on the task of combating and redefining anti-Semitism. Irwin Cotler, the McGill University human rights scholar and parliamentarian who would become Canada's Minister of Justice, gave several influential speeches on this topic early in the new millennium. Cotler compared traditional Jew-hatred with its newer iterations, explaining that "[t]raditional anti-Semitism denied Jews the right to live as equal members of society, but the new anti-Jewishness denies the right of the Jewish people to live as an equal member of the family of nations."[24] In April 2002, Swedish Deputy Prime Minister Per Ahlmark identified the new anti-Semitism, which he argued was directed against a "collective Jew":

> [C]ompared to most previous anti-Jewish outbreaks, this one is directed less toward individual Jews. Instead, its attacks focus on the collective Jew—the State of Israel. Such attacks spark a chain reaction of assaults on individual Jews and Jewish institutions. We certainly could say that in the past the most dangerous antisemites were those who wanted to make the world *Judenrein*, or free of Jews. Today, the most dangerous antisemites might be those who want to make the world *Judenstaatrein*, free of a Jewish state.[25]

In December 2002, the Organization for Security and Cooperation in Europe's (OSCE's) Porto Conference expressed concern with racist incidents targeting both Muslims and Jews. The OSCE was a useful post-War international forum, which included the United States, much of Europe, and Russia among its members. Formed after the Second World War, it provided a forum for reshaping the new (post-War) Europe, especially with respect to shaping European states' human rights commitments.[26] In June 2003, the OSCE explicitly agreed to oppose anti-Semitism, but Jewish advocates were concerned that OSCE participants failed to recognize that anti-Semitism was coming from new directions.[27]

The First European Union Definition

Jewish community advocates complained to officials of the European Union Monitoring Centre for Racism and Xenophobia, a precursor to Europe's Fundamental Rights Agency. The European Council had established the EUMC in 1997 in order to provide reliable and comparable data on human rights violations that could be used in developing responsive measures and enforcement strategies. Beate Winkler, the EUMC's then-director, held a series of meetings with European Jewish Congress officials, and agreed to commission a series of reports on anti-Semitism in each EUMC member state.[28] The Centre for Research on Anti-Semitism (ZfA) in Berlin analyzed the reports and issued a composite analysis, which was leaked to the press in December 2003. Unfortunately, the ZfA's report was badly received, because it assigned much of the blame for resurgent anti-Semitism to young Muslim males. In the European Union, this issue temporarily overshadowed the question of how anti-Semitism should be defined or understood.

In March 2004, the EUMC responded to a measurable spike in European anti-Semitism by issuing a report with the deceptively bland title, "Manifestations of Antisemitism in the EU 2002–2003."[29] The EUMC's controversial report was intended to raise awareness about the resurgence of anti-Semitism, to facilitate the development of measures to counter it, and to develop a theoretical foundation to support European trans-national governmental data-gathering. In other words, the report was supposed to resolve disagreements about what constitutes anti-Semitism in a political context in which the presence or absence of anti-Semitism was highly contested.

The EUMC report was initially criticized for its discussion of the ethnic composition of the people responsible for the resurgence of anti-Semitism in Europe. The Monitoring Centre had been taken to task for suppressing the ZfA report. In its March 2004 report, the EUMC provided a more nuanced analysis, but the press release announcing its issuance blamed the resurgence primarily on "young, disaffected white Europeans," rather than the young Muslim men whom the EUMC's commissioned experts had held responsible.[30] In the brouhaha surrounding whether the EUMC was whitewashing Muslim involvement, the larger issue, which initially went unnoticed, was the troubling definition of anti-Semitism upon which the EUMC relied.[31]

As we have seen, the EUMC embraced a conception of the figural Jew that is based on seven stereotypical traits: deceptiveness, strangeness, hostility, greed, corruption, conspiratorial power, and deicidal murderousness. For this reason, the EUMC concluded that the "core" of anti-Semitism consists of "any acts or attitudes that are based on the perception of a social subject (individual, group, institution or state)" as "the ('deceitful', 'corrupt', 'conspiratorial', etc.) Jew."[32] The EUMC argued that this construction far exceeds the sort of generalizations that we all practice in everyday life. Rather, it is a "closed belief system" with "no exit door," because every argument about anti-Semitism is seen as an expression of Jewish power and conspiratorial control.[33]

When the EUMC turned to the question of anti-Zionism, it applied this notion of the figural Jew. "If we turn to the crucial question of defining the point where anti-Israeli and anti-Zionist expressions are to be considered as anti-Semitism," the EUMC explained, "then we would conclude, on the basis of our definition of antisemitism, that anti-Israeli or anti-Zionist attitudes and expressions *are* antisemitic in those cases where Israel is seen as a representative of 'the Jew,' i.e. as a representative of the traits attributed to the anti-Semitic construction of 'the Jew.'"[34]

"But what if the opposite is the case," the EUMC queried, "and Jews are perceived as representatives of Israel?" At first blush, this would seem to be the case where killers like Mohamed Merah say that they are acting out of hatred for Israel target Jews or to avenge actions that it is supposed to have taken toward Palestinians. "If we stick to our definition," the EUMC logically concluded, "then, strictly speaking, we would have to qualify hostility to Jews as 'Israelis' only then as antisemitic if it is based only underlying perception of Israel as 'the Jew.'"[35] The converse would also be true under the EUMC's then definition. "If this is not the case," the EUMC continued, "then we would have to consider hostility towards Jews as 'Israelis' as *not* antisemitic, because this hostility is not based on the antisemitic stereotyping of Jews."[36]

History has not been kind to the EUMC's first definitional effort. Critics denounced the effort as misconceived and convoluted. In a devastating critique, Kenneth Stern explained that the EUMC would recognize anti-Semitism if a Jew is assaulted in the streets of Paris because the attacker perceives Israelis as conspiratorial, greedy, or slimy, and views French Jews as stand-ins for Israelis. However, the EUMC definition would fail to discern anti-Semitism if the same unfortunate French Jew is assaulted because the attacker is angry about the Israeli government and attacks the Jew as a proxy for Israel. From a practical point of view, this was an untenable distinction. As Stern explains, circumstances overtook the old EUMC definition, demonstrating in dramatic fashion why it was inadequate to the task for which it had been devised:

> Five days after the report was released, a Montreal Jewish elementary school was firebombed. A note left behind indicated that the attack was in retaliation for Israel's assassination of a Hamas leader—presumably, not antisemitism according to the EUMC definition. The functional equivalent would be declaring the lynching of a young African American man in the 1960s racist if the motivating factor was a belief that blacks were shiftless or lazy or were destroying the white gene pool, but not if the same victim was swinging from the same magnolia tree and the murderer was motivated by dislike of the Voting Rights Act of 1964.[37]

The 2004 EUMC definition was quickly discredited. More significantly, the definition's two central features came into disrepute. First, it had focused on the perpetrator's mental state. In doing so, it had not merely emphasized individual attitudes or emotions; rather, it had taken a more abstract approach, isolating the figural qualities generated by anti-Semitic ideology. This approach proved inadequate to the task of identifying, monitoring, and addressing particular incidents of anti-Jewish hatred and violence. Worse, it generated a standard under which most forms of anti-Israel animus would appear to be excluded, even if they resulted in violence against individual non-Israeli Jews. In the aftermath of the Montreal firebombing, this standard fell out of favor.

Natan Sharansky's 3-D Test

Given that anti-Zionism is *in some cases* anti-Semitic, the challenge has been to formulate a definition, or a set of standards, for determining which anti-Zionist actions or expressions are anti-Semitic and which are not. In the wake of the debacle that was the EUMC's initial effort to define anti-Semitism, attention swung toward what we have called "praxeological definitions." That is to say, practitioners and scholars alike engaged in a concerted effort to develop guidelines for determining which actions could be deemed anti-Semitic and which not.

Fortunately, a clever template was at hand. In February 2004, the month prior to the EUMC's initial failed effort, Natan Sharansky published a short but influential *Jerusalem Post* opinion piece announcing what he called the "3D Test" for distinguishing between anti-Semitism and mere criticism of Israel.[38] Sharansky, a child chess prodigy who had gone on to become the most famous of the old Russian refuseniks, was by this time a prominent Israeli parliamentarian, human rights activist, party leader, and minister. At the time, he held the post of Minister for Jerusalem and Diaspora Affairs. Sharansky's words carried great weight internationally, and his essay would be reprinted, reposted, and discussed around the world. Sharanky's test was intended to draw boundary lines between anti-Semitism and "legitimate" criticism of Israel. He argues that these criteria are distilled from standards that had historically been used to identify classical anti-Semitism before the popular anti-Jewish animus was displaced onto the Jewish state.

Sharansky's 3D Test proposes that hostility toward Israel may be considered anti-Semitic when it deploys *demonization, double standards*, or *delegitimization*. This use of three "D" words was mnemonically inspired, and the essay has become a classic. Sharansky "test" may lack sufficient rigor to be used, without modification, for governmental or scholarly purposes, but scholarly rigor would be too much to ask of such short-hand standards. The more important point is that this test provides a useful and accessible means of understanding the problem, as opposed to a fully developed solution.

Demonization

Demonization refers to the ascription of supernatural characteristics toward the Jewish state. The term is frequently misused in contemporary discourse to describe particularly biting or extreme criticisms, especially if they portray their object in an especially negative light. For example, Israel's supporters sometimes insist that the Jewish State is demonized by unjustifiably harsh criticism. But "demonization" means something much more specific. It references the age-old canard that Jews harbor demonic or evil powers. This trope was widespread, for example, in medieval Christian Europe, where it was related to the deicide myth, and appears to have reemerged in the Arab world in the wake of the 1967 war.

Sharansky's point is that Israel's enemies often characterize the state in similar terms, which reflects a cultural transfer to Israel of long-standing anti-Jewish characterizations:

> Whether it came in the theological form of a collective accusation of deicide or in the literary depiction of Shakespeare's Shylock, Jews were demonized for centuries as the embodiment of evil. Therefore, today we must be wary of whether the Jewish state is being demonized by having its actions blown out of all sensible proportion.[39]

In other words, it is an example of how Israel (or "Israel") is often perceived as the collective embodiment of the figural Jew—the "collective Jew," that is, as Per Ahlmark put it. This can be seen in much contemporary Middle Eastern discourse. For example, during the spring of 2013, various commentators observed that at least a couple of influential Iranians had lately warned of the Jewish powers of sorcery. One powerful Iranian cleric, Mehdi Taeb, reportedly lectured seminarians on April 20, 2013, that Zionists have used ancient Jewish sorcery against them in the past and that worse could be expected:

The Jews are currently subjecting us to an unprecedented trial. As you read in the Koran, [King] Solomon ruled the world . . . The Jews have the greatest powers of sorcery, and they make use of this tool. All the measures that have been brought against us originate with the Zionists. . . . So far, they have not used the full [scope of] their sorcery against us. Sorcery was the final means to which they resorted during the Ahmadinejad era, but they were defeated.[40]

Sharansky's demonization criterion gains persuasive force by the transparent use of this ancient anti-Jewish trope in diatribes directed against Israel and Zionists.

Double Standards

Sharansky's second "D" stands for *double standards*. This refers to the application of different standards or evaluative measures to assess the behavior of Jewish people or the State of Israel. The gist here is that it is discriminatory to evaluate similar conduct by dissimilar measures. Sharansky argues that Israel is criticized by more stringent standards than are other countries, just as Jews have historically been so criticized. "When criticism of Israel is applied selectively," Sharansky explains, "when Israel is singled out by the United Nations for human rights abuses while the behavior of known and major abusers, such as China, Iran, Cuba, and Syria, is ignored; when Israel's Magen David Adom, alone among the world's ambulance services, is denied admission to the International Red Cross—this is anti-Semitism."[41]

Based on empirical research, sociologist Sina Arnold has identified five distinct double standards employed by American progressives in their criticisms of Israel:

- The "double standard of *salience*," by which Israel's conflicts garner vastly more public attention than other comparable international disputes;
- The "double standard of *state foundation*," by which Israel's establishment is characterized as violent and hostile, while violence in the early history of other nations is downplayed or ignored altogether;

- The "double standard of *state formation*," by which Israel's political arrangements are portrayed as archaic while similar structures are not;
- The "double standard of *self-understanding*," which criticizes Israel's ethno-religious characteristics while disregarding similar characteristics among other states; and, finally,
- The "double standard of *self-determination*," which recognizes a right of self-government for Palestinians but not necessarily for Israelis or, alternatively, which recognizes the validity of Palestinian feelings of frustration or anger under the present political circumstances while declining to recognize the validity of such feelings among Israelis.[42]

One might add the double standard of *punishment*, which singles Israel out for boycotts, divestment, and sanctions that are not urged upon other states that have substantially worse human rights records.

Double standards are often conflated with the broader category of *adverse treatment*. This can be seen, for example, in this observation by a prominent scholar: "The use of different standards concerning Jews . . . was often so obvious that it was self-understood, for instance, when Jews were confined to living in certain parts of a town, were not free to wear the clothes they wanted, and could not work in most professions." A restriction on the residential options or clothing choices available to Jews is a form of adverse treatment. By contrast, if one criticized Jewish housing or clothing more harshly than similar items owned by others, this would exemplify *double standards*. The concept of double standards merits special attention because it is so frequently observed, especially in international treatment of the State of Israel.

Delegitimization

Sharansky's third criterion is *delegitimization*. Here again, Sharansky draws this criterion from a longstanding form of anti-Jewish hostility that has been transferred to the Jewish state. *Delegitimization* refers to efforts to deny Israel the legitimacy given to other states. "In the past," Sharansky explains, "anti-Semites tried to deny the legitimacy of the Jewish religion, the Jewish people, or both. Today, they are trying to deny the legitimacy of the Jewish state, presenting it, among other things, as the last vestige of colonialism."[43] Like virtually all modern commentators, Sharansky is careful to distinguish between *delegitimization* and ordinary criticism of Israeli policies. "While criticism of an Israel policy may not be anti-Semitic," he explains, "the denial of Israel's right to exist is always anti-Semitic. If other peoples have a right to live securely in their homelands, then the Jewish people have a right to live securely in their homeland."[44]

As Sharansky articulates this indicium, it is merely a particular example of *double standards*, perhaps with occasional overtones of demonization. Nevertheless, it is possible to overstate the widespread character of this criterion. Some commentators, for example, insist that Jews "alone among all peoples of the world" are told that they do not have a right to a separate state in their own homeland. This argument is surely overstated, particularly with respect to such counter-examples as the Basques, the Chechens, the Kurds, and various indigenous peoples of North America. If one can imagine non-discriminatory arguments against these peoples' requests for collective self-governance, then perhaps such arguments claims can be made against Jews as well. To say that the arguments would be unpersuasive is not to demonstrate that they would be anti-Semitic. For this reason, it must be stressed that Sharansky's criteria should not be considered to be unrebuttable rules.

Sharansky's 3D Test would ultimately become the backbone of the most important modern definitions of anti-Semitism. Before this could be possible however, Western public authorities needed to understand anti-Semitism more clearly, including both its protean character and its relationship to anti-Israelism, and had to create a mechanism through which the fruits of new scholarship could be distilled.

The Berlin Declaration

On April 28–29, 2004, the OSCE convened its second conference on anti-Semitism in Berlin at the invitation of the German Foreign Minister Joschka Fischer. The two-day conference drew over 800 participants, including representatives of the organization's 55 member states, its 10 partner states, and many non-governmental organizations. The goal was to develop an agreed-upon course of practical action by OSCE's participating states to counter the upsurge in anti-Semitism.

Today, the conference is best remembered for the so-called "Berlin Declaration," a summary of the proceedings formally read out by Bulgarian Foreign Minister Solomon Passy, who was then the OSCE's Chairman in Office.[45] The Berlin Declaration was notable for several advances.[46]

As a conceptual matter, the Declaration firmly endorsed the proposition that anti-Semitism had assumed new characteristics during the postwar period. This was a major development at a time when some commentators argued that anti-Semitism had been extinguished during the Second World War and that contemporary incidents were related primarily to Israel rather than to the history of Jew-hatred. The Declaration explicitly recognized "that anti-Semitism, following its most devastating manifestation during the Holocaust, has assumed new forms and expressions, which, along with other forms of intolerance, pose a threat to democracy, the values of civilization and, therefore, to overall security in the OSCE region and beyond."[47]

Significantly, the Declaration acknowledged that anti-Semitism is sometimes directed at Jewry as a collective body. This is important, because certain forms of hostility toward Israel have targeted Israel as a collective Jew. In acknowledging that anti-Semitism sometimes targets Jewish collectivity, the Declaration provided a substantial advance toward understanding the relationship between anti-Semitism and anti-Israelism. The Declaration explained that the assembled nations were concerned "in particular that this hostility toward Jews—as individuals or collectively—on racial, social, and/or religious grounds, has manifested itself in verbal and physical attacks and in the desecration of synagogues and cemeteries."

The Declaration also established various mechanisms for analyzing, monitoring, and combating anti-Semitism. Broadly, the Declaration commits the OSCE's member states to combat anti-Semitism within the OSCE region. The OSCE's Warsaw-based Office for Democratic Institutions and Human Rights (ODIHR) was tasked with promoting good practices to respond to anti-Semitism and advising member nations on their efforts to fight anti-Semitism. Moreover, the Declaration tasked the ODIHR to work with the EUMC, other government entities, and NGOs, to find better ways to assess and monitor anti-Semitic incidents in OSCE countries. This was to be an important impetus for renewed efforts to define anti-Semitism during the fall-out from the EUMC's failed 2004 definition.

The International Working Definition

In response to the Berlin Declaration and the debacle of the 2004 EUMC definition, a number of anti-Semitism scholars participated in creating a new definition of anti-Semitism later that year. Kenneth Stern coordinated this effort, which incorporated contributions by historians Dina Porat, Yehuda Bauer, and others. Their draft definition begins as follows: "Antisemitism is hatred toward Jews because they are Jews and is directed toward the Jewish religion and Jews individually or collectively. More recently, antisemitism has been manifested in the demonization of the State of Israel."[48] This version relies too much on the Jews-as-Jews formulation but had the virtue of emphasizing idea of *collective* anti-Semitism and, more specifically, the relationship between anti-Semitism and animus toward the State of Israel. The most important aspect of this draft definition was however its practicality.

In hindsight, the advantage of this definition lay in the praxeological examples that it provided. These included some examples of long-standing anti-Semitic defamations, such as notions of global Jewish conspiracy, as well as more modern examples such as Holocaust denial. More ambitiously, the new definition also included several examples relating to the State of Israel. Echoing Sharansky's 3D Test, this definition includes the application of double standards and delegitimation of the Jewish state, as well as Holocaust inversion.[49] When the EUMC scrapped its controversial 2004 definition of anti-Semitism, largely under pressure from American Jewish organizations, this draft definition would become a model for the EUMC's next efforts to forge a workable definition of anti-Semitism.

The EUMC took that fateful step on January 28, 2005, informally issuing the International Working Definition, which became known as the "EUMC Working Definition of Anti-Semitism" or the "International Working Definition." Like all of its predecessors, this definition reflected its time, its place, and its social and political environment. This International Working Definition is not a theoretical or academic work, like its predecessors, but rather a practical tool for government officials and civil rights activists to use in identifying anti-Semitism.[50] It was a "working document" in this pragmatic sense, but it was also a working definition in the additional sense that it was considered to be a work-in-progress as opposed to a final statement approved by the European Union's political leadership. For this reason, formal endorsement was neither sought nor obtained.

The purpose of the new working definition, in its framers' words, was to "provide a practical guide for identifying incidents, collecting data, and supporting the implementation and enforcement of legislation dealing with anti-Semitism." The Working Definition was the joint product of the EUMC, the ODHIR, the American Jewish Congress, the American Jewish Committee, other major Jewish organizations, and various scholars.[51] The American Jewish Committee's Rabbi Andrew Baker negotiated the details of the definition with then–EUMC Director Beate Winkler. The International Working Definition closely resembles Kenneth Stern's draft definition, especially in its praxeological approach and its use of examples relating to the State of Israel.

The International Working Definition provides several recent examples of anti-Semitism in public life, the media, schools, the workplace, and religious institutions that relate to this collectivity, including the following:

- Making mendacious, dehumanizing, demonizing, or stereotypical allegations about Jews as such or the power of Jews as collective—such as, especially but not exclusively, the myth about a world Jewish conspiracy or of Jews controlling the media, economy, government, or other societal institutions
- Accusing Jews as a people of being responsible for real or imagined wrongdoing committed by a single Jewish person or group, or even for acts committed by non-Jews.
- Denying the fact, scope, mechanisms (e.g., gas chambers) or intentionality of the genocide of the Jewish people at the hands of National Socialist Germany and its supporters and accomplices during World War II (the Holocaust).
- Accusing the Jews as a people, or Israel as a state, of inventing or exaggerating the Holocaust.

- Accusing Jewish citizens of being more loyal to Israel, or to the alleged priorities of Jews worldwide, than to the interests of their own nations.[52]

These examples demonstrate the EUMC's insight that the putatively political or anti-Israeli cast of much anti-Israelism shrouds significant continuities with antecedent forms of the "longest hatred." In addition, the Working Definition provides the following examples of "the ways in which anti-Semitism manifests itself with regard to the State of Israel taking into account the overall context":[53]

- Denying the Jewish people their right to self-determination . . .
- Applying double standards by requiring of it a behavior not expected or demanded of any other democratic nation.
- Using the symbols and images associated with classic anti-Semitism (e.g., claims of Jews killing Jesus or blood libel) to characterize Israel or Israelis.
- Drawing comparisons of contemporary Israeli policy to that of the Nazis.
- Holding Jews collectively responsible for actions of the state of Israel.

The Working Definition emphasizes that criticism of Israel similar to that leveled against other countries does not constitute a form of anti-Semitism.[54]

The criteria by which anti-Semitic criticisms of Israel may be recognized include the use of classic anti-Semitic stereotypes, such as the demonization of Jews or the Jewish state; the use of double standards for Israel versus all other nations, including denial of national self-determination only to the Jews; and holding Jews collectively responsible for Israeli policy. What these criteria have in common is that they all indicate when facially anti-Israeli expressions are in fact an expression of an underlying anti-Jewish animus.

The Working Definition has been widely applauded and enormously influential. Shortly after its issuance, ODHIR integrated the definition into its educational materials.[55] In June of 2004, the OSCE prominently referenced the Working Definition at its Cordoba conference.[56] Since then, numerous national and international bodies have used the definition, cited it, or recommended using it, ranging from parliamentary bodies to governmental agencies to nongovernmental organizations to the UK National Union of Students. Law enforcement agencies in several countries have found it useful in training police officers on hate crimes, whether or not directed against Jews.[57] The Working Definition has been translated into at least 33 languages.[58]

The International Working Definition also received some deference in the courts. Six months after the EUMC announced the definition, for example, a Lithuanian court found that the editor of *Respublika*, a Vilnius newspaper, had published material that illegally propagated "national, racial and religious enmity," by asserting a global Jewish plot to rule mass media, financial institutions, and the world at large. The judicial decision cited the International Working Definition and found that the *Respublika*'s text exhibited the hallmarks of anti-Semitism enumerated by the International Working Definition.[59]

The Inter-Parliamentary Coalition for Combating Antisemitism, an international body composed of legislators from dozens of countries, has urged public officials to endorse the definition. For example, the Inter-Parliamentary Coalition's London Declaration urged that governments to expand their use of the International Working Definition for national and international regulatory purposes and law enforcement training. More specifically, the Coalition's Ottawa Protocol on Combating Antisemitism, which this author participated in drafting, admonishes universities to use the International Working Definition as a foundation for education, orientation, and training.[60] The U.S. Department of State adopted the International Working Definition during the George W. Bush administration, determining that it "provides an adequate initial guide by which anti-Semitism can eventually both be defined and combated."[61] At my recommendation, the U.S. Commission on Civil Rights similarly adopted the Working Definition at that time.[62] The Obama administration continued to use the definition, promoting it through the State Department's Office to Monitor and Combat Global Antisemitism, before formulating its own definition.

The UCU Rejection and Fraser Litigation

In May 2011, the Congress of the UCU debated a motion to formally disassociate the union from the International Working Definition, denouncing the Working Definition as a tool "to silence debate about Israel and Palestine on campus."[63] During the course of debate, Ronnie Fraser, a Jewish delegate to the UCU, presented an impassioned criticism of the motion and argued that the mood of the Congress that produced it was itself laden with the very problem that it was intended to address. Fraser's emotional plea quickly circulated around the globe:

> I, a Jewish member of this union, am telling you, that I feel an antisemitic mood in this union and even in this room.
>
> I would feel your refusal to engage with the EUMC definition of antisemitism, if you pass this motion, as a racist act. . . .
>
> You may disagree with me. You may disagree with all the other Jewish members who have said similar things.
>
> You may think we are mistaken. But you have a duty to listen seriously.
>
> Instead of being listened to, I am routinely told that anyone who raises the issue of antisemitism is doing so in bad faith. . . .[64]

The UCU ignored Fraser's pleas, passing the motion on May 30, 2011. Leaders of the Anglo-Jewish community quickly condemned the union's action as the "last straw" in a pattern of UCU actions hostile to the Jewish people. Jeremy Newmark and Jon Benjamin, then the respective heads of England's Jewish Leadership Council and the Board of Deputies of British Jews, both decried the UCU as "institutionally racist."[65]

In response, Fraser filed the lawsuit against the UCU described above, charging the trade union with a pattern of anti-Jewish discrimination and harassment, including its action in adopting this motion. While the *Fraser* case was pending, the UCU endorsed an alternative definition. Rather than attempting a different praxeological definition, with a new set of examples, the UCU's move was to redefine anti-Semitism in terms of a fixed set of characteristics. In February 2012 the UCU produced a leaflet entitled "Anti-Semitism," which endorses a definition of anti-Semitism offered by Brian Klug. Klug's short definition, as adopted by the UCU, is as follows: "At the heart of anti-Semitism is the negative stereotype of 'the Jew': sinister, cunning, parasitic, money-grubbing, mysteriously powerful, and so on. Antisemitism consists in projecting this figure onto individual Jews, Jewish groups, and Jewish institutions."

The problem with Klug's UCU definition is that it is simultaneously too theoretical and also un-theoretical. It is too theoretical in the sense that it that, like all ideological definitions, it lacks sufficient concrete detail and factual grounding to be useful for practitioners. When a hooligan hurls a rock through a Hillel building or destroys a Holocaust memorial or sets fire to a Sukkah or assaults a Jewish student, it is seldom possible to determine whether the figural Jew motivates him. If he is apprehended, he may claim that he is protesting Israel's treatment of Palestinians. The perpetrator's deepest intentions are usually opaque, certainly to others and possibly also to himself, which is why praxeological definitions have been devised. At the same time, it is un-theoretical in the sense that it misconstrues the role of ideology in the formulation of the figurative Jew. As we saw in the last chapter, the figural "Jew" is not a single negative stereotype, as Klug insists, nor even a fixed and finite series of stereotypes, but rather a screen on which an endless number of contradictory images may be presented. In this sense, the "Jew" is the "Don Quixote" that Frederic Jameson observed "is not really a character at all, but rather an organizational device that permits Cervantes to write his book, serving as a thread that holds together a number of different types of anecdotes together in a single form."[66] "The Jew," whether individually or as a stand-in for the collective "Israel," fulfills a common narrative device, bringing consistency to an overarching ideological system by unifying into a cohesive narrative the experiences of, for example, moral decadence, economic deterioration, political frustrations, and collective humiliation.[67] For these reasons, Klug's definition is not an adequate substitute for the Working Definition for either theoretical or practical purposes.

From International Working Definition to U.S. State Department Definition

The European Union has not recently afforded the International Definition the respect that it has elsewhere received. Neither the EUMC nor its successor agency, the European Union's Fundamental Rights Agency, has ever formally endorsed the definition. Rather, the agency's

Executive Director issued it without formal review by her political overseers. This gave the document a peculiar vulnerability to the winds of political change. In 2013, as we have seen, the Fundamental Rights Agency took the Working Definition down from its website during the course of renovations.[68] Although the agency downplayed the significance of its action, it provoked strong international responses from the Jewish community and elsewhere.

Political scientist Amy Elman has observed that Jewish communal professionals had overestimated the significance of the agency's action in posting the Working Definition to its website.[69] Elman is almost certainly correct. If so, however, then these same professionals have no less overestimated the significance of the agency's action in taking it down. That is to say, the International Definition was never an officially adopted statement of the European Union, even when it appeared on the FRA's website. But if posting the document was not an official act of adoption, then removing it was not an official act of rejection.

Within the United States, the status of the Working Definition is not as important as in Europe or in other parts of the world, because in 2010 the Obama Department of State established its own official definition of anti-Semitism. The State Department definition, which has been widely distributed under the department's imprimatur, is essentially a modified, improved, and abridged version of the Working Definition, which makes some elements of Natan Sharansky's 3D definition more explicit.[70] Adopted under Special Envoy Hannah Rosenthal, it is now the federal government's authoritative current statement on the issue. It is decidedly not a "working definition," but rather the Department's official position on the issue. In the United States, the State Department definition should be considered the official final version for which the Working Definition was a first draft.

The State Department definition borrows the Working Definition's description of anti-Semitism as "a certain perception of Jews, which may be expressed as hatred toward Jews. Rhetorical and physical manifestations of anti-Semitism are directed toward Jewish or non-Jewish individuals and/or their property, toward Jewish community institutions and religious facilities."[71] It then provides the following additional specific examples of "the ways in which anti-Semitism manifests itself with regard to the state of Israel," which it wisely emphasizes must take into account "the overall context":

DEMONIZE ISRAEL:

- Using the symbols and images associated with classic anti-Semitism to characterize Israel or Israelis
- Drawing comparisons of contemporary Israeli policy to that of the Nazis
- Blaming Israel for all inter-religious or political tensions

DOUBLE STANDARD FOR ISRAEL:

- Applying double standards by requiring of it a behavior not expected or demanded of any other democratic nation
- Multilateral organizations focusing on Israel only for peace or human rights investigations

DELEGITIMIZE ISRAEL:

- Denying the Jewish people their right to self-determination, and denying Israel the right to exist[72]

While most of this is taken verbatim from the Working Definition, the example about blaming Israel for political and inter-religious tensions is new. Like the EUMC, and nearly all other authorities, the State Department properly stresses that many criticisms of Israel are not anti-Semitic. "*However,*" the definition emphasizes, in what has become a nearly universally adopted caveat, "*criticism of Israel similar to that leveled against any other country cannot be regarded as anti-Semitic.*"[73] The definition then provides familiar contemporary examples, quoted in full below:

- Calling for, aiding, or justifying the killing or harming of Jews (often in the name of a radical ideology or an extremist view of religion).
- Making mendacious, dehumanizing, demonizing, or stereotypical allegations about Jews as such or the power of Jews as a collective—especially but not exclusively, the myth about a world

Jewish conspiracy or of Jews controlling the media, economy, government or other societal institutions.
- Accusing Jews as a people of being responsible for real or imagined wrongdoing committed by a single Jewish person or group, the state of Israel, or even for acts committed by non-Jews.
- Accusing the Jews as a people, or Israel as a state, of inventing or exaggerating the Holocaust.
- Accusing Jewish citizens of being more loyal to Israel, or to the alleged priorities of Jews worldwide, than to the interest of their own nations.[74]

These examples are also largely drawn from the Working Definition, but they provide one important improvement. The first example (about killing or harming Jews) adds the word "often," thus encompassing the killing and harming of Jews even when it is not motivated by a radical ideology.

The State Department definition has not received nearly as much attention as it deserves. Since it was not developed in close consultation with Jewish communal organizations or anti-Semitism scholars, the groups that have supported the Working Definition have not championed it to the same extent. It is less innovative in that it is so pervasively and obviously indebted to the Working Definition and to Sharansky. Nevertheless, the State Department definition is formally and officially the position of the United States, at least with respect to foreign policy.

Office for Civil Rights Investigations

In higher education cases before OCR, as discussed in the Introduction, federal investigators must be guided by an understanding of what it means for a Jewish student to face anti-Semitism—such as the one that the State Department's definition affords. For several years, OCR struggled over whether it should investigate any anti-Semitism allegations whatsoever, given that its jurisdiction extended to racial and ethnic discrimination but not religion. Now that OCR has established that it will address anti-Semitism, the question is whether it can grasp anti-Semitic incidents that are brought to their attention, especially when they relate in some fashion to hostility against the State of Israel. Policy is one thing but enforcement another.

As we have seen, the Zionist Organization of America complained to OCR in 2004, while I was the head of that agency, that Irvine had maintained a hostile environment for Jewish students over the prior three to four years. In a nutshell, ZOA alleged that anti-Israel activists had harassed, threatened, and assaulted Jewish pro-Israel students; that they had destroyed a Holocaust memorial; that they repeatedly vandalized property including defacing posters announcing Jewish communal events; and that they had regularly hosted campus speakers who denigrate Jews and Israelis.

The earliest of these allegations were encompassed within ZOA's 2004 complaint to OCR. OCR had submitted its 2004 complaint shortly after I had announced that OCR would adopt a policy of protecting Jewish students against anti-Semitic incidents based on ethnic or ancestral discrimination. As we have seen, OCR dismissed ZOA's 2004 complaint because OCR's leadership in the years immediately following my departure denied that Jews should be protected from discrimination under Title VI of the Civil Rights Act. Specifically, OCR dismissed as time-barred ZOA's allegations that anti-Israel activists destroyed a Holocaust memorial and made harassing comments to Jewish students, such as "dirty Jew," "fucking Jew," "go back to Russia," "burn in Hell," "slaughter the Jews," "take off that pin" (bearing flags of Israel and the United States) "or we'll beat your ass."[75] OCR conceded however that other claims were timely filed, such as intimidation of Jewish students by Arab and Muslim students; defacement of an Israel flag on a student's dormitory room door; and allegations of anti-Semitic speeches and activities stretching across annual anti-Israel protest events held from May 2001 through at least May 2007. OCR found that some of these statements were offensive to Jewish students but concluded that they were nevertheless inactionable because they were based on the students' political views rather than their national origin.[76]

At the same time that OCR affirmed its prior dismissal of ZOA's 2004 complaint (*Irvine I*), it also dismissed a companion case (*Irvine II*). Like its predecessor, *Irvine II* addresses the University of California at Irvine, but it describes only new matters brought to its attention subsequent to the filing of ZOA's 2004 complaint.[77] Specifically, in *Irvine II*, OCR addressed nine 2007 conflicts that ZOA had brought to its attention a few years after filing its 2004 *Irvine I* complaint.[78] Some of the incidents as recounted by OCR do not amount to much. For example, one Jewish student reports that friendship with Muslim students in her dormitory frayed after they disagreed about a lecture by historian Daniel Pipes. As the argument coarsened, the students exchanged accusations of "racism" and "anti-Semitism." When the Jewish student stopped speaking to the Muslim students, the Muslims stopped speaking to her. This led to tensions and "unwelcoming looks." The Jewish student asked to be moved to another dormitory, and the university complied. OCR unsurprisingly found the unwelcoming looks to be insufficient basis for a federal lawsuit.

Other incidents were rougher. Muslim students presented an event entitled "Israel: Apartheid Resurrected." Jewish students argued that this spectacle exacerbated the campus' anti-Jewish atmosphere, and they were probably correct. OCR countered that even "rough and discordant expressions" are protected by the First Amendment's guaranty of free speech.[79] This is also correct.[80] As it happens however the notion that the "Israel: Apartheid" event included only political speech as opposed to hateful expressions was difficult to sustain. The truth came out when a rabbi came to attend the event and was loudly taunted, "Don't you have somebody's money to steal?"[81] This slur reflects the deeper, age-old anti-Jewish stereotypes underlying much anti-Israel agitation. OCR analyzed this statement, finding it to be "offensive." At the same time however the agency found rather that it was not, standing on its own, sufficiently serious to justify the finding of a violation by Irvine. This finding was odd, since the allegation unquestionably was not standing on its own. Rather, it was included with a myriad of other troubling allegations not only in *Irvine II* but also in the *Irvine I* complaint from which it had been artificially separated. OCR gave no reason for why the incident should be viewed in isolation, when it is so obvious part of a larger pattern of anti-Jewish incidents on campus.

In other incidents, anti-Israel activists did not resort to explicit anti-Jewish stereotypes, but their actions nevertheless reflected anti-Jewish hostility. For example, several students repeatedly cursed a female Jewish student in obscene terms and called her "whore" and "slut" for wearing a pro-Israel t-shirt to an event sponsored by the Muslim Student Union and expressing disagreement with the Union's invited speaker. Similarly, a Muslim student repeatedly pushed a camera in the face of a Jewish Israeli-American student reporter, who wore an "I love Israel" t-shirt, as she tried to interview Ward Churchill. The student told OCR that MSU members often placed cameras in the faces of individuals with "pro-Israel or politically conservative views" in order to intimidate them.

The *Irvine* case presents difficult challenges, because some of the hostility directed at Jewish students appears to be politically motivated, especially as Zionist Jews and conservative speakers were apparently mistreated in a similar manner. Nevertheless, harassment of those who express love for Israel unavoidably creates a hostile environment for Israeli students. Moreover, as we saw in the last chapter, it may also be viewed as a form of irrational ethnic trait discrimination against Jewish Americans. The harassment was based on the students' sense of connectedness to the State of Israel. This has a political dimension, as the students recognized, but it is also deeply intertwined with age-old elements of Jewish ethnic, cultural, and religious identity.

OCR's disposition of the Irvine cases as well as its similarly unsympathetic treatment of other anti-Semitism cases have led some observers to worry that OCR's doors are no longer open to Jewish complainants. In fact, OCR continues to recognize that harassment of Jewish students may violate federal civil rights law, even if this recognition is difficult to discern in recent cases. OCR also acknowledges that certain hostilities toward Israel may violate the rights of Jewish students. This can be seen in a presentation that Deputy Assistant Secretary Seth Galanter prepared for the 2012 annual convention of the American-Arab Anti-Discrimination Committee.[82] Galanter offers the following hypothetical as an example of a case in which OCR would exercise Title VI jurisdiction:

> College students who attend a speech and rally sponsored by a campus group that is known for its support of Israel's policies towards the Palestinians are heckled with shouts of "Zionist" and "Murderer" as they arrive at the rally, are hit by rocks thrown as they enter the rally, and later receive threatening notes under their dorm room doors.

The notes read: "Dear Zionist—For your support of Israel and complicity in its crimes we will hunt you down the way the Nazis hunted your Jewish ancestors."[83]

This is an important presentation, because it demonstrates OCR's recognition that some seemingly political activities directed against Israel's supporters in fact constitute federal civil rights violations. At first blush, the key to this hypothetical is the reference to "your Jewish ancestors." As the notes to Galanter's presentation indicate, this language suggests "that the students were targeted because of their real or perceived Jewish ancestry."[84] Galanter emphasizes that the fact that "the students may also have been targeted because of their perceived support for Israel (the only evidence thereof being the students' attendance at this event) does not deprive OCR of jurisdiction."[85] In fact, if anything it should reinforce that jurisdiction, insofar as the hypothetical statement exemplifies the State Department's insight that anti-Semitism includes "accusing Jews . . . of being responsible for real or imagined wrongdoing committed by . . . the state of Israel."

Investigators should determine whether students are mistreated in ways that meet established conduct-based definitions of anti-Semitism such as the U.S. Department of State definition. They would find countless examples. A few months after September 11, 2001, Muhammad al-Asi lectured students at the University of California at Irvine that, "We have a psychosis in the Jewish community that is unable to co-exist equally and brotherly with other human beings. You can take a Jew out of the ghetto, but you cannot take the ghetto out of the Jew, and this has been demonstrated time and time again."[86] This is the "certain perception of the Jews" to which the State Department and Working Definition refer.

Starting around that time, fliers appeared around that campus picturing the Star of David dripping with blood and equating Israeli Jews with Nazis.[87] This is what the State Department definition calls an expression "drawing comparisons of contemporary Israeli policy to that of the Nazis." At another lecture, students were told that Jews use the media to brainwash gentiles, that there is a "psychosis" in the Jewish community, and that Jews must be "rehabilitated." Here we see what the State Department calls "making . . . stereotypical allegations about Jews ... especially ... about ... Jews controlling the media." In March 2004, a Jewish student was called "dirty Jew," reviving yet another old anti-Jewish stereotype.[88] In 2010, during Apartheid Week, Malik Ali publicly lectured UCI Jewish students that "you Jews are the new Nazis," reinforcing once again the anti-Semitic practice that the State Department definition calls "drawing comparisons of contemporary Israeli policy to that of the Nazis."[89]

That same year, 63 UCI faculty members published a letter saying that they "are deeply disturbed about activities on campus that foment hatred against Jews and Israelis" including "the painting of swastikas on university buildings, the Star of David depicted as akin to a swastika, a statement (by a speaker repeatedly invited by the Muslim Student Union) that the Zionist Jew is a party of Satan, a statement by another MSU speaker that the Holocaust was God's will, the tearing down of posters placed by the student group Anteaters for Israel, and the hacking of their web site." The professors intimated that some "community members, students, and faculty indeed feel intimidated, and at times, even unsafe."[90] Other faculty disagreed and issued opposing statements, but these incidents nevertheless echo the State Department definition and the Working Definition. We have explained that such standards should be applied as rebuttable presumptions, rather than bright-line tests, since surrounding contextual information may indicate that some actions are not what they initially seem. While the accused would have a right to be heard, it is difficult to imagine any persuasive defense to the anti-Jewish rhetoric and actions in which anti-Israel activists engaged for several years at Irvine.

Israel as the "Collective Jew"

The State Department definition, the International Working Definition, and Sharanky's 3-D Test all recognize that some animus directed at Israel may properly be described as "anti-Semitic." These definitions view Israel as the collective Jew or, in Irwin Cotler's mordant language, the "Jew among nations." As we have seen, negative attitudes toward Israel strongly correlate with hostility toward Jews. But why is it appropriate to discern anti-Semitism in certain forms of anti-Israel hostility?

Broadly speaking, there are four ways in which anti-Israel hostility may properly be considered anti-Semitic, which we might identify as the *Intentionality, Tacitness, Memetics,* and *Ethnic Trait* principles. The *Intentionality Principle* provides that some critics of Israel consciously use as Israel as a pretext to express anti-Jewish animus. The *Tacitness Principle* provides that other critics of Israel, who are not consciously aware that they hold negative attitudes toward Jews, use Israel to express unconscious resentment of Jews. The *Memetics Principle* provides that some anti-Israelism is anti-Semitic in the sense that it arises from a climate of opinion that is hostile to Jews, regardless of the conscious or unconscious beliefs of individual speakers. Finally, the *Ethnic Trait Principle* provides that certain form of hostility toward Israel are anti-Semitic in the sense that it causes foreseeable harm to Jews based on a trait that is central to Jewish identity.

The Intentionality Principle

The *Intentionality Principle* provides that negative treatment of Israel is anti-Semitic if it is based on hatred of Jews, provided that "hatred of Jews" is understood in the chimerical manner described in the last chapter. This proposition is largely uncontroversial. The more difficult question concerns when, as a factual matter, the treatment is so motivated. As we have seen, there are many cultural reasons why intentional acts of anti-Semitism are mischaracterized in terms of other, distinct phenomena, such as ethnic conflict. On the other hand, some morally innocent actions are mistaken for anti-Semitism.

References to "Israel" or "Zionism" frequently form a cultural code or pretext for a form of discrimination that is less socially acceptable or persuasive in some social circles or cultures. There is widespread agreement, for example, that Soviet propaganda operated in this manner during the Cold War and that right-wing extremists employ a similar vocabulary today.[91] There is greater controversy on the extent to which current left-wing and Islamist anti-Zionist propaganda is similar. In some cases, the connection is overt. For example, at a May 2002 political protest at San Francisco State University, pro-Palestinian activists shouted at pro-Israel Jewish students and faculty, "Hitler didn't finish the job," "F—— the Jews," and "Die, racist pigs."[92] Similar chants and taunts have been heard at several California public universities since then.

Nevertheless, many strong critics of Israel do not consciously hold negative attitudes toward Jews or will not admit to them. For example, in a recent poll commissioned by the Anti-Defamation League, 43% of Netherlanders reported negative attitudes toward Israel but only 5% said that they accepted six or more of the anti-Semitic statements about which they were asked.[93] This divergence is unusual, but it is worth noting, as are its many possible explanations. The six-or-more-statements standard may be unduly stringent, given that 20% of Netherlanders believe that Jews talk too much about what happened to them in the Holocaust, 17% believe that Jews have too much power in the business world, and 16% say that Jews don't care what happens to anyone but other Jews.[94] Alternatively, it may be that many Netherlanders have developed negative attitudes toward Israel for reasons that are entirely unrelated to Israel's Jewish character. It is also possible that Netherlanders are reluctant to disclose anti-Semitic attitudes in light of the shame that some Europeans still feel in the wake of the Holocaust. Finally, some Europeans may have subconscious negative attitudes toward Jews that they are unwilling to admit even to themselves.

The Tacitness Principle

The *Tacitness Principle* posits that some hostilities may be motivated by *unconscious* or *tacit* anti-Jewish prejudice. This notion is familiar to social scientists. It is now well-established in the psychological literature that white Americans harbor far more anti-black racial prejudice than they are consciously aware of. In the same way, when researchers ask students to grade identical essays by two students, they assign lower grades to the one with a Jewish-sounding name.[95] In North America and Western Europe, racism and anti-Semitism are often repressed, since they are socially stigmatized, but they have not disappeared.[96]

In an important Rutgers University study of college students, researchers confirmed that hostility to Israel often reflects unconscious anti-Semitism.[97] The Rutgers researchers utilized sophisticated psychological devices to smoke out anti-Semitic beliefs among subjects who insisted that they were not prejudiced. First, they convinced some of the students that the researchers would know if they were lying, making subterfuge futile. Psychologists have various techniques for convincing subjects that they have this ability, and the techniques had previously been successful in identifying other hidden beliefs and prejudices. Second, and equally importantly, they caused some of the students to think about their own mortality by asking them to write about their deaths. Other students, who formed a control group, would be made to think about an examination instead. The idea, known as "Terror Management Theory," is that prejudices emerge when people are reminded of their own death (known as "mortality salience").[98]

The researchers found that those students who expressed hostility toward Israel were also more likely to express negative attitudes toward Jews. In addition, students expressed far more hostility toward Israel and Jews when they believed that the researchers would know if they were lying, especially if they were first made to think about their own demise. This phenomenon was, it turns out, unique to Jews and Israel. For example, when students were subjected to the same conditions, they did not urge greater sanctions on other countries that are said to violate human rights, such as Russia or India. The students, apparently, felt free to express their views on Russia or India, regardless of whether they knew the truth would out. Similarly, the students did not express more hostility toward Palestinians when they were subjected to similar conditions.

Intuitively, these results could be explained in either of two ways. The students might, under ordinary circumstances, conceal their actual negative attitudes toward Jews and Israel for fear of appearing anti-Semitic. Or instead they may fear only that their concerns about Israel's human rights policy could be misconstrued as anti-Semitic. This might be called the "Butler Hypothesis," since it reflects Judith Butler's familiar concern that anti-Israel activists are intimidated from expressing their true beliefs about Israel's human rights policies. The researchers disproved the Butler Hypothesis in two ways. First, they determined that students who were forced to think about their own death were significantly more likely to disclose negative attitudes toward Israel when they believed that their lies would be detected. By contrast, when they were only made to think about an exam, they showed no such discrepancies when they believed their views were transparent. Second, the researchers determined that when students' negative attitudes toward Israel increased (under mortality salience), they also expressed negative attitudes toward Jews. The researchers concluded that the students were not so much afraid of being mistaken for anti-Semitic; rather, their core prejudices emerged under extreme conditions, and the students understood deep down the ugliness of those beliefs.

The students understood in their hearts that their hostility to Israel reflected an underlying anti-Semitism, and they knew enough to hide those views under ordinary circumstances. Plainly put, the research demonstrated that people who argue "that there is no connection between anti-Semitism and hostility toward Israel are wrong."[99] On the other hand, the Rutgers study also confirms that some anti-Israel attitudes are not associated with any amount of anti-Semitism. Some people disapprove of Israel's conduct, whether rightly or wrongly, for reasons that are unrelated to their attitudes toward Jews. This stands to reason, since it is precisely the fact that some people dislike Israel for innocent reasons that permits anti-Semites to camouflage their true beliefs under the cover of anti-Israelism.

The Memetics Principle

The *Memetics Principle* provides that even where anti-Semitism cannot be detected, either consciously or unconsciously, on an individual basis, it may nevertheless circulate within a social group. After repeated usage of long periods of time, some common tropes such as the blood libel have come to transmit cultural information about Jews even when the speaker is unaware of their impact. Similarly, some speakers transmit anti-Jewish cultural stereotypes and defamations, without either conscious or unconscious intent, as when they use the term "Jew" as a verb denoting sharp business practices or as a noun denoting a person of unscrupulous character. Some criticism of Jews, individually or collectively, includes such units of cultural transmission or *memes*.

This may be seen in the recent controversy over a costume worn by the singer Macklemore. Macklemore, a Grammy Award-winning artist, faced accusations of anti-Semitism after wearing a fake bowl-cut wig, beard and hooked nose while performing his hit song "Thrift Shop" at Seattle's Experience Music Project. Critics charged that Macklemore's attire presented a stereotypical version of Jewish male appearance. Macklemore apologized profusely, insisting that he had assembled the costume spontaneously and without any intention to appear Jewish or to reinforce anti-Jewish stereotypes.[100] The Anti-Defamation League accepted Macklemore's apology. Actor Seth Rogan, however, responded with a skeptical tweet: "@macklemore really?? Because if I told someone to put together an anti Semitic Jew costume, they'd have that exact shopping list."[101] Rogan and the ADL might both be right. It is entirely possible that Macklemore randomly assembled his wardrobe without giving a thought to Jewish perceptions. Nevertheless, a famous singer who appears at a prominent venue wearing a cheap beard and an enormous prosthetic nose while singing about a thrift shop will reinforce a strong set of cultural stereotypes.

Bernard Harrison, the English philosopher, has elegantly described how contemporary anti-Semitism often permeates what he calls the "climate of opinion," even while those most in its thrall may be unaware of its influence. In Harrison's theory, a climate of opinion is not the work of an individual mind, either conscious or unconscious. Rather, it is formed from a "multitude of spoken and written items—books, articles, news items, . . . lectures, stories, in-jokes, stray remarks—of equally multitudinous authorship."[102] Individual speakers buy into it, rather than developing it themselves. When enough people in a subculture buy into a climate of opinion, that climate becomes dominant in the subculture. When a climate of opinion becomes dominant, it is difficult for members of the subculture to think outside of its terms.[103] Harrison describes negative attitudes toward Israel, replete with anti-Jewish stereotypes and defamations, as forming a dominant subculture in some Western social circles. Hostilities directed at Israel may revive ancient anti-Jewish stereotypes, tropes, or memes, in ways that threaten non-Israeli Jews, both currently and in the future. This is frequently said, for example, of the frequent invocation of blood libels against Israel, or the widespread dissemination of anti-Semitic literature such as *The Protocols of the Elders of Zion*. The U.S. Commission on Civil Rights announced in 2006 that on many American university campuses "anti-Israeli or anti-Zionist propaganda has been disseminated that includes traditional anti-Semitic elements, including age-old Jewish stereotypes and defamations."[104] The Commission added that these stereotypes have "included, for example, ant-Israel literature that perpetuates the medieval blood libel of Jews slaughtering Jews for ritual purpose, as well as anti-Zionist propaganda that exploits ancient stereotypes of Jews as greedy, aggressive, overly powerful, or conspiratorial."[105] Similarly even some of Israel's strongest critics concede that some anti-Israel criticism traffics in classic anti-Semitic stereotypes. Judith Butler, for example, acknowledges that some criticisms of Israel "do employ antic-Semitic rhetoric and argument and so must be opposed absolutely and unequivocally."[106]

The cultural transmission of such memes can exacerbate public negative attitudes toward Jews. Troublingly, the Rutgers study demonstrated that hostility toward Israel may color social attitudes toward Jews. "Although not specifically predicted by our original model," the Rutgers researchers wrote, "we also found evidence that the effects of mortality salience on anti-Semitism were partially mediated by hostility toward Israel."[107] In other words, just as some people are motivated by Jew-hatred to oppose Israel, others are led to dislike Jews as a result of the way that they view Israel. This is consistent with recent findings about the impact of contemporary right-wing political movements on the resurgence of anti-Semitism in Hungary. For example, studies have shown that anti-Semitism correlates, in some times and places, with certain attitudes such as general xenophobia, nationalism, law-and-order conservatism, and anomie. Sociologist András Kovács' recent research in Hungary shows however that these attitudes do not yield the same intensity of anti-Semitic attitudes in every region and social milieu. The differences correlate with the degree of the Jobbik party's support in each respective region and group. From this, Kovács tentatively concludes that support for Hungary's far-right Jobbik party is not the result of anti-Semitism, but rather that attraction to such politics is a factor that mobilizes attitudes that people have about Jewish people.[108] In other words, one of the main functions of such parties is to forge a common political identity for people who, for different reasons, have turned against mainstream political institutions and toward anti-establishment groups that capitalize on pseudo-revolutionary resentments. These groups may seize upon anti-Israel hostility for a variety of reasons, although their tendency is to sustain and generate negative attitudes toward Jews.

At American universities, especially in humanities and social sciences departments, the phenomenon may be more multilayered, since anti-Semitism is advanced through a complex interaction of three forces rather than two: contemporary intellectual trends, anti-Zionism, and anti-Semitism. As we have seen, a loose conglomeration of intellectual trends, such as post-colonialism, post-structuralism, post-modernism, and Marxism, has shaped generations of professors in these disciplines. These movements are often stitched together and made cohesive by a unifying ideology of anti-Zionism. In this way many of these professors have become almost reflexively disposed to perceive Israel in a highly critical way, to oppose Israel's policies, and even to call for the Jewish state's elimination.[109] This in turn advances anti-Semitism, not only in the sense that anti-Semitic memes and motifs are contained within these political stances, but also in the sense that anti-Jewish elements are part of the ideological package that many American academics embrace as a part of their socialization, much as Hungarian Jobbik party members are inculcated with a right-wing version of the same prejudice.

The Ethnic Traits Principle

The Intentionality, Tacitness, and Memetics principles demonstrate respectively that some hostility toward Israel should be considered anti-Semitic because of the speakers' conscious or unconscious mental states or because of the cultural information they transmit. The *Ethnic Traits Principle* by contrast focuses on the foreseeable impact of this hostility on reasonable Jewish listeners or targets. This principle provides that some extreme abuse of Israel should be condemned as anti-Semitic because it is objectively offensive to Jews. The rationale is that a sense of connection to Israel is a trait closely related to the Jewish people. Under this argument, if hostility to Israel is sufficiently offensive to reasonable Jewish people, it does not matter whether the speaker or perpetrator intended offense, or was subconsciously biased, or used language that carried demonstrably anti-Jewish memes. Regardless of intent, bias, or mimetics, abuse of Israel may be profoundly offensive to Jews because of the intimate relationship between a person's Jewish identity and that person's sense of attachment to Israel.

Ronnie Fraser advanced a version of the Jewish Traits Principle in his unsuccessful case against the UCU. In that case, which we discussed briefly in the last chapter, Fraser had sued the UCU for harassment under the U.K. Equality Act of 2010 based on resolutions that the UCU had adopted against Israel as well as the union's decision to abandon the International Working Definition. Fraser argued that significant, repeated anti-Zionist political activity by the UCU created a hostile environment for anglo-Jewish lecturers like himself. As the court also characterized Fraser's case, it was based in part on the Jewish Traits Argument, to wit: Fraser "has a strong attachment to Israel. This attachment is a non-contingent and rationally intelligible aspect of his Jewish identity. It is an aspect of his Jewish identity. It is an aspect, that is, of his race and/or religion."[110]

In a widely criticized opinion, the tribunal denied Fraser's claims, finding *inter alia* that that attachment to Israel is not sufficiently central to Jewish identity for the UCU's hostility against that state to amount to harassment of Jews.[111] Indeed, the tribunal found that this attachment is not "intrinsically part of Jewishness":

> It seems to us that a belief in the Zionist project or an attachment to Israel or any similar sentiment cannot amount to a protected characteristic. It is not intrinsically a part of Jewishness and, even if it was, it could not be substituted for the pleaded characteristics, which are race and religion or belief.[112]

With little reasoning or historical analysis, the tribunal mistakenly concluded that Fraser's attachment to Israel is "not intrinsically a part of Jewishness." In denying the connection between Jewishness and the land of Israel, the tribunal makes a colossal historical mistake. Jews have been intimately associated with the land of Israel for 3,000 years and have made Jerusalem the focus of Jewish literature and liturgy.

Although this connection is not exclusively religious, it can be seen most closely in religious practice. Jewish synagogues traditionally face toward Jerusalem. "If I forget thee Oh Jerusalem," reads one of the most famous Jewish psalms, "let my right hand wither, let my tongue stick to my palate if I do not remember you, if I do not set Jerusalem above my greatest joy."[113] The "Amidah," a silent prayer integral to all

Jewish religious services, contains this blessing: "Return to Your city Jerusalem in mercy, and establish Yourself there as you promised . . . Blessed are you Lord, builder of Jerusalem." Observant Jews recite this prayer thrice daily, every day of their lives, while facing Jerusalem. At the end of the ritual meal (or *seder*) enjoyed during the Passover holiday, even secular Jews outside of Israel recite, "Next year in Jerusalem." There are few traits more intrinsic to any group than Jewry's longstanding attachment to Israel and, especially, Jerusalem.[114]

If the *Fraser* case had been brought in an American court, the question of Jewry's "intrinsic" ties to Israel might be framed in terms of irrational ethnic trait discrimination. That is to say, an American Fraser might argue that severe, persistent, pervasive hostility toward Israel creates a hostile environment for Jewish Americans, whether in the workplace or the campus or the schoolyard, based on a Jewish ethnic or religious trait, that is, a sense of connection to Israel. In racial and ethnic discrimination cases, however, courts have not been as liberal as they have been with respect to sex and gender stereotypes. It is often said that current American civil rights law permits employers (and by extension educators) to engage in irrational trait discrimination against members of ethnic or racial groups unless the trait is immutable.[115]

In the stringent sense once adopted by the U.S. Supreme Court, "immutability" is considered to be solely determined at birth.[116] Applying this sense of "immutability," United States courts have not, therefore, generally forbade workplace requirements that employees wear unbraided hairstyles to work,[117] cut their hair short,[118] speak only English at work,[119] or shave their beards, even if these practices impair traits closely associated with certain identity groups. Although litigants have argued that each of these requirements irrationally discriminates based on a trait associated with their respective groups, the courts have held these traits to be "mutable."[120] Under the same logic, one might argue that a commitment to Israel is not an immutable characteristic of Jewish identity in the way that, for example, skin color or deafness may be considered immutable. Since the Court, however, has not revisited the concept of immutability since 1986, some scholars have speculated that it is now extinct, at least in this formulation.[121] The demise of the concept would be little mourned, as commentators have frequently argued that it relies upon outmoded biological conceptions of human difference or that it fails to account for the most frequent forms of bias in contemporary society.[122]

In the meantime, the modern trend has been to understand "immutability" more broadly if not to disregard it altogether. Under this emerging new conception, a trait is immutable if it is "so fundamental to the identities or consciences of its members that members either cannot or should not be required to change it."[123] This is a normative idea of immutability, based more on moral judgments about what *should not* be changed than on biological judgments about what *cannot* be altered. Indeed, one federal court of appeals has been surprisingly explicit in explaining that immutable characteristics can indeed be changed, defining immutable characteristics as those "such as race, gender, or a prior position, status, or condition, or characteristics that are capable of being changed but are of such fundamental importance that persons should not be required to change them, such as religious beliefs."[124]

Under this more modern formulation, some have argued that traits such as religion or pregnancy, which may appear mutable at first blush, are in fact immutable based on their connection to personal or group identity.[125] Thus, certain physical restrictions such as deafness are now considered immutable even where the disabled person could ameliorate the restriction, for example through surgery, but chooses not to because the condition is too closely connected to their identity.[126] Stanford law professor and former federal appellate judge Michael McConnell, for example, has argued that: "It would come as some surprise to a devout Jew to find that he has 'selected the day of the week in which to refrain from labor,' since the Jewish people have been under the impression for some 3,000 years that this choice was made by God."[127] To be sure, there are some Jews who reject the Jewish religion, but this does not necessarily render the religion a "mutable" characteristic for those who steadfastly adhere to it. The same may be said of the commitment to Israel, which has a similarly long and deep a history with the Jewish people.

To the extent that the immutability principle imports such normative considerations, it surely encompasses the Jewish commitment to Israel. Indeed, for many Jews, a commitment to Israel is so intrinsic to their religious belief as to be the paradigmatic case of a characteristic that a people should not be required to change. For those Jews who embrace Israel as a part of their Jewish identity, although not necessarily for religious reasons, the argument is nearly as strong: the commitment is one of multi-generational duration, shared historically by many members of the group, inscribed centrally in the group's common literature and tradition, and pervasive of the culture. For this reason, an American court following the modern trend should find that Jewish attachment to Israel is an immutable trait of the Jewish people.

Jewish Hostility Toward Israel

The *Ethnic Traits* argument, framed in the context of American civil rights law, provides that a sense of connectedness to Israel is of such fundamental importance that Jewish persons should not be required to disavow it. This does not imply that all Jews share this sense, nor even that all Jews should share it. Moreover, it certainly does not imply that Jews (or others) are precluded from criticizing Israeli policy. People often most vigorously criticize those to whom they feel closest, including family members. Nevertheless, some opponents argue that this sense of connectedness is inconsistent with forms of political expression to which they feel compelled by their own sense of Jewishness. This criticism misconstrues the Ethnic Traits Argument. As we have seen, deafness is now considered an immutable trait even where the disabled person could eliminate the trait through surgery. This is because members of the relevant group consider the trait to be closely connected to their identity. There may be some disabled people who disagree, and some may undertake surgery to eliminate the condition. The presence of some dissenters within the group is altogether conventional and does not, without more, deny the existence of an immutable group trait.

In a recent intervention, Judith Butler attempts to refute the Ethnic Trait Principle along these lines.[128] Butler argues that Jews must contest what she calls the "hegemonic control Zionism exercises over Jewishness" in order to challenge "the colonial subjugation Zionism has implied for the Palestinian people."[129] That is to say, she believes that her Jewish values compel her to criticize Israeli policy toward Palestinians and argues that she is impaired from doing so by the prevailing view that Jewish identity is closely connected to Israel. "In fact," Butler argues, "one would not be concerned with the first hegemonic move (Jewish = Zionist) if one were not primarily concerned with ending the history of subjugation."[130] In other words, Butler's political commitment to improving the situation of the Palestinian people, as she sees it, gives weight and urgency to the question of Jewry's relationship to Israel.

It is beyond the scope of this volume to consider whether the values Butler identifies are recognizably Jewish, whether they support the particular criticisms she describes, or whether it is really incumbent upon any Jew to advance the arguments she crafts. What is clear, however, is that these points, even if properly established, would not demonstrate that hostility toward Israel is never anti-Semitic. That is to say, they do not address whether such criticisms are intended to harm Jews, whether they are coded or pretextual, whether anti-Jewish animus is unconscious or tacit, whether they are stereotypical or defamatory (of Jews), or whether they espouse Jewish collective responsibility. Butler's arguments address only the Jewish Traits argument, and they do so unpersuasively. Butler shows at best that *her* political commitments require her to criticize Israel, and she argues that these values have a pedigree among Jewish thinkers of a certain intellectual disposition. To be sure, Judaism has long embraced a role for dissenters. But this hardly disproves the deep sense of connection to Israel that Jews as a group have expressed since ancient times. Indeed, Butler's repetitive, almost compulsive attention to Israel only reinforces the integral relationship that Israel has to the Jewish identities even of her harshest critics.

Jewish Anti-Zionism

Like Butler, many who dispute the connection between anti-Semitism and anti-Zionism often observe that some of Israel's sharpest critics are Jewish.[131] The presence of these Jewish anti-Zionists has been used to rebut accusations of anti-Semitism on the ground that a Jewish person cannot be an anti-Semite.[132] This is, for example, the crux of Cameron Kerry's argument that his brother John cannot be anti-Semitic because Jewishness and persecution are in his "DNA"—an argument that is entirely empty whether the secretary of state's heart is pure or not. More broadly, many find it difficult to fathom that any member of a stigmatized group, whether Jewish, black, or gay, could harbor hatred for their own group. In fact, however, we now know that Jewish anti-Semitism, black racism, and gay heterosexism are not oxymoronic.[133]

This phenomenon can be partly explained on the ground that some Jews absorb anti-Israel and even anti-Jewish attitudes tacitly as a function of their choice of ideologies. Like anyone else, Jews often adopt broad worldviews that resonate with them across a range of issues and then maintain views and behavior that follow from these over-arching ideologies.[134] If they choose to embrace certain progressive ideologies, they may adopt the positions on Israel that come with the package, even if these positions are based upon anti-Jewish stereotypes. Moreover, insofar as anti-Israel attitudes have become part of this "package deal," they have become a cultural code marking their adherents as belong to a particular subcultural milieu.[135] Some scholars argue that this "collective identity" approach best explains anti-Zionist attitudes among progressive Jews, become it averts the need for psychological and speculative concepts such as "Jewish self-hatred."[136] The concept of *Jewish self-hatred* is now considered impolitic in some circles, just as there are other circles in which its existence is beyond question.

A full treatment of this issue, however, cannot ignore the reality that Jews, like members of other persecuted groups, sometimes embrace the perceptions of their group that circulate within the larger society. Members of many persecuted groups have come to embrace the perceptions of their group that circulate within the larger society. As with any toxin, the principle of respiratory inspiration applies to anti-Semitism: If you can smell it, you have already inhaled it. It has entered your body. That is to say, no person can be fully immune to the viruses that circulate unseen around them. The power of common prejudices, the "persuasive wisdom of what 'everyone knows,'" can cause members of any minority group to believe even the worst that others say about them.[137] "It is a mistake," as Niza Yanay writes, "to believe that one can be free of hatred in a society that promotes an ideology of hatred, as much as one cannot transcend racism in a society with a tradition of racism."[138] Just as there are Jewish anti-Semites, there are indeed many Jewish critics of Israel, including some whose criticisms are devoid of anti-Semitism and others whose criticisms are not. It should go without saying that a statement or action is no less anti-Semitic merely because a Jewish person utters it. On the other hand, just as there are Jewish anti-Semites, there are many Jewish critics of Israel, including some whose criticisms are devoid of anti-Semitism and others whose criticisms are not.

Self-hatred is in this sense nothing more than the tendency of some stigmatized group members to accept the distorted perceptions that their reference group (i.e., the social group that they see as defining their own group) has developed as a reality.[139] In sociological terms, the power of chimerical animus is often strong enough to bring some in-group members within its ambit.[140] Gordon Allport explained self-hatred as a "subtle mechanism" through which a victim comes to agree with his persecutors and to see his group their eyes. He observed, for example, that a Jew "may hate his historic religion . . . Since he cannot escape his own group, he does in a real sense hate himself—or at least the part of himself that is Jewish."[141] Indeed, members of persecuted groups have powerful incentives to reject the markers of their otherness. In anti-Semitic environments, this has generated efforts to deny or escape from Jewish origins in environments that attach stigma or inferiority to Jewishness.[142] In such cases, Jewish self-hatred reflects a persecuted group's identification with its aggressor.

Jewish self-hatred is complex, because causality flows in both directions. While Jews undoubtedly are influenced by animus directed at the figural Jew, Jews have also provided some of the materials that have been used against them. This arises in part from traditions of self-criticism within Jewish culture. The vocabulary of self-abuse in Hebrew literature, from the time of the Prophets to the present, is unparalleled except in the most virulent anti-Semitic propaganda. In addition, those Jews who have come to identify with their persecutors in intensely anti-Semitic environments have been among the harshest antagonists of the Jewish community. This can be seen in the experience of medieval Spain. After the anti-Jewish massacres in 1391, Jews converted to Christianity in large numbers, and converts (*conversos*) were among the leaders calling for degradation, segregation, and persecution of their own former brethren.[143] As author Arthur Schnitzler wrote in fin de siècle Austria, "Anti-Semitism did not succeed until the Jews began to sponsor it."[144] This is not to say that Jews are responsible for anti-Semitism but rather that Jewish sources have frequently provided the tools with which it has been formed.

At the end of his classic treatise on *Jewish Self-Hatred*, Sander Gilman writes that "one of the most recent forms of Jewish self-hatred is the virulent opposition to the existence of the State of Israel."[145] Jewish progressive and intellectuals are often responsible for some of the most virulent criticism of Israel. Noam Chomsky, Norman Finkelstein, Ilan Pappé, and Jacqueline Rose, for example, have been among Israel's most unrelenting critics. A few left-wing Jewish organizations, such as Jewish Voices for Peace, have been formed largely to criticize the State of Israel or to urge others to take actions hostile to the Jewish state. Judith Butler has participated in conferences and panel discussions that have been characterized as containing or advancing anti-Semitic elements. For example, Butler participated in the March 2007 conference on "Alternative Histories within and beyond Zionism" at the University of California at Santa Cruz.[146] Tammi Rossman-Benjamin analyzed that notorious conference as advancing the following arguments:

> Zionism is a form of racism; Israel is an apartheid state; Israel commits heinous acts crimes against humanity, including genocide and ethnic cleansing; Israel's behavior is comparable to that of Nazi Germany; Jews exaggerate the Holocaust as a tool of Zionist propaganda; Israel should be dismantled as a Jewish state; morally responsible people should actively oppose the Jewish state by, for instance, supporting divestment campaigns.[147]

There is an extent to which collective self-criticism reflects a healthy propensity for internal self-examination, free dissention, and unfettered debate, just as there is a point at which it becomes unhealthy. Yehuda Bauer described the Jewish tendency toward internecine conflicts in an interview with *Ha'aretz*: "It starts with the struggle between the Hasidim and their opponents; between the true prophets and the false prophets; in the splitting of the United Kingdom into two rival kingdoms that fought each other; in the disputes between Sadducees and Pharisees; between Hellenizers and Hasmoneans; between the religious establishment and the various zealots before the Great Revolt [against the Roman Empire], and so on."[148] As Bauer argues, this quality has had an important role in the continuity of the Jewish people. Argumentation gives vitality to a people and can drive cultural change. There are moments at which the debate between Zionists and anti-Zionists appears to fall within this tradition. But if Bauer is right, this does not mean that neither side of the current debate over Zionism is wrong. Nor does it mean that this debate is healthy, only that it is arises from a Jewish trait that has served an evolutionary function.

In fact, Judaism's internecine quarrels and self-criticisms have provided the grist for anti-Jewish ideology since ancient times. This can be seen from the earliest Jewish religious texts, such as the Psalmist, who developed the stereotype of Jewish hypocrisy that became so influential in early Christian and Muslim texts.[149] "And they flattered him with their mouth," the Psalmist wrote, "with their tongues they lied to him, while their heart was not straight with him, / And they kept no faith with his covenant."[150] Since ancient times, anti-Jewish ideologues have simultaneously praised Jewish prophecy and despised Jewry, accusing Jews of stubborn resistance to and persecution of those who arose within them to chastise and enlighten them.[151] "You stubborn people," John admonished, "Can you name a single prophet your ancestors never persecuted? They killed those who foretold the coming of the Upright One, and now you have become his betrayers, his murders."[152]

In many cases, Jewish dissidents have stressed their Jewish origins in order to support projects hostile to the Jewish people. In this way, they have responded to an assimilationist fantasy, whether in medieval Spain or on contemporary California university campuses: "Become like us—abandon your difference—and you may be one with us."[153] Thus, for example, Jews were among the first medieval polemicists to write against Judaism, and they stressed their Jewish origins in doing so.[154] Over the centuries, anti-Jewish polemicists within the Jewish community have used the authority of their Jewish background to legitimize virtually every anti-Jewish canard, from blood libel to international Jewish conspiracies.[155] In recent years, this has been seen in the popular reception of self-critical voices within the Jewish community, from Noam Chomsky to Norman Finkelstein to Judith Butler.[156]

Conclusion

The General Definition

At this point, it should be clear that a complete definition of anti-Semitism must account for its ideological, attitudinal, and practical qualities; its continuities, discontinuities, and repetitive structure within Western cultures; its connections to analogous phenomena; its chimerical quality; and its role in the construction of individual and collective Jewish identity. That is to say, it must account for the participation of anti-Semitic discourses and practices in the construction of the "the *Jews*," individually and collectively. This process is equally critical to the understanding of anti-Semitism and to the development of means of counteracting what might be called anti-Semitism's chimerical core.

There are many reasons to define a term like anti-Semitism, and it is appropriate to develop different definitions for these different purposes. As we have seen, some definitions are less useful than others, due to conceptual problems that limit their utility. It may be the better part of valor simply to describe the characteristics exhibited by effective definitions rather than to suggest that a single definition could uniquely capture all the insights that a definition of anti-Semitism should encapsulate. The best definitions of anti-Semitism, in our estimation, reflect the following insights:

Anti-Semitism consists of negative attitudes toward the Jewish people, individually or collectively; conduct that reflects these attitudes; and ideologies that sustain them. In other words, it means hostility toward Jews, including thoughts that are not acted upon and actions that are not fully thought out. As a set of attitudes, it ranges from mild disdain to virulent loathing. As a form of conduct, it embraces hostility toward individual Jews, Jewish institutions, and Jewish collectivity. As an ideology, it provides a way to make sense of the entire world and all of history, not just the relatively small territory occupied by the descendants of Jacob.

The ideology of anti-Semitism can be articulated in various ways. Sometimes it is conceived in opposition to the perceived Jewish "religion" and at other times against an imagined Jewish "race." In the end, anti-Semitism is not about race or religion. Rather, it is a process of working up Jews into a distorted image of "the *Jews*." Whether this image borrows from racial or religious ideas is ultimately immaterial. Nevertheless, it bears mentioning that anti-Semitism characteristically constructs a figure of "the *Jews*" that is commonly characterized, at least in its extreme forms, by the related phenomena of demonization and bestialization.

The ideology of anti-Semitism is remarkable for the extent to which it has recurred over the course of three millennia in very different places and cultures. In our view, anti-Semitism should be understood as a repetitive process that responds to similar needs or conflicts in widely different periods. At an individual level, anti-Semitism may be understood as a projection onto "the *Jews*" of despised traits that the anti-Semite identifies in herself and represses only to see it return in distorted form. This repression may be a pathology to which certain people are subject or as a normal element of assimilation into a culture. At a societal level, anti-Semitism may reflect underlying social conflicts, such as the subordination of certain peoples to major powers (such as the Roman Empire at its height) that are too dangerous to engage directly.

Anti-Semitism has similarities with other forms of aversion, but it also has distinctive attributes. Anti-Semitism resembles other animosities in its structure, functions, and characteristics, but is unique in its range, virulence, and repetitiveness. Anti-Semitism's most remarkable quality is the extent to which it provides a nodal point around which other ideological elements, including other forms of aversion, are stitched together into an apparently coherent worldview. The peculiar feature of anti-Semitism is not a "certain perception of the Jews" but rather the repetitive process by which Jews are worked up into different versions of "the *Jews.*"

In today's political context, the definition of anti-Semitism most frequently arises in disputes concerning whether certain hostilities toward Israel should be considered "anti-Semitic." The best definitions emphasize that many criticisms of Israel are not anti-Semitic. At the same time, they recognize that animus toward Israel may be anti-Semitic in some circumstances, often characterized by the presence of double standards, demonization, or delegitimization. More precisely, hostility toward Israel may be considered anti-Semitic when any of the following four conditions are met. First, it may be associated with conscious anti-Semitism. In some cases, it may be a pretext or ruse to conceal conscious animosity toward Jews. Second, it may arise from tacit or unconscious animosity toward Jews. Third, it may arise from and advance a climate of opinion that is hostile to Jews, regardless of the perpetrator's own mental state. Fourth, it may irrationally discriminate against Jews based on a group trait that is deeply or immutably connected to Jewish identity.

To conclude in this manner would however seem like something of an evasion since the chief lessons of the preceding chapters can in fact be reduced to a single general definition. The precise terms of the definition may be less important than the thinking that went into it. In this sense the broader definition consists of this entire volume and not just the one sentence in which its message is encapsulated. If one were however to distill the lessons of this volume into one general definition of anti-Semitism, that definition would read as follows:

> Anti-Semitism is a set of negative attitudes, ideologies, and practices directed at Jews as Jews, individually or collectively, based upon and sustained by a repetitive and potentially self-fulfilling latent structure of hostile erroneous beliefs and assumptions that flow from the

application of double standards toward Jews as a collectivity, manifested culturally in myth, ideology, folklore, and imagery, and urging various forms of restriction, exclusion, and suppression.

This definition is, as best I can assess, the least vulnerable to the various challenges that definitions of anti-Semitism have historically faced. Since different kinds of definitions are devised for the different purposes for which the word is used, it is appropriate to supplement the general definition with more specific tools employed for particular purposes, such as the State Department and International Working Definitions.

In light of this discussion, are we now better able to address the specific recent controversies that were described in the Introduction? For example, do we have a means of resolving the controversy surrounding Günter Grass's poem, "What Must Be Said"? Have we provided tools by which law enforcement could more effectively and quickly analyze a crime such as *Les Barbares*' attack on Ilan Halimi? Do we have a better understanding of Mohamed Merah's murderous rampage? Could this knowledge guide the investigation of federal agents, such as the OCR investigators who must investigate allegations of anti-Semitism on American college and university campuses? Can we now better see the BDS movement for what it is?

Rereading Günter Grass and the *Harvard Crimson*

To begin with, how should we now reread Günter Grass's controversial poem, "What Must Be Said" in light of this analysis? As we observed in the Introduction, this Nobel laureate's controversial poem triggered considerable controversy for its heavy-handed criticism of Israel. Under the definition of anti-Semitism offered by *Webster's Third International Dictionary*, this poem would be considered anti-Semitic simply because it criticizes the Jewish state. No reputable authority would support that definition today. Under the opposite categorical definition, no criticism of Israel could be considered anti-Semitic, even if its author is a former member of German Waffen SS. This definition is as untenable as is *Webster's Third's*. In order to determine whether "What Must Be Said" reflects what we have called "a set of negative attitudes, ideologies, and practices directed at Jews as Jews, individually or collectively," we must use a more refined instrument.

The State Department definition and the International Working Definition provide a surprisingly useful aid to analyzing Grass's poem, even though they were certainly not devised for literary purposes. Both definitions alert us to the presence of double standards, and Grass does appear to apply different standards to Israel than to the rest of the world. But the larger issue is that of stereotypes. Here again, both definitions prove useful. The International Working Definition observes that anti-Semitism "frequently charges Jews with conspiring to harm humanity" and that "it is often used to blame Jews for 'why things go wrong.'"[1] More directly, the State Department definition notes that anti-Semitism blames Israel "for all inter-religious and political tension."[2] This is precisely how we must understand Grass's lament that Israel threatens not only the extermination of the Iranian people but also the entirety of world peace and indeed all of life itself.

Grass's accusation that Israel "endangers an already fragile world peace" must be read in the context of an ideology in which Jews are conceived as the central danger to humanity. More specifically, the poem exemplifies what the International Working Definition calls the "mendacious, dehumanizing, demonizing, or stereotypical allegations about Jews as such or the power of Jews as collective." "What Must Be Said" resonates with medieval stereotypes of the Jews as a wealthy, powerful, menacing, and controlling collectivity, demanding the sacrifice of others to their own greed. More deeply, Grass's poem follows in a long European tradition, exemplified by the *Protocols,* of conceiving Jewry as a fundamental threat to human existence. The is what we (following Helen Fein) mean by the "latent structure of hostile erroneous beliefs and assumptions that flow from the application of double standards toward Jews as a collectivity, manifested culturally in myth, ideology, folklore, and imagery." In this context, Grass's poem must be understood as anti-Semitic, whatever his personal intentions were in writing it.

It must be acknowledged that Grass might have written other things about Jewish people that would not be anti-Semitic even if they reinforced comparable stereotypes. For example, he could have observed that Janet Yellen, the chair of the Board of Governors of the United

States Federal Reserve System, has enormous influence over international financial institutions. Alternatively, he could have criticized disgraced former financier Bernie Madoff for his mendacity and greed. In both cases, he would have associated a particular Jewish individual with qualities that are stereotypically attributed to the Jewish people as a whole. In both cases, he would have spoken truthfully. For reasons explained in Chapter Five, the fact that Madoff really is a crook and Yellen a powerful banker does not prove that statements about their respective crookedness or influence are not anti-Semitic. There are undoubtedly some anti-Semites who use Yellen's power or Madoff's criminality as proof of their own distorted ideology. Yet the hypothetical comments about Yellen and Madoff may be based entirely on valid observations about his conduct and her position, rather than on a "latent structure of hostile erroneous beliefs and assumptions." Our definition of anti-Semitism does not insist on falsehood, but it does exclude realistic assumptions or observations. True statements about Yellen and Madoff are generally not anti-Semitic because they are based on realistic observations and not just because they also turn out to be true. In the same way, Grass's poem is anti-Semitic not so much because it implies mistaken facts but rather because it rests upon stereotypes that are unreasonable and hateful.

Similarly, Grass might have criticized the Jewish state in other ways that would not have been anti-Semitic. As we have seen, much controversy surrounded Harvard University's decision to host a conference on the so-called "one-state solution" to the Israel-Palestine conflict. We have criticized the *Harvard Crimson* for suggesting without evidence that the discussion at this conference would not be anti-Semitic. It is all too easy to imagine ways in which speakers at such a conference might engage in anti-Semitic discourse. On the other hand, there is nothing inherently anti-Semitic about the concept of a one-state solution. Indeed, one prominent writer has recently supported the idea of a one-state solution from a robustly Zionist perspective.[3] Unlike Grass however the Zionist author does not indulge in anti-Jewish stereotypes or memes. Some activists have argued that Palestinian one-state solutions are necessarily anti-Semitic because they would endanger the Jewish character of the Jewish state. Others argue that such solutions are anti-Semitic because they would endanger the physical security of Israeli Jews. These arguments ignore that there are arguments in favor of a one-state solution that are not based on antipathy toward the Jewish people. There may be strong policy counter-arguments against these positions, but that does not make them anti-Semitic.

Grass's poem is anti-Semitic because it is based upon "a set of negative attitudes, ideologies, and practices directed at Jews as Jews," in this case "collectively" embodied in the State of Israel, based not upon verifiable observations but rather upon the same "latent structure of hostile erroneous beliefs and assumptions" that has historically supported anti-Semitic rhetoric.

Decoding the Barbarians

Are we now similarly better equipped to handle the Ilan Halimi case that stymied the French police? As we saw in Chapter One, French authorities were unable to predict the *Les Barbares'* cruelty because they failed to acknowledge that anti-Semitism motivated their crime. If we were in their shoes, would we similarly resist the conclusion to which the evidence clearly led? Were we to use an ideological definition, we might be similarly misled. During much of the investigation, it was impossible to determine that the gang members viewed "the *Jews*" in chimerical fashion. Rather, some information suggested that the Barbarians targeted a Jewish victim because they believed that Jews have sufficient resources to pay a substantial ransom. At first blush, it appeared that Halimi was targeted as a Jew but not because he conforms to a preconceived notion of the figural Jew. Instead, it initially looked as though he was targeted because the *Barbares* presumed Jews to be wealthy.

Although the International Working Definition was initially devised as an aid to law enforcement, it may remain too closely tied to ideology to be helpful in such matters. The Working Definition encompasses "calling for, aiding, or justifying the killing or harming of Jews in the name of a radical ideology or an extremist view of religion."[4] In retrospect, we can see that the Barbarians were indeed acting on a radical anti-Semitic ideology. While the crime was ongoing however it was not yet clear what ideology held the kidnappers in its thrall, nor was it clear whether the criminals were acting on what the Working Definition calls "a certain perception of the Jews." In this sense, the Working Definition is useful to us in this case only in retrospect, but it would not have been helpful in real time to French law enforcement, because it retains too closely tethered to the perceptions that anti-Semites have of Jewish people. The U.S. State Department definition includes subtly different language that turns out to be decisive. This definition adopts the same provision that we have seen above but softens it with the addition of one critical word: "often" (together with a set of parentheses). The Department's relevant provision thus encompasses "calling for, aiding, or justifying the killing or harming of Jews (*often* in the name of a radical ideology or an extremist view of religion)."[5] The Halimi case shows how difficult it can be to determine establish that a particular anti-Semitic incident is motivated by a radical ideology. Implicit in this definition is that they are being harmed as Jews, which was certainly the case with Halimi.

By contrast, consider the widely discussed argument that anti-Semitism explains the surprising defeat of U.S. House of Representatives Majority Leader Eric Cantor in his 2014 primary reelection bid. Those national figures who contributed to his defeat, such as radio commentators Laura Ingraham and Glenn Beck, certainly harmed a prominent Jew. But there is little or no evidence to suggest that Cantor's Jewishness, as opposed to his position on immigration reform, had anything to do with their actions. For this reason, the accusations of anti-Semitism were baseless. With the State Department's critical emendation, the definition now encompasses the "killing or harming of Jews" *whether it is in the name of a radical ideology or not*. Whatever else one might say of the Barbarians, they were guilty of this (and Glenn Beck was not). In hindsight, as we consider the evidence that has accumulated since the *Barbares*' trial, it is now clear that the perpetrators were indeed motivated by typical anti-Jewish delusions. At the time however it should have been sufficient to ascertain that the *Barbares* specifically sought to harm and kill Jews. The State Department definition alone does so.

Returning to Toulouse

What of Mohamed Merah? As we saw in the Introduction, the Toulouse murderer massacred Jewish children in cold blood saying he wanted "to avenge Palestinian children." Many commentators assume that Palestinian solidarity politics motivate such attacks, whether the perpetrators are as explicit as Merah or not. As we have learned from Günther Jikeli's research (Chapter Five), young French immigrant Muslim men like Merah are more likely to hate Israelis because they are Jewish, rather than to hate Jews because many Jews support Israel. We should not assume that this was Merah's own motivation. But we should also not conclude that Merah was motivated only by politics merely because his self-justifying statements could be interpreted this way.

We have seen that anti-Semitism may be directed at Jews "individually or collectively." The Working Definition provides that it is anti-Semitic to hold "Jews collectively responsible for the actions of the state of Israel." Here again the State Department's definition is decisive. The State Department adds the critical italicized terms to this example of anti-Semitism that it shares with the Working Definition: "Accusing Jews as a people of being responsible for real or imagined wrongdoing committed by a single Jewish person or group, *the State of Israel*, or even for acts committed by non-Jews."[6] The implicit wisdom in these definitions is that it should not matter for practical purposes whether Merah murdered his victims because he was holding them collectively responsible for Israel's actions or not, since holding individuals collectively responsible for the actions of others is an indicator of prejudice. As a matter of fact, Merah likely saw his victims as Jews first and foremost, with all of the distorted misperceptions common to the anti-Semitic point of view. But his actions should be identified as anti-Semitic even if this could not be shown.

The analysis would be more difficult if Merah had acted on a reasonable belief that his victims had been complicit in actual crimes. Two years after the Toulouse massacre, 29-year-old French citizen Mehdi Nemmouche allegedly entered the Jewish Museum of Belgium and shot an Israeli couple, Mira and Emanuel Riva, dead with a Kalashnikov assault rifle.[7] While most commentators immediately assumed that the act was anti-Semitic, others disagreed. Some commentators, including Tariq Ramadan, raised the possibility that the Rivas might have been hit in a targeted killing. They argued the killer's actions, as caught on video cameras, resembled that of a professional, as opposed to a random murderer, and that the Rivas both worked for Israeli governmental agencies.⁸ As we have seen, Ramadan also argued that Merah is not anti-Semitic, and we have concluded that his argument about Merah is unconvincing. Nevertheless, if Nemmouche had killed the Rivas in response to actions that they had personally undertaken, then he would still be a murderer but not necessarily an anti-Semite.

Reopening the Irvine Investigation

What of OCR? As we have seen, OCR investigated allegations that anti-Israel activists repeatedly and severely harassed Jewish students at the University of California at Irvine over a period of several years. In the end, OCR rejected these claims, finding that they did not amount to discrimination on the basis of national origin, that is to say, of Jewish ethnicity or ancestry. OCR was wrong. In order to understand its error, consider the agency's account of even a few of the allegations that it concedes were timely filed:

> OCR's investigation determined that during these events many speakers criticized Israel, its governmental policies, its treatment of the Palestinians, and Jews throughout the world who support Israel. Most speakers distinguished opposition to Zionism from opposition to Jews. Other speakers did not do so, yet their criticism of Jews was focused on their perceived support of Israel. OCR's investigation also revealed that some speakers made broad generalizations about Jews, which were offensive to Jewish students. In addition, during these events, there were often symbols utilized that were offensive to the Jewish students, such as mock check points; green armbands; and a poster that contained a picture of a wall on which was painted a swastika, an equal sign, and a Star of David. Several students interviewed by OCR stated that they were deeply offended and, in some instances, intimidated and harassed by these events.⁹

After a full investigation, OCR determined that "although offensive to the Jewish students, the speeches, articles, marches, symbols and other events in question were not based on the national origin of the Jewish students, but rather based on opposition to the policies of Israel."¹⁰

When we read OCR's resolution letter closely, we can see that OCR has failed to grasp the nature of anti-Semitism. In the language quoted above, OCR begins with its determination that "many speakers criticized Israel, its governmental policies, its treatment of the Palestinians, and Jews throughout the world who support Israel." The State Department and International Working definitions, like nearly all reputable authorities, emphasize that "criticism of Israel similar to that leveled against any other country cannot be regarded as anti-Semitic." Nevertheless, they demonstrate that some criticism of Israel is also hostile to Jews.

OCR next observed that most of the Irvine speakers "distinguished opposition to Zionism from opposition to Jews." As we have seen, this is a common rhetorical device among anti-Zionists. Such self-serving protestations cannot be accepted uncritically, since they frequently mask anti-Semitic sentiment. As we have also seen, some anti-Zionists advance anti-Semitic positions, despite their contrary assertions, in the sense that they harbor tacit anti-Semitism, advance anti-Jewish tropes, or engage in irrational ethnic trait discrimination. Significantly, OCR also noted that other speakers did not distinguish between opposition to Zionism from opposition to Jews. In other words, these speakers assailed all Jewish people and not just Israelis or Zionists. OCR should have seen this as clear evidence that the expressions at issue were anti-Semitic and not just anti-Zionist. Nevertheless, OCR was swayed by its finding that "their criticism of Jews was focused on their perceived support of Israel." This amounts to holding "Jews collectively responsible for the actions of the state of Israel," which the Working Definition provides as an example of anti-Semitism. More specifically, it is an example of the form of anti-Semitism that the State Department has described as "accusing Jews as a people of being responsible for real or imagined wrongdoing committed by . . . the State of Israel."

Given its ultimate disposition of the case, it is surprising that OCR acknowledges that "some speakers made broad generalizations about Jews, which were offensive to Jewish students." One should not be too quick to draw conclusions here. After all, some offensive statements may be constitutionally protected. Additionally, it is possible that some Jewish students are unusually thin-skinned. The fact that some Jewish students found the generalizations to be offensive does not necessarily mean that a reasonable person standing in their shoes would agree. But OCR does not find the statements to be constitutionally protected, nor does it deny that they are objectively as well as subjectively offensive. In particular, it is conspicuous that OCR recognizes the use of symbols . . . that were offensive to the Jewish students," including the "poster that contained a picture of a wall on which was painted a swastika, an equal sign, and a Star of David." As we saw in Chapter Six, the State Department and Working Definitions both instruct that "drawing comparisons of contemporary Israeli policy to that of the Nazis" is a form of anti-Semitism. In short, the facts as OCR describes them include classic examples of behavior that the State Department has established to be anti-Semitic. OCR misconstrued the facts gathered in its own investigation, largely because it lacks a clear understanding of the meaning and scope of anti-Semitism. Such misunderstandings could be dispelled if OCR correctly applies the definition of anti-Semitism established by its sister agency, the Department of State.

Understanding BDS

What then of BDS? The BDS movement appears at first blush to be based on human rights objectives. To be sure, these demands are framed in terms of a "Palestinian solidarity" narrative. Terms such as "occupation" and "colonization" are politically contested, as is the putative right of Palestinian return. One could argue that neither term is apposite to the current situation in Israel. Yet the decision to frame the issue in a manner advantageous to one side of the dispute may be based on strategic and political considerations, rather than ethnic animus. Some Jewish leaders argue the proposal for a Palestinian right of return is anti-Semitic. They point out that if all Palestinians were to return to their families' pre-1948 homes, the demographic shift within Israel could destabilize the Jewish state, with uncertain consequences for Israeli Jews.[11] Whatever the merits of this analysis, it does not prove that the underlying claim is anti-Semitic. Rather, the Palestinian people may seek a right of return for reasons that have less to do with a hatred of Jews than with a desire for their own collective advancement.

Many commentators have argued that BDS is anti-Semitic based on some version of Natan Sharansky's 3D test. For example, the Statement of Jewish Organizations on Boycott, Divestment, and Sanctions (BDS) Campaigns Against Israel argues that the campaign is anti-Semitic on the grounds that it "demonizes Israel or its leaders, denies Israel the right to defend its citizens or seeks to denigrate Israel's right to exist."[12] This is a valid approach. The problem though is that these tests establish presumptions rather than bright-line tests. The BDS movement's pervasive use of double standards for Israel surely requires explanation. But explanations may be available. For example, if a BDS advocate is Palestinian, she may retort that she is exclusively focused on Israel's perceived faults because they impact so directly on her own personal experiences. This rationale may be pretextual, given ADL's recent survey finding that 93% of West Bank and Gaza residents harbor anti-Semitic attitudes. Nevertheless, the pretextual character would need to be demonstrated rather than merely assumed.

The Origins of BDS

The difficulty in applying standards to BDS is that it is not obvious what BDS is, when it began, or what it stands for. The conventional explanation is that the BDS campaign began on July 9, 2005. On that date, over 100 Palestinian organizations issued the "Palestinian Civil Society Calls for Boycott, Divestment and Sanctions against Israel Until it Complies with International Law and Universal Principles of Human Rights."[13] This so-called Palestinian "Call" justified itself based on allegations of ethnic cleansing and racial discrimination. The Call's three explicit objectives were to end Israel's "occupation and colonization" of "all Arab lands," to recognize the equal fundamental rights of Israel's Arab-Palestinian citizens, and to promote a proposed Palestinian right of return to their former homes and properties.[14] If we are to understand BDS, the conventional narrative goes, we must start with these three innocent-sounding objectives. Unfortunately, the conventional narrative is not entirely convincing. Indeed, it is not clear that these three rationales are more than contemporary window-dressing on a movement with long prehistory and rather unsavory connections.

To begin with, if the BDS campaign really began with the 2005 Call of Palestinian civil society, then we would expect to find no BDS efforts in 2003, 2003, or 2004. In fact, these were boom years for the BDS campaign. During this period, there were numerous calls to boycott or divest from Israel, including Palestinian boycott calls during each of those three years.[15] By October 2002, for example, more than 50 campuses were circulating divestment petitions.[16] From this perspective, the 2005 Call appears less as the impetus to the BDS movement than as an effort by Palestinian civil society institutions to assume control of the BDS narrative, articulating its aims in a publicly palatable manner.

In fact, the BDS movement can be traced back at least to the 2001 World Conference Against Racism, Racial Discrimination, Xenophobia and Related Intolerance (Durban I), which was held in Durban, South Africa. The conference's NGO Forum was attended by 8,000 representatives from as many as 3,900 nongovernmental organizations. Its "Meeting in Solidarity with the Palestinian People" yielded an NGO plan of action that called for "complete and total isolation of Israel as an apartheid state as in the case of South Africa which means the imposition of mandatory and comprehensive sanctions and embargoes, the full cessation of all links (diplomatic, economic, social, aid, military cooperation and training) between all states and Israel."[17]

When the BDS movement is interpreted in light of Durban I, a different image appears. That conference was significant not only for its human rights objections to Israel but also for its widespread anti-Semitism.[18] Flyers were distributed that praised Adolf Hitler and expressed remorse that he had not prevailed. Copies of *Protocols of the Elders of Zion* were distributed.[19] Posters were hung that described how the Jews make their bread with the blood of Muslims and that depict a rabbi with the *Protocols of the Elders of Zion* under his arm and an Israeli army cap on his head.[20] When someone asked an unpopular question about procedure, the crowd booed and shouted, "Jew, Jew, Jew."[21] This was also the conference at which then–Iranian President Mahmoud Ahmadinejad notoriously accused "Zionist circles" of conspiring to undermine the conference's goals.[22] To the extent that BDS is seen as an outgrowth of this conference, its motivations may more complicated.

But BDS's origins are still more complicated. Well-established, state-sponsored efforts had been continuously enforced throughout the existence of the State of Israel and even before. In 1945, the 22-nation Council of the Arab League, founded the previous year, had called for an economic boycott of Jewish goods and services in the British-controlled mandate territory of Palestine: "Jewish products and manufactured goods shall be considered undesirable to the Arab countries."[23] All Arab "institutions, organizations, merchants, commission agents and individuals" were called upon "to refuse to deal in, distribute, or consume Zionist products or manufactured goods."[24] Three years later, following the war establishing Israel's independence, the League formalized its boycott against the state of Israel, broadening it to include non-Israelis who maintain economic relations with Israel or who are perceived to support it.[25] Some Arab League member states and entities have formally withdrawn from the boycott, or at least some aspects of it, either through peace treaties, or other diplomatic agreements, or as a result of diplomatic relations, but the boycott largely remains in place.[26]

The Arab boycott (1945 to the present) did not come out of nowhere. From 1933 to 1945, Nazi propagandists transmitted anti-Semitic propaganda to Arabs and Muslims in the Middle East and North Africa.[27] This included Arabic-language shortwave radio programs broadcast seven days per week during this period, as well as millions of printed items.[28] This propaganda combined selective readings of the Koran, Nazi critiques of Western imperialism, and anti-Jewish themes in Islam. Nazi officials considered anti-Semitism and anti-Zionism to be the best means of entrance into Arab and Muslim hearts and minds.[29] Nazi ideology would continue to influence both Arab nationalists and religious extremists throughout the Middle East, including among Palestinian leaders, for decades afterward.[30] When the Arab League began its anti-Jewish boycott, it was "filled with ex-Axis collaborators."[31] During the early years of the Arab League boycott, affinity for National Socialism in the Arab world continued unabated.[32]

These efforts echoed an earlier anti-Jewish boycott in Germany. On April 1, 1933, two months after coming to power in Germany, the Nazis set the pattern for future anti-Jewish boycotts when they conducted, as their first nationwide action against Jews, a temporary boycott against Jewish businesses and professionals.[33] As Lucy S. Dawidowicz has observed, Adolf Hitler's contribution was to formalize, rationalize, and channel the impulses behind hooligan attacks on stores owned by German Jews, into "'meaningful' political action."[34] It is important to recall that the Nazis did not justify the Nazi boycott on Jewish racial or religious issues, any more than later efforts did. Rather, the Nazis justified their anti-Jewish boycott in the rhetoric of their era as a response to the anti-German propaganda that Jewish people as well as foreign journalists, were allegedly spreading in the international press.[35] For this reason, German soldiers insisted they were defending Germans from Jewish aggression, rather than attacking Jews for racial reasons. The Stormtroopers' battle-cry was, "Germans! Defend yourselves! Do not buy from Jews!"[36] This ushered in the Nazi's nationwide campaign against the entire German Jewish population. Just a week later, for example, the Nazis passed a law barring civil service employment to non-"Aryans."[37] Like the yellow star that Jews were later forced to wear, the Nazi boycott was the first systematic national socialist mechanism to strip Jews of the "normalization" that had come with emancipation. The culmination of these efforts was the program of systematic extermination.

Like Hitler's Nazi boycott, the Durban I and Palestinian Call formalized, systematized, and justified the sporadic boycotts and anti-Jewish attacks that preceded them. The primary strategy of BDS leadership is to reject Israel's "normalization," defined as the treatment of Israel as a "normal" state with which business as usual can be conducted.[38] The Palestinian Campaign for the Academic and Cultural Boycott of Israel (PACBI) insists they oppose normalization on political rather than racial grounds. Indeed, their public statements speak of resistance to putative Palestinian oppression, rather than of any essentially malevolent characteristics of the Jewish people. Nevertheless, this anti-normalization effort echoes prior anti-Jewish boycotts. It also provides a dark rejoinder to the early Zionist thinkers, who had argued that a Jewish state could solve the problem of anti-Semitism by giving the Jewish people, who had long been haunted by their statelessness, a sense of normalcy.

Analyzing the BDS Campaign

Nowadays, it is largely indisputable that the Nazi boycott was a conscious, intentional, anti-Semitic action, perhaps a paradigmatic case of anti-Semitic action, even if it was justified in the language of its time as a response to Jewish aggression. In retrospect, it is now also clear that the Arab League boycott, which was at a minimum a forerunner to the modern BDS campaign, has sometimes been a more general boycott of Jews, even if it is formally a boycott of the State of Israel. Indeed, Bernard Lewis has remarked that "the way in which the boycott of Israel, operated by all member states of the Arab League, was put into effect" is "[p]erhaps the clearest indication of the way in which the war against Israel was generalized to be a war against the Jews."[39] This can be seen, for example, in various examples in which Arab states canceled cultural events or rejected ambassadorial credentials based on Jewish rather than Israeli or Zionist connections.[40]

But is this true of the modern BDS movement too? To the extent that the BDS campaign is equated with the 2005 Call, its aims appear to be based on human rights concerns. Nevertheless, the first signatory to the Call is the Council for the National and Islamic Forces in Palestine, an organization that includes Hamas and other terrorist groups that are unambiguously motivated by hatred of Jews.[41] To be sure, one cannot attribute the views of any one signatory to the document it signed. But neither can one ignore the presence among the signatories of some who are clearly anti-Semitic.

There seems to be widespread agreement that conscious antipathy to Jews fuels at least some of the growth of the BDS movement. There can be little question of anti-Jewish animus, for example, when BDS activists call Jewish University of Michigan students "kike" and "dirty Jew" or spit on a Jewish University of California at Santa Barbara student for wearing a Star of David necklace.[42] Similarly, it is unquestionably anti-Semitic for BDS activists to engage in or support Holocaust denial, as some have done.[43] This is unquestionably anti-Semitic.

Other critics of Israel, who may not be *consciously* aware that they harbor negative attitudes toward Jews, nevertheless denigrate Israel to express *unconscious* resentment of Jews. No studies specifically examine the incidence of tacit or unconscious anti-Semitic views among members of the BDS movement. Based on the existing research it is fair to extrapolate that unconscious anti-Semitism is substantially higher among BDS advocates than among the general population. One can glean also signs of unconscious anti-Semitism in certain verbal slips among Israel's most stringent critics. For example, unconscious hostility is an obvious alternative explanation for comments interpreted as "stupid or hostile," such as "You mean there are some good Jews—I mean Israelis?"[44] This is similar to the situation of composer Mikis Theodorakis, who insisted that he suffered from a "slip of the tongue," when in the middle of excoriating Israel, he accidentally said, "I must point out that I am an anti-Semite."[45]

Whether BDS advocates are aware of it or not, they often spread anti-Jewish stereotypes, images, and myths. For example, BDS advocates within Protestant church groups equate Palestinian suffering with Jesus Christ's suffering, referring to the so-called "Israeli government crucifixion system."[46] Such tropes revive the anti-Semitic deicidal accusation that Jews killed Jesus. In some cases, the cultural transmission of these memes colors the social environment in substantial ways. This can also be seen in the way that some academics advocate for anti-Israel resolutions within academic associations. This can be seen for example in how some members of the Modern Language Association (MLA) argued for a proposed resolution to censure Israel.[47] Professor Alessio Lero of Temple University argued that the MLA's harsh focus on Israel is justified because of what Lero called "the humongous influence that Jewish scholars have in the decision making process of Academia in general."[48] Lero's comment is an example of what the State Department definition calls "stereotypical allegations about Jews as such or the power of Jews as a collective—especially but not exclusively, the myth about a world Jewish conspiracy or of Jews controlling the media, economy government or other societal institutions."[49] That is to say, whatever Lero's true attitudes about Jews, the effect of his statement was to reinforce stereotypical allegation about Jewish conspiratorial control.

At around the same time, Lero added on his Facebook page that "6 million? Mh . . . we all know [or should know] that the counting of Jews is a bit controversial."[50] This comment appears opaque, but if we recognize the abbreviation "Mh" as gamer jargon for "maphack," which is a form of cheating in online games, then its meaning can be easily decoded.[51] The gist of the message is thus that Jews are deliberately miscounting or exaggerating the extent of the Holocaust in order to "game" or obtain an unfair disadvantage in debates about Israel. Such comments, often characterized as "Holocaust minimization," are similar to Holocaust denial in that they rely upon stereotypes of the Jews as a powerful, conspiratorial cabal able to perpetuate a grand hoax on the world at large in order to attain sinister purposes. The State Department definition and the Working Definition explain that "accusing the Jews as a people, or Israel as a state, of inventing or exaggerating the Holocaust" is a form of anti-Semitism.

In the same MLA discussion, Professor Elizabeth Jane Ordóñez of the Metropolitan State University of Denver argued that "Zionist attack dogs" invariably block efforts to seek justice for Palestinians, adding that the "Zionist lobby railroads its way through Congress, universities, and civil society."[52] When some of Ordóñez's peers objected to her wording, Professor Basem L. Ra'ad of Al-Quds University defended her, observing that, "'Zionist attack dogs' was probably used metaphorically" and that it may be "severe" but that it is "not far from the truth."[53] The problem is that her "severe" comments have the same pedigree as Lero's. Here again, this is what the State Department characterizes as "stereotypical allegations . . . about Jews controlling the media, economy, government or other institutions." It has overtones of what the Working Definition calls "accusing Jewish citizens of being more loyal to Israel, or to the alleged priorities of Jews worldwide, then to the interests of their own nations." Here again, it hardly matters whether Ordóñez, Ra'ad, or Lero harbor anti-Semitic intent. Their comments are anti-Semitic regardless of intent, because they both rely upon and reinforce the "latent structure of hostile erroneous beliefs and assumptions that flow from the application of double standards toward Jews as a collectivity, manifested culturally in myth, ideology, folklore, and imagery."

Finally, some abuse of Israel by the BDS campaign is profoundly offensive to Jews because of the intimate relationship between a person's Jewish identity and that person's sense of attachment to Israel. Indeed, for many Jews, a commitment to Israel is intrinsic to their religious belief or cultural identity. This commitment has enjoyed multi-generational duration, shared historically by many members of the group, inscribed in a common literature and tradition, and pervasive of the culture. The *Ethnic Traits* principle provides that no group should face discrimination based on this kind of trait. This does not imply that all Jews do share or should this trait. Nevertheless, the many

Jews who do share this deeply felt commitment are unjustly injured by the hostile environments that BDS advocates sometimes create for them.

To be clear, some statements about Israel are not anti-Semitic even though many Jewish people take offense. As we saw in the Introduction, many prominent Israelis were offended by Secretary John Kerry's warning that Israel risks facing a widespread boycott if it does not enter into a peace agreement with the Palestinian Authority. For purposes of analyzing this statement, we will take Kerry at his word that he meant neither to threaten Israel nor to justify the boycott. It is true that Kerry remarked to the Trilateral Commission, some time after his comments about a possible boycott, that if Israel does not enter into a deal with the Palestinian Authority quickly it will either cease to be a Jewish state or become "an apartheid state." The apartheid allegation is sometimes an example of what we have called the "latent structure of hostile erroneous beliefs and assumptions that flow from the application of double standards toward Jews as a collectivity." Giving Kerry the benefit of the doubt however, he appears not to be stereotyping Israel but rather engaging in a hyperbolic effort at prognostication. In urging Israel to pursue his diplomatic recommendations, Kerry was not engaging in ethnic trait discrimination. He was instead aggressively pursuing a diplomatic resolution that may be wise or unwise, fruitful or unfruitful, politic or impolitic, but which bears none of the hallmarks of anti-Semitism.

The BDS Response

Needless to say, BDS leaders reject the notion that their movement is anti-Semitic, going so far as to insist that it is anti-Semitic to oppose them. The argument proceeds through three claims: BDS cannot be anti-Semitic because BDS criticizes Israel, and criticizing Israel is not the same as criticizing all Jews. Not all Jews identify with Israel, and Israel should represent Jews and non-Jews equally. And some Jews actually support BDS, so it is anti-Semitic to say that BDS is anti-Semitic. Each of these claims presents a kernel of truth in distorted fashion. It is true that criticizing Israel is not the same as criticizing all Jews, that many Jews do not identify with Israel, and that some Jews enthusiastically support BDS. But none of these propositions supports the conclusions that BDS' supporters draw from them.

Omar Barghouti cogently expresses the first claim, that is, that BDS cannot be anti-Semitic unless all Jews and Israel are one. "Arguing that boycotting Israel is intrinsically anti-Semitic is not only false," the BDS movement's principal spokesman argues, "but it also presumes that Israel and 'the Jews' are one and the same."[54] Barghouti likens this to the notion that boycotting a self-defined Islamic state like Saudi Arabia, because of its horrific human rights record, would of necessity be Islamophobic. We will put aside the obvious problem with Barghouti's example, which is that no one boycotts Saudi Arabia because of its horrific human rights record, even if they insist on boycotting Israel for its much stronger human rights record, and this application of double standards may itself be anti-Semitic. At a deeper level, Barghouti misunderstands the argument that he tries to refute. No one argues that BDS is anti-Semitic on the grounds that Israel and "the Jews" are the same. Those who argue that BDS is anti-Semitic typically observe that BDS uses double standards to denounce Israel, while demonizing and delegitimizing Israel as anti-Semites traditionally tried to do with the Jewish people. The argument is not that Israel and the Jewish people actually are the same but rather that hateful misperceptions of Israel reflect prior misperceptions of the Jewish people.

Judith Butler articulates the second claim, that is that BDS cannot be anti-Semitic because some Jews do not identify with Israel:

> Only if we accept the proposition that the state of Israel is the exclusive and legitimate representative of the Jewish people would a movement calling for divestment, sanctions and boycott against that state be understood as directed against the Jewish people as a whole. Israel would then be understood as co-extensive with the Jewish people. There are two major problems with this view. First, the state of Israel does not represent all Jews, and not all Jews understand themselves as represented by the state of Israel. Secondly, the state of Israel should be representing all of its population equally, regardless of whether or not they are Jewish, regardless of race, religion or ethnicity.[55]

Butler is unquestionably right to assert that many Jews do not consider themselves to be "represented by the state of Israel." Indeed, many Jews do not identify with Israel even in the weaker sense that they consider Israel to be their homeland. But no one argues to the contrary. And it would be too much to expect this of any ethnic traits argument. To say that a sense of connection with Israel is a deeply held Jewish trait is not to imply that every Jew shares the same sense of conviction. This can be seen by analogy to the sort of ethnic traits claims that are made on behalf of other groups. Those who attack Spanish language speakers harm Hispanics, even if some Hispanics do not speak Spanish and many Spanish speakers are not Hispanics. The same is true of the harm that hostility to Israel inflicts on Jews. In both cases, the animus is directed at a trait that is, as an American court has characterized such socially immutable traits, "so fundamental to the identities or consciences of its members that members either cannot or should not be required to change it."[56]

The U.S. Campaign for the Academic Boycott of Israel articulates the third claim on its web site, namely, that BDS cannot be anti-Semitic because many Jews support it and indeed that it is anti-Semitic to identify Jews with Zionism:

> Zionism is a political movement that is by no means supported by all Jews, many of whom support and advocate for boycott, divestment and sanctions and the end of Zionism itself. Indeed, what is really anti-semitic is the attempt to identify all Jews with a philosophy that many find abhorrent to the traditions of social justice and universality that Judaism enshrines.[57]

As we have seen however, it does not matter whether "all" Jews embrace Zionism, since the ethnic traits argument does not require unanimity. The fact that some Jews deny their own sense of connection to Israel may be the exception that proves the rule. Finally, some will argue that it is wrong to charge BDS with anti-Semitism, since this is tantamount to censorship. But that argument infers too much about the ramifications of identifying something as anti-Semitic. Some forms of anti-Semitism entail constitutionally protected free speech. Nothing discussed in this chapter should be construed to support the idea that arguments for BDS should be banned by law. Although some BDS actions are prohibited by law, this does not imply that must be illegal to urge their adoption.

The Bottom Line on BDS

Commentators tend to draw opposite conclusions from BDS's ugly history and noble-sounding goals. Some assume that it is nothing more than a continuation of its Arab League and Nazi predecessors, while others deny that a human rights movement could be prejudiced. Neither argument is entirely convincing. The pre-Nazi, Nazi, Arab League, and BDS boycotts all share common elements: they seek to deny Jewish legitimacy or normalcy as a punishment for supposed Jewish transgressions. The BDS campaign, like its Nazi predecessor, rationalized and justified sporadic efforts that had preceded it. To be sure, these various campaigns began at very different times, places, and cultures. While there are continuities among them, there are also discontinuities. These boycotts, like other campaigns against Jewish people, must be understood as a repetitive series of incidents that serve the same underlying function, namely, a low-risk expression of anxieties about modernity's destabilizing tendencies. This is as true of the Arab League Boycott and the Palestinian BDS Call as it was for their Nazi antecedent. The fact that the contemporary BDS movement is dressed up in the language of human rights does not differentiate it from its predecessors, which also used the rhetoric of their respective times to establish the common theme.

The modern BDS campaign is anti-Semitic, as its predecessors were, because some of its proponents act out of conscious hostility to the Jewish people; others act from unconscious or tacit disdain for Jews; and still others operate out of a climate of opinion that contains elements that are hostile to Jews and serve as the conduits through whom anti-Jewish tropes and memes are communicated; while all of them work to sustain a movement that attacks the commitment to Israel that is central to the identity of the Jewish people as a whole. This does not imply that all BDS proponents are anti-Semites. All available empirical research confirms that some of Israel's strongest critics are not motivated by prejudice. Their reasons may be convincing or unconvincing, logical or illogical. But they are not anti-Semitic.

Nevertheless, it ought to give them pause to realize that, for whatever reasons, they are participating in a boycott that has deeply unsavory roots and ramifications. It is not coincidental that the world's only Jewish state is subjected to greater scrutiny and pressure than most of the world's other nations. Nor is it coincidental that current efforts to boycott the Jewish state resemble the nearly constant efforts that have been made to boycott Jewish businesses since well before Israel's establishment. The historical record is clear that many and perhaps all of these efforts have been based, in no small part, on the basest forms of human bigotry. Some BDS advocates may be ignorant of this history, but this only makes them unwitting agents in a process by which hatred articulates itself across time. Moreover, they are allying themselves with others who consciously seek to undermine Israel for reasons of sheer hatred. In this respect, they resemble the lady who accidentally married a Nazi while professing the deepest aversion to anti-Semitism.[58]

The aptest metaphor may be to the American poll tax. Poll taxes were implicit preconditions on the exercise of the ability to vote. Like boycott resolutions, poll taxes were sometimes described in race-neutral terms. Nevertheless, these taxes emerged in the late nineteenth-century American South as part of the Jim Crow laws. Some white Southerners intentionally adopted poll taxes to disenfranchise African Americans; others purported to support the tax for race-neutral reasons, such as revenue-raising, but were at least unconsciously prejudiced against blacks; still others acted upon and reinforced a racist climate of opinion, regardless of their personal mental states; and all of them acted to sustain a system that disenfranchised black voters. Under these circumstances, it would be possible to describe the poll tax as a neutral revenue-raising scheme and to emphasize the pure motives on which some of its proponents acted. One might even abhor the false or exaggerated claims of discrimination that have been made against some of these proponents. But this would miss the point of the taxes, which were a peculiarly effective means of marginalizing and delegitimizing an entire people. The institution was racist, through and through, whether all of its supporters were bigots or not.

The Way Forward

Given the ambiguities that surround the definition of anti-Semitism, this topic is best approached with humility, discretion, and caution. In view of the practical stakes, however, it must also be addressed with boldness and courage. This means not only that accusations of bias should not be taken lightly but also that the accusers must be taken seriously. For American civil rights enforcement agencies, the way forward it clear. Whatever else they may do to address resurgent anti-Semitism, the first step should be to adopt the State Department's definition. Such definitions unavoidably have conceptual limitations, but these can be overcome by using working definitions as supplements to more comprehensive definitions, such as the one presented in these pages.

For those people of good will who wish to grapple with pressing issues of public affairs without being accused—rightly or wrongly—of vile prejudice, the issue is both simpler and more complex than it may have seemed at the start. It is more complex, because the categorical approaches to which some still cling are non-starters. It will not do either to sweep all criticisms of Israel into the anti-Semitism bin or to exclude them altogether. Even Sharansky's 3D test provides only the beginning of a proper analysis and not a shortcut to the solution. There is no authoritative list of words or phrases that are always or never anti-Semitic. Rather, each word, phrase, or deed must be measured against its speaker's intent, its tacit meaning, its cultural significance, et cetera. Nevertheless, the task is also simpler than some assume, because the meaning of anti-Semitism is subject to reasonable definition.

NOTES

Introduction
1. *BBC News Europe*, Obituary, "Toulouse Gunman Mohamed Merah" (Mar. 22, 2012), http://www.bbc.co.uk/news/world-europe-17456541.
2. Dan Bilefsky, "Personal Angst Powered Killer's Arsenal in France," *The New York Times* (Mar. 29, 2012), http://www.nytimes.com/2012/03/30/world/europe/personal-angst-powered-killers-arsenal-in-france.html. In other words, they argue that it is anti-Semitic to argue that anti-Israeli hostility is anti-Semitic, because this argument falsely equates Israel's supposed wrong-doing with the Jewish people.
3. French President Nicolas Sarkozy was one conspicuous exception.
4. Tariq Ramadan, Press Release, "Behind the Toulouse Killings" (Mar. 22, 2012), http://www.tariqramadan.com/Behind-the-Toulouse-Shootings,11913.html?lang=fr.
5. Omar Dakhane, "Reactions to the Toulouse murderer in Algeria," *Jerusalem Post* (Mar. 28, 2012), http://blogs.jpost.com/content/reactions-toulouse-murderer-algeria.
6. Jewish Telegraphic Agency, "Toulouse Massacre Encouraged More French Anti-Semitic Attacks, Report Says" (June 4, 2012), http://www.jta.org/news/article/2012/06/04/3097226/toulouse-massacre-encouraged-more-french-anti-semitic-attacks-report-says.
7. The Associated Press, "White House Struggles With Obama Comment on Paris Attack," *The New York Times* (Feb. 10, 2015), http://www.nytimes.com/aponline/2015/02/10/us/politics/ap-us-obama-france-attacks.html?_r=0.

8. Jonathan Chait, "Administration Turns Obama Anti-Semitism Gaffe Into Epic Blunder," New York Magazine (Feb. 10, 2015), http://nymag.com/daily/intelligencer/2015/02/obama-anti-semitism-gaffe-becomes-epic-blunder.html.
9. Ibid.
10. Günter Grass, "What Must Be Said," *Süddeutschen Zeitung* (Apr. 4, 2012), translated and reprinted in *Pulse* (Apr. 17, 2012) (trans. Michael Keefer and Nica Mintz), http://pulsemedia.org/2012/04/07/what-must-be-said/.
11. Jacob Heilbrunn, "Is Gunter Grass An Anti-Semite?," *The National Interest* blog (Apr. 4, 2012), http://nationalinterest.org/blog/jacob-heilbrunn/gunter-grass-anti-semite-6734.
12. Barak Ravid, "Netanyahu slams Gunter Grass for Controversial Israel Poem," *Ha'aretz* (Apr. 5, 2012), http://www.haaretz.com/news/diplomacy-defense/netanyahu-slams-guenter-grass-for-controversial-israel-poem-1.422881?.
13. Jerry Haber, "Goldberg Slipping on Grass," *The Magnes Zionist* (Apr. 10, 2011), http://www.jeremiahhaber.com/2012/04/goldberg-slipping-on-grass.html.
14. Ulrich Rippert, "Defend Günter Grass!," *World Socialist Web Site* (Apr. 7, 2012), http://www.wsws.org/index.shtml.
15. Josef Joffe, "Gunter Grass's Tin Ear," *The Wall Street Journal* (Apr. 17, 2012).
16. Antony Lerman, "Günter Grass, Antisemitism and the Inflation of Evil," *Open Democracy* (Apr. 16, 2012), http://www.opendemocracy.net/antony-lerman/g%C3%BCnter-grass-antisemitism-and-inflation-of-evil.
17. Ben Cohen, "The Big Lie Returns: How Anti-Semites are Asserting Their Right to Define 'Anti-Semitism'—and Why the Culture is Allowing Them to Do It," *Commentary* (Feb. 2012), pp. 13, 19.
18. *Carto v. Buckley*, 649 F. Supp. 502, 509 (S.D.N.Y. 1986) (discussing *Liberty Lobby v. National Review*, No. 79-3445, slip op. at 10 (D.D.C. April 20, 1983)). Significantly, United States court cases that address the meaning of "anti-Semitism" typically do so in the context of defamation rather than anti-discrimination claims. That is to say, their concern is not whether to penalize the alleged anti-Semite but rather whether to require the accuser to pay damages to the accused. This is partly because the term "anti-Semitism" rarely appears in anti-discrimination statutes, while it is sometimes used in contested accusations.
19. Graeme Paton, "Pupils Asked 'Why Do Some People Hate Jews?' in GCSE exam," *The* (UK) *Telegraph* (May 24, 2012), http://www.telegraph.co.uk/education/educationnews/9288585/Pupils-asked-why-do-some-people-hate-Jews-in-GCSE-exam.html.
20. Zygmunt Bauman, *Modernity and the Holocaust* (Ithaca, NY: Cornell University Press, 1989), p. 62.

21. Walter Laqueur, *The Changing Face of Antisemitism: From Ancient Times to the Present Day* (Oxford: Oxford University Press, 2006), p. 1 (emphasis added).
22. Adam LeBor, "Exodus: Why Europe's Jews Are Fleeing Once Again," *Newsweek* (July 29, 2014), http://www.newsweek.com/2014/08/08/exodus-why-europes-jews-are-fleeing-once-again-261854.html.
23. Anti-Defamation League (ADL), "ADL Global 100" (May 2014), website maintained by ADL, http://global100.adl.org.
24. Kantor Center for the Study of Contemporary European Jewry, *Antisemitism Worldwide 2012: General Analysis* (Tel Aviv: Tel Aviv University, 2013).
25. For the best general survey, see Leonard Dinnerstein, *Antisemitism in America* (New York: Oxford University Press: 1994).
26. "ADL Global 100," USA country survey, at http://global100.adl.org/#country/usa.
27. Gilad Atzmon, quoted in "Israeli Author Says Anti-Semitism Is Just a Myth," *World Bulletin* (Feb. 8, 2014), http://www.worldbulletin.net/news/128479/israeli-author-says-anti-semitism-is-just-a-myth; retweeted @GiladAtzmon, "Israeli author says anti-Semitism is just a myth ☐http://www.worldbulletin.net/interviews-in-depth/128479/israeli-author-says-anti-semitism-is-just-a-myth . . .," (Feb. 9, 2014).
28. U.S. Department of State, *Contemporary Global Antisemitism: A Report Provided to the United States Congress* (Mar. 2008), http://www.state.gov/documents/organization/102301.pdf.
29. European Union Fundamental Rights Agency, *Antisemitism—Summary Overview of the Situation in the European Union 2001–2005*, Updated version, Dec. 2006, p. 22, EUMC, Vienna, http://fra.europe.eu/fraWebsite/attachments/Antisemitism_Update_2006.pdf.
30. Alain Badiou, "Uses of the Word Jew," in *Polemics* (London: Verso, 2006), pp. 158–159.
31. Kenneth L. Marcus, "The Definition of Antisemitism," in Charles Asher Small, ed., *Global Antisemitism: A Crisis of Modernity* (Leiden: Brill, 2013), p. 97.
32. Leo Strauss, *Jewish Philosophy and the Crisis of Modernity: Essays and Lectures in Modern Jewish Thought* (New York: State University of New York Press, 1997), quoted in Anthony Julius, *Trials of the Diaspora: A History of Anti-Semitism in England* (Oxford: Oxford University Press, 2010), p. xliii.
33. Gavin I. Langmuir, *Toward a Definition of Antisemitism* (Berkeley, CA: University of California Press, 1990), p. 351.
34. Dina Porat, "Historical Perspective," in Dina Porat and Kenneth Stern, *Defining Antisemitism*, 2005, available at: www.tau.ac.il/Anti-Semitism/asw2003-4/porat.htm.
35. Ibid.

36. Rifat N. Bali, "Antisemitism in Turkey: From Denial to Acknowledgement, From Acknowledgement to Discussion of its Definition," in Dina Porat and Esther Webman, compilers, *The Working Definition of Antisemitism—Six Years After: Unedited Proceedings of the 10th Biennial Seminar on Antisemitism* (Tel Aviv: Kantor Center for the Study of Contemporary European Jewry, 2012), http://kantorcenter.tau.ac.il/sites/default/files/proceeding-all_6.pdf., p. 1.
37. Florette Cohen, Lee Jussim, Kent D. Harber, and Gautam Bhasin, "Modern Anti-Semitism and Anti-Israel Attitudes," *Journal of Personality and Social Psychology* 97 (2009), pp. 290–306.
38. American Psychological Association Resolution on Anti-Semitic and Anti-Jewish Prejudice (Adopted by the APA Council of Representatives, August 2005/Amended August 2007), http://www.apa.org/about/policy/antisemitic.pdf.
39. Ibid.
40. Ibid.
41. Robert Wistrich, *A Lethal Obsession: Anti-Semitism from Antiquity to the Global Jihad* (New York: Random House, 2010), p. 496.
42. Ibid., p. 631.
43. Anthony Julius, *Trials of the Diaspora: A History of Anti-Semitism in England* (Oxford: Oxford University Press, 2010), p. xlvi.
44. Wendy Brown, "We Are All Democrats Now," in Giorgio Agamben et al., *Democracy in What State?* (New York: Columbia University Press, 2011), p. 44, Kindle Loc 472 of 1334.
45. Neil J. Kressel, *"The Sons of Pigs and Apes": Muslim Antisemitism and the Conspiracy of Silence* (Washington, D.C.: Potomac Books, 2012), pp. 144, 145.
46. Wistrich, *Lethal Obsession*, p. 322.
47. David Hirsh, "Accusations of Malicious Intent in Debates about the Palestine-Israel Conflict and about Antisemitism: The Livingstone Formulation, 'Playing the Antisemitism Card' and Contesting the Boundaries of Antiracist Discourse," *Transversal* 2010:1, pp. 47–76; Lesley Klaff, "Political and Legal Judgment: Misuses of the Holocaust in the UK," *Journal for the Study of Antisemitism* 5:1 (2013), pp. 45, 53–54.
48. Wistrich, *Lethal Obsession*, p. 400.
49. Ibid., p. 341.
50. Ruth Wisse, *No Joke: Making Jewish Humor* (Princeton, NJ: Princeton University Press, 2013), p. 1.
51. Ibid., p. 3.
52. Jerome A. Chanes, "Jewish Involvement in the American Public-Affairs Agenda," in Norman Linzer, David J. Schnall, and Jerome A. Chanes, eds., *A Portrait of the American Jewish Community* (Santa Barbara, CA: Praeger, 1998), pp. 177, 178.

53. Ian Buruma, "The Freedom to Offend," *The New Republic* (Sept. 4, 2006), p. 23.
54. Roger Cohen, "The BDS Threat," *The New York Times* (Feb. 10, 2014).
55. Lahav Harkov, "Bayit Yehudi MK: Kerry Pressure on Israel has Anti-Semitic Undertones," *Jerusalem Post* (Jan. 30, 2014), http://www.jpost.com/Diplomacy-and-Politics/Bayit-Yehudi-MK-Kerry-pressure-on-Israel-has-anti-Semitic-undertones-339879 (quoting Motti Yogev from the Bayit Yehudi Party).
56. Bradley Burston, "Could You Be a Closet Anti-Semite? Let the Settlers' New 'John Kerry Test' Be Your Guide," *Ha'aretz* (Feb. 4, 2014) (quoting Adi Mintz).
57. Cameron Kerry, "The DNA of My Brother, John Kerry," Yedidut Ahronot, translated and posted on the U.S. Embassy Tel Aviv Facebook page, February 14, 2014, https://www.facebook.com/U.S.EmbassyTelAvivIsrael/photos/a.10150104442655622.318765.530099406 21/10152192872940622/?type=1&theater.
58. Yaakov Kirschen, "Antisemitism and the Power of Cartoons," (lecture, Yale University, New Haven, CT, Oct. 14, 2009), quoted in Kressel, *Sons of Pigs and Apes*, p. 15.
59. Kenneth Lasson, "In an Academic Voice: Antisemitism and Academic Bias," *Journal for the Study of Antisemitism* 3:2 (2011), pp. 394–397.
60. Anthony Julius, *Trials of the Diaspora: A History of Anti-Semitism in England* (Oxford: Oxford University Press, 2010), p. xliv.
61. Elisabeth Young-Bruehl, *The Anatomy of Prejudices* (Cambridge, MA: Harvard University Press, 1996), p. 3.
62. Ibid.
63. Ibid., p. 4.
64. Wistrich, p. 68.
65. See Jewish Telegraphic Agency, "Italian Judge Says Cartoonist is No Anti-Semite" (Apr. 27, 2012), http://www.jta.org/news/article/2012/04/27/3094096/italian-judge-says-cartoonist-is-no-anti-semite.
66. Peter Wallsten, "Center for American Progress, Group Tied to Obama, under Fire from Israel Advocates," *The Washington Post* (Jan. 19, 2012), http://www.washingtonpost.com/politics/center-for-america-progress-group-tied-to-obama-accused-of-anti-semitic-language/2012/01/17/gIQAcrHXAQ_story.html.
67. Dina Porat and Kenneth Stern, *Defining Antisemitism*, 2005, available at: www.tau.ac.il/Anti-Semitism/asw2003-4/porat.htm, quoting European Union Monitoring Center, "Manifestations of Antisemitism in the EU 2002–2003" (Vienna, 2004), p. 237, http://eumc.eu.int/eumc/as/PDF04/AS-Main-report-PDF04.pdf.
68. Ibid.
69. Ibid.

70. Ibid.
71. Ibid.
72. European Forum on Antisemitism, Working Definition of Antisemitism, http://www.european-forum-on-antisemitism.org/working-definition-of-antisemitism/english.
73. Dina Porat, "The International Working Definition of Antisemitism and Its Detractors," *Israel Journal of Foreign Affairs* 5:3 (2011), p. 2.
74. Dina Porat and Esther Webman, "Introduction," in Porat and Webman, *Working Definition of Antisemitism—Six Years After*, p. 1.
75. Ibid.
76. Ibid.
77. Inter-parliamentary Coalition for Combating Antisemitism, The Ottawa Protocol on Combating Antisemitism, http://www.antisem.org/archive/ottawa-protocol-on-combating-antisemitism/.
78. Porat, "International Working Definition of Antisemitism and Its Detractors," pp. 1–2.
79. Rex Weiner, "Line Between Anti-Israel and Anti-Semitic Protests Splits AJC: Group's Top Ranks Divided Over How To Respond to Campus Demonstrations," *The Jewish Daily Forward* (Aug. 16, 2011), http://forward.com/articles/141386/line-between-anti-israel-and-anti-semitic-protests/#ixzz23obD2EW5.
80. Cary Nelson, AAUP President, and Kenneth Stern, American Jewish Committee Anti-Semitism on Campus," http://www.aaup.org/AAUP/about/officers/let/antisemitism.htm.
81. Jonathan S. Tobin, "The Reality of Campus Anti-Semitism: An Exchange," *Commentary Contentions* (Apr. 4, 2011), http://www.jidaily.com/N1bwd/r.
82. Weiner, "Line Between Anti-Israel and Anti-Semitic Protests."
83. This section draws from Kenneth L. Marcus, "California's First Amendment Follies," *The Algemeiner* (Sept. 12, 2012), http://www.algemeiner.com/2012/09/12/californias-first-amendment-follies/.
84. Richard "Rick" D. Barton and Alice Huffman, *University of California Jewish Student Campus Climate Fact-Finding Team Report & Recommendations* (Oakland, CA: University of California President's Advisory Council on Campus Climate, Culture, & Inclusion 2012), http://www.universityofcalifornia.edu/news/documents/campus_climate_jewish.pdf.
85. California House Resolution 35 (2011-201), http://leginfo.legislature.ca.gov/faces/billTextClient.xhtml?bill_id=201120120HR35.
86. The constitutionally vulnerable portion of the resolution provides as follows: "WHEREAS, While these actions are important steps, strong leadership from the top remains an important priority so that no administrator, faculty, or student group can be in any doubt that anti-Semitic activity will not be tolerated in the classroom or on campus,

and that no public resources will be allowed to be used for anti-Semitic or any intolerant agitation."
87. Dina Porat, ed., *Anti-Semitism Worldwide 2013: General Analysis* (Tel Aviv: Kantor Center for the Study of European Jewry at Tel Aviv University, 2014), http://kantorcenter.tau.ac.il/sites/default/files/Doch_2013.pdf.
88. Jewish Telegraphic Agency (JTA), "EU Drops its 'Working Definition' of Anti-Semitism," JTA website (Dec. 5, 2013), http://www.timesofisrael.com/eu-drops-its-working-definition-of-anti-semitism/.
89. Ibid.
90. U.S. Department of State, Special Envoy to Monitor and Combat Anti-Semitism, Fact Sheet, "Defining Anti-Semitism" (June 8, 2010), http://www.state.gov/j/drl/rls/fs/2010/122352.htm.
91. Ibid.
92. Kenneth L. Marcus, "Jurisprudence of the New Anti-Semitism," *Wake Forest University Law Review*, pp. 371–430 44 (Summ. 2009).
93. Kenneth L. Marcus, *Jewish Identity and Civil Rights in America* (New York: Cambridge University Press, 2010).
94. Kenneth L. Marcus, "The New OCR Antisemitism Policy," *Journal for the Study of Antisemitism*, pp. 479–91 2 (2011).
95. Details of the investigation were obtained from OCR through a Freedom of Information Act and are detailed in Kenneth L. Marcus, "Whitewashing Antisemitism at the University of California–Irvine," *Journal for the Study of Antisemitism* 2:1 (2010), pp. 13–48.
96. As discussed in *Jewish Identity*, the head of OCR's San Francisco office believed at the time of his investigation that a hostile environment for Jewish students had formed at Irvine but that Irvine's administrative response was sufficiently effective to meet federal standards. Later on, as he continued to monitor the situation, he revised his opinion, realizing in light of subsequent events that Irvine's responses had not been sufficient to prevent a recurrence of these incidents and that anti-Semitic incidents did in fact persist.
97. Marcus, *Jewish Identity*, p. 17.
98. Ibid., pp. 17–18.
99. The Associated Press, "Israel's Netanyahu Calls Boycotters 'Anti-Semites,'" *The New York Times* (Feb. 17, 2014), available at: http://www.nytimes.com/aponline/2014/02/17/world/middleeast/ap-ml-israel-boycott.html?partner=rss&emc=rss&_r=0.
100. Abraham H. Foxman, "An Open Letter on Academic Freedom and University Responsibility," Anti-Defamation League website, http://www.adl.org/assets/pdf/press-center/NYT-Ad.pdf.
101. U.S. Campaign for the Academic Boycott of Israel (USACBI), "FAQ's," USACBI web site, http://www.usacbi.org/faqs/
102. *Webster's Third New International Dictionary*, 1966, p. 96.

103. David Hirsh, "Defining Antisemitism Down: The EUMC Working Definition and Its Disavowal By the University & College Union," *Fathom* (Summer 2013), p. 11.

Chapter 1

1. Craig S. Smith, "Torture and Death of Jew Deepen Fears in France," *New York Times* (Mar. 5, 2006), http://www.nytimes.com/2006/03/05/international/europe/05france.html?_r=1&ei=5070&en=f19c5a316fe2a7cc&=&emc=eta1&adxnnlx=1141830098-cdfGOKcgFCRtjqWZlANf7g;cx-1142226000;amp=&pagewanted=all.
2. Ariane Bernard and Craig S. Smith, "French Officials Now Say Killing of Jew Was in Part a Hate Crime," *New York Times* (Feb. 23, 2006), http://www.nytimes.com/2006/02/23/international/europe/23paris.html?_r=2&oref=slogin.
3. Ibid.
4. Jewish Telegraphic Agency, "Murdered Man's Mother Blames Police," (Apr. 2, 2009), http://www.jta.org/news/article/2009/04/02/1004194/murdered-teens-mother-blames-police.
5. Smith, "Torture and Death of Jew Deepen Fears in France."
6. Ibid.
7. It also bears mentioning that the initial deniers included some Jewish community notables like Théo Klein, former head of the Council of Jewish Institutions of France. Robert Wistrich, *A Lethal Obsession: Anti-Semitism from Antiquity to the Global Jihad* (New York: Random House, 2010), p. 341.
8. Jewish Telegraphic Agency, "Anti-Semitic Videos to Keep Halimi Killer in Jail for 7 More Years," (Feb. 18, 2013).
9. Phyllis Goldstein, *A Convenient Hatred: The History of Antisemitism* (Brookline: Facing History and Ourselves, 2012), p. 7.
10. Quoted in Nathan Zuckerman, *The Wine of Violence: An Anthology of Anti-Semitism* (New York: Association Press, 1947), p. 13.
11. Jean-Paul Sartre, *Anti-Semite and Jew*, trans. George C. Becker (New York: Schocken Books, 1995), p. 10.
12. Carole Nuriel, "History and Theoretical Aspects," in Dina Porat and Esther Webman, compilers, *The Working Definition of Antisemitism—Six Years After: Unedited Proceedings of the 10th Biennial Seminar on Antisemitism* (Tel Aviv: Kantor Center for the Study of Contemporary European Jewry, 2012), http://kantorcenter.tau.ac.il/sites/default/files/proceeding-all_6.pdf, p. 1 (emphases added). For its primary definition, the venerable *Oxford English Dictionary* defines anti-Semitism as "[h]ostility and prejudice directed against Jewish people."
13. Albert S. Lindesmann and Richard S. Levy, "Introduction," to *Antisemitism: A History* (Oxford: Oxford University Press, 2010), p. 1.

14. Kenneth L. Marcus, *Jewish Identity and Civil Rights in America* (New York: Cambridge University Press, 2010), p. 37.
15. The blood libel began in Norwich, England, in 1144 and has often used been used, over the centuries, as a preparation for the mass-murder of Jews. Wistrich, *Lethal Obsession*, pp. 19, 88–90. Today a quarter of young Muslim men in England, France, and Germany insist that Jews kill children or that Israelis kill children (often using "Jews" and "Israelis" interchangeably) when asked to present their views on the Middle East conflict. Günther Jikeli, "Antisemitism among Young European Males," in Alvin H. Rosenfeld, *Resurgent Antisemitism: Global Perspectives* (Bloomington: Indiana University Press, 2013), pp. 280–281. Even in the United States, those critics who choose to portray the State of Israel negatively often use analogs of the blood libel. This can be seen, for example, in images of the Star of David dripping with blood that have been posted at the University of California at Irvine and elsewhere. Kenneth Lasson, "In an Academic Voice: Antisemitism and Academic Bias," *Journal for the Study of Antisemitism* 3:2 (2011), pp. 349–405; Kenneth L. Marcus, "The Resurgence of Antisemitism on American College Campuses," *Current Psychology* 26:3–4 (2007), pp. 206, 210.
16. Georg Christoph Berger Waldenegg, *Antisemitismus: "Eine gefährliche Vokabel"? Diagnose eines Wortes* (Vienna: Böhlau, 2003), p. 94.
17. Zygmunt Bauman, *Modernity and the Holocaust* (Ithaca, NY: Cornell University Press, 1989), p. 34 (emphasis added).
18. Berel Lang, "Self-Description and the Anti-Semite: Denying Privileged Access," in The Vidal Sassoon International Center for the Study of Antisemitism, Annual Report (1999), reprinted in Ron Rosenbaum, ed., *Those Who Forget the Past: The Question of Anti-Semitism* (New York: Random House, 2004), pp. 91, 95.
19. Jocelyn Hellig, *The Holocaust and Antisemitism: A Short History* (Oxford: OneWorld, 2003), p. 74.
20. "'Anti-Semitic' French Envoy Under Fire," BBC, (Dec. 20, 2001), http://news.bbc.co.uk/2/hi/europe/1721172.stm.
21. Abraham H. Foxman, *Never Again? The Threat of the New Anti-Semitism* (New York: Harper Collins, 2003), p. 14.
22. Judith Butler, *Excitable Speech: A Politics of the Performative* (New York: Routledge, 1997), p. 16.
23. Ibid.
24. Kenneth Stern, "Proposal for a Redefinition of Antisemitism," in Dina Porat and Kenneth Stern, *Defining Antisemitism* (Tel Aviv: Tel Aviv University, 2005), www.tau.ac.il/Anti-Semitism/asw2003-4/porat.htm.
25. Mel Gibson, Statement, "Gibson Asks Jews for Help to Find 'Appropriate Path To Healing,'" *Access Hollywood* (Aug. 1, 2006), http://www.accesshollywood.com/gibson-asks-jews-for-help-to-find-appropriate-path-to-healing_article_1069.

26. Barry Oringer, "Terrorism Chic," *Pacific News Service* (May 9, 2002), reprinted in Ron Rosenbaum, ed., *Those Who Forget the Past: The Question of Anti-Semitism* (New York: Random House, 2004), pp. 286.
27. Edward H. Kaplan and Charles A. Small, "Anti-Israel Sentiment Predicts Anti-Semitism in Europe," *Journal of Conflict Resolution* 50:4 (2006), pp. 548–561.
28. Berel Lang, "Self-Description and the Anti-Semite: Denying Privileged Access," in The Vidal Sassoon International Center for the Study of Antisemitism, *Annual Report* (1999), reprinted in Rosenbaum, ed., *Those Who Forget the Past*, pp. 91, 95.
29. Ibid.
30. Ibid.
31. George E. Simpson and Milton Yinger, *Racial and Ethnic Minorities*, 4th ed. (New York: Harper & Row, 1972), p. 253 (emphasis added).
32. Michael Lerner, *The Socialism of Fools: Anti-Semitism and the Left* (Oakland: Tikkun Books, 1992), p. 1.
33. Kenneth S. Stern, *Antisemitism Today: How It Is the Same, How It Is Different, and How to Fight It* (New York: American Jewish Committee, 2006).
34. Dina Porat, "The International Working Definition of Antisemitism and Its Detractors," *Israel Journal of Foreign Affairs* 5:3 (2011), p. 6.
35. Waldenegg, *Antisemitismus*, pp. 53–54.
36. Kenneth Stern, "Proposal for a Redefinition of Antisemitism," in Dina Porat, "Historical Perspective," in Dina Porat and Kenneth Stern, *Defining Antisemitism*, 2005, www.tau.ac.il/Anti-Semitism/asw2003-4/porat.htm.
37. Ibid.
38. Ibid.
39. Ibid.
40. Cf. McDonnell Douglas Corp. v. Green, 411 U.S. 792 (1973).
41. Hannah Arendt, "Antisemitism," in *The Jewish Writings*, ed. Jerome Kahn and Ron H. Feldman (New York: Schocken, 2007), p. 49.
42. Steve Cohen, "That's Funny, You Don't Look Anti-Semitic" (1984), posted to *That's Funny, You Don't Look Anti-Semitic*, http://you-dont-look-anti-semitic.blogspot.com/2007/01/anti-semitism.html.
43. Jean-Paul Sartre, *Anti-Semite and Jew*, trans. George C. Becker (New York: Schocken Books 1995), p. 17 (emphasis added).
44. András Kovács, "Antisemitic Prejudice and Political Antisemitism in Present-Day Hungary," *Journal for the Study of Antisemitism* 4:2 (2013), pp. 443, 446.
45. David Nirenberg, *Anti-Judaism: The Western Tradition* (New York: W.W. Norton, 2013), p. 3.
46. Sartre, *Anti-Semite and Jew*, p. 17.
47. Nirenberg, *Anti-Judaism*, pp. 181–182.

48. Ibid., p. 181.
49. "The Testament of an Anti-Semite," in Moshe Zimmermann, *Wilhelm Marr* (Oxford: Oxford University Press, 1986), p. 151, quoted in Anthony Julius, *Trials of the Diaspora: A History of Antisemitism in England* (Oxford: Oxford University Press, 2010), p. 21.
50. Norman Cohn, *Warrant for Genocide: The Myth of the Jewish World Conspiracy and the Protocols of the Elders of Zion* (London: Serif, 1967).
51. Hannah Arendt, *The Origins of Totalitarianism* (New York: Schocken Books, 1948), p. 3.
52. T. W. Adorno, Else Frenkel-Brunswik, Daniel J. Levinson, and R. Nevitt Sanford, *The Authoritarian Personality*, Studies in Prejudice Series, vol. 1 (New York: American Jewish Committee, 1950), p. 71 (1950) (emphasis omitted).
53. Helen Fein, "Dimensions of Antisemitism: Attitudes, Collective Accusations, and Actions," in Helen Fein, ed., *The Persisting Question: Sociological Perspectives and Social Contexts of Modern Antisemitism* (Berlin/New York: Walter de Gruyter, 1987), p. 67 (emphases omitted).
54. Nirenberg, *Anti-Judaism*, p. 471.
55. Julius, *Trials of the Diaspora*, p. xlii.
56. Ibid., p. xliv.
57. Ibid.
58. Robert S. Wistrich, *From Ambivalence to Betrayal: The Left, the Jews, and Israel* (Lincoln: University of Nebraska Press, 2012), pp. 70–92. Paul Berman has argued, in response to this point, that anti-Semitism may claim a St. Paul as well.
59. Steven Beller, *Antisemitism: A Very Short Introduction* (Oxford: Oxford University Press, 2007), p. 2.
60. Susan Sontag, "Illness as a Metaphor," in *Illness as a Metaphor and AIDS and its Metaphors* (New York: Anchor Books, 1990), p. 87.
61. Paul Johnson, "The Anti-Semitic Disease," *Commentary* (June 2005), http://www.commentarymagazine.com/viewarticle.cfm/the-anti-semitic-disease-9904.
62. Alvin Johnson, "The Rising Tide of Anti-Semitism," *Survey Graphic: Magazine of Social Interpretation* (Feb. 1939), http://newdeal.feri.org/survey/39a01.htm.
63. Julius, *Trials of the Diaspora*, p. 27.
64. Ruth Wisse, "The Anti-Semite's Pointed Finger," *Commentary* (Nov. 2010), pp. 24, 27.
65. Ruth Wisse, "Holocaust, or War Against the Jews?," in Michael Brown, ed., *Approaches to Antisemitism: Context and Curriculum* (American Jewish Committee and the International Center for University Teaching of Jewish Civilization, 1994) p. 24.
66. Steven Beller, *Antisemitism: A Very Short Definition* (Oxford, 2007), pp. 2–3.

67. Nirenberg, *Anti-Judaism*, p. 113, quoting John Chrysostom, *Discourses against Judaizing Christians*, trans. Paul W. Hawkins (Washington, DC: Catholic University Press of America Press, 1979), p. 1.1.4, 1.4.4.
68. Sontag, "Illness as a Metaphor," p. 83.
69. Kenneth L. Marcus, "Accusation in a Mirror," *Loyola University Chicago Law Journal* 43 (Winter 2012), pp. 357–393. Such inversions have been explained, in Freudian terms, on the grounds that anti-Semites like other oppressors tend to project their disowned impulses onto the target population, in this case, the Jewish people. By this explanation, the anti-Semitic superego tends to repress unconscious desires which are seen as diseased, and these same desires are later projected onto the figure of "the *Jew*." Thus, as Wistrich observes, Christian anti-Semites over the centuries commonly fantasied the Jew as a *persecutor* of Christians. Similarly, the figure of the eternal Jew may project anti-Semitic ambitions for the sort of malevolent millenialism expressed in the idea of the *Tausendjähriges Reich* (thousand-year realm).
70. Wolfgang Ischinger, German Ambassador to United States, Letter to Editor, *Commentary* (Oct. 2005), http://www.commentarymagazine.com/viewarticle.cfm/anti-semitism-11126.
71. Thomas Szasz, Letter to Editor, *Commentary* (Oct. 2005), http://www.commentarymagazine.com/viewarticle.cfm/anti-semitism-11126.
72. Kober v. Kober, 16 N.Y.2d 191, 196 (N.Y. 1965).
73. Ibid. at 197.
74. Ibid.
75. Tony Judt, *Postwar: A History of Europe Since 1945* (New York: Penguin Books, 2006).
76. William E. Nelson, *The Legalist Reformation: Law, Politics, and Ideology in New York, 1920–1980* (Chapel Hill, NC: University of North Carolina Press, 2001), p. 233.
77. Allison Hope Weiner, "Mel Gibson Apologizes for Tirade after Arrest," *New York Times* (July 30, 2006), http://www.nytimes.com/2006/07/30/us/30gibson.html.
78. Mel Gibson, Statement, printed in Access Hollywood, "Gibson Asks Jews For Help To Find 'Appropriate Path To Healing,'" (Aug. 1, 2006), http://www.accesshollywood.com/gibson-asks-jews-for-help-to-find-appropriate-path-to-healing_article_1069.
79. Ibid.
80. Ibid.
81. Anti-Defamation League, Press Release, "ADL Welcomes Mel Gibson's Apology to the Jewish Community" (quoting Foxman statement) (Aug. 1, 2006), http://www.adl.org/PresRele/ASUS_12/4862_12.htm.
82. Slavoj Žižek, *In Defense of Lost Causes* (London: Verso, 2008), p. 38.
83. Ibid.

84. Max Horkheimer and Theodor W. Adorno, *Dialectic of Enlightenment: Philosophical Fragments*, ed. Gunzelin Schmid Noerr, trans. Edmund Jephcott (Stanford, CA: Stanford University Press, 2002),
85. Léon Poliakov, *The History of Anti-Semitism*, vol. 2, *From Mohammed to the Marranos*, trans. Natalie Gerardi (New York: Vanguard Press, 1973), p. vii.
86. Žižek, *In Defense of Lost Causes*, pp. 39–40.
87. Butler, *Excitable Speech*, p. 34.
88. Ibid.
89. Nirenberg, *Anti-Judaism*, p. 2.
90. Ibid, p. 6. Nirenberg does not use the term anti-Semitism here, because he reserves the term for a more limited sense, but he is writing about a phenomenon fairly characterized as "anti-Semitism" within at least some of the definitions considered in this volume.
91. Žižek's readers may be pardoned if they misinterpret Žižek as suggesting that anti-Semitism is itself a healthy ideology. After all, the Slovenian philosopher, who is sometimes photographed with pictures of Stalin in the background, is fond of presenting himself in ways that give monstrously false impressions. Žižek would likely characterize the notion that anti-Semitism is itself a healthy ideology as an example of going one step too far in the right direction.
92. This divergence is explored at greater length in David Seymour, "Adorno and Horkheimer: Enlightenment and Antisemitism," *Journal of Jewish Studies* 51:2 (Autumn 2000), pp. 297–312.

Chapter 2

1. Slavoj Žižek, *The Sublime Object of Ideology* (London: Verso, 1989), p. 128.
2. In an alternative definition, which adds an ethnic category while preserving the same basic structure, *Merriam-Webster* provides that anti-Semitism may consist of (any) "hostility toward or discrimination against Jews as a religious, ethnic, or racial group." Merrium-Webster.com (concise encyclopedia), http://www.merriam-webster.com/dictionary/anti-semitism?show=0&t=1356096652 (emphasis added).
3. Albert S. Lindemann and Richard S. Levy, "Conclusion: Not the Final Word," to *Antisemitism: A History* (Oxford: Oxford University Press, 2010), pp. 259–263.
4. Steven Beller, *Antisemitism: A Very Short Introduction* (Oxford: Oxford University Press, 2007).
5. Gordon Allport, *The Nature of Prejudice* (Reading, MA: Addison-Wesley, 1954; New York: Anchor, 1958).
6. Wistrich, *Antisemitism*, p. vx.

7. Walter Laqueur, *The Changing Face of Anti-Semitism: From Ancient Times to the Present Day* (Oxford: Oxford University Press 2006), p. 21.
8. Georg Christoph Berger Waldenegg, *Antisemitismus: "Eine gefährliche Vokabel"? Diagnose eines Wortes* (Vienna: Böhlau, 2003), p. 23.
9. Ibid., p. 24.
10. Hannah Arendt, "Antisemitism," in *The Jewish Writings*, ed. Jerome Kohn and Ron H. Feldman (New York: Schocken, 2007), p. 111 note 2.
11. Quoted in Robert Wistrich, *A Lethal Obsession: Anti-Semitism from Antiquity to the Global Jihad* (New York: Random House, 2010), p. 117.
12. *The Jewish Encyclopedia,* vol. 1 (1901), http://www.jewishencyclopedia.com/articles/1603-anti-semitism.
13. Quoted in Dina Porat, "Historical Perspective," in Dina Porat and Kenneth Stern, *Defining Antisemitism* (2005), www.tau.ac.il/Anti-Semitism/asw2003-4/porat.htm.
14. Quoted in Dina Porat, "Historical Perspective."
15. Didi Herman, *An Unfortunate Coincidence: Jews, Jewishness and English Law* (Oxford: Oxford University Press, 2011), pp. 14–15.
16. See Edward Said, *Orientalism* (New York: Vintage, 1979).
17. William Meijs and Susan Blackwell, "Loaded Words: Evolving Interpretations of 'Anti-Semitic' and 'Anti-Semitism' in Dictionary Definitions and in Public Discourse," *Variéng: Studies in Variation, Contacts and Change in English 6: Methodological and Historical Dimensions of Corpus Linguistics* (2011), http://www.helsinki.fi/varieng/series/volumes/06/meijs_blackwell/.
18. European Union Monitoring Centre, "Manifestations of Antisemitism in the EU 2002–2003" (Vienna, 2004), p. 12, http://fra.europa.eu/sites/default/files/fra_uploads/184-AS-Main-report.pdf. As we will see, this report became controversial for entirely unrelated reasons.
19. Laqueur, *Changing Face of Anti-Semitism*, pp. 21–22; Bernard Lewis, *Semites and Anti-Semites: An Inquiry into Conflict and Prejudice* (New York: W.W. Norton & Co., 1986), p. 117; Wistrich, *Antisemitism*, p. xvi.
20. Lewis, *Semites and Anti-Semites*, p. 16.
21. Jeffrey Herf, *Nazi Propaganda for the Arab World* (New Haven, CT: Yale University Press, 2009), pp. 15–35.
22. Gavin Langmuir, *Toward a Definition of Antisemitism* (Berkeley: University of California Press, 1990), p. 311.
23. Berger Waldeneff has demonstrated this point at great length. See Georg Christoph Berger Waldenegg, *Antisemitismus*, pp. 97–110.
24. See, e.g., European Union Monitoring Centre, "Manifestations of Antisemitism in the EU 2002–2003," p. 11.
25. Berger Waldenegg, *Antisemitismus*, p. 29.
26. Paul Reitter, *On the Origins of Jewish Self-Hatred* (Princeton, NJ: Princeton University Press, 2012), p. 1.

27. Joint Committees I (on Constitutional, Presidency of the Council of Ministers and Interior Affairs) and III (on Foreign and European Union Affairs), *Final Report of the Fact-Finding Inquiry on Anti-Semitism* (Oct. 14, 2011), p. 8 [hereinafter, the "Italian Parliamentary Report"].
28. Swiss Federal Commission Against Racism, website, "Anti-Semitism," accessed August 19, 2013, http://www.ekr.admin.ch/themen/00023/00025/index.html?lang=en.
29. Bachman v. St. Monica's Congregation, 902 F.2d 1259, 1260–1261 (7th Cir. 1990).
30. For the author's view on the idea of a Jewish "race," see Kenneth L. Marcus, *Jewish Identity and Civil Rights in America* (New York and Cambridge: Cambridge University Press, 2010).
31. Langmuir, *Toward a Definition of Antisemitism*, p. 313.
32. "The Statement of Race," quoted in Jon Entine, *Abraham's Children: Race, Identity and the DNA of the Chosen People* (New York: Grand Central Publishing, 2007), pp. 250–251.
33. Pierre-André Taguieff, *The Force of Prejudice: On Racism and Its Doubles*, trans. and ed. Hassan Melehy (Minneapolis: University of Minnesota Press, 2001), p. 21.
34. Amartya K. Sen, *Identity and Violence* (New York: Norton, 2006). For example, a person may be a woman, African American, Roman Catholic, Caribbean immigrant, and medical doctor, but racism reduces her to one group identity.
35. Pierre Bordieu, *Sociology in Question*, trans. Richard Nice (London: Sage, 1993), p. 177.
36. Zygmunt Bauman, *Modernity and the Holocaust* (Ithaca, NY: Cornell University Press, 1989).
37. For an illustration of how some anti-Jewish prejudices do not essentialize the "Jew," see Daniel Jonah Goldhagen, *The Devil That Never Dies: The Rise and Threat of Global Antisemitism* (New York: Little, Brown & Co., 2013), pp. 56–57.
38. Benjamin Isaac, "The Ancient Mediterranean and the Pre-Christian Era," in Albert S. Lindemann and Richard S. Levy, *Antisemitism: A History* (Oxford: Oxford University Press, 2010), pp. 34–46.
39. Ibid., p. 36.
40. Robert Wistrich, *A Lethal Obsession: Anti-Semitism from Antiquity to the Global Jihad* (New York: Random House, 2010), pp. 92–93.
41. Ibid., p. 238.
42. Ibid.
43. Ibid.
44. Ibid., p. 244.
45. Richard Landes and Steven T. Katz, "Introduction: The Protocols at the Dawn of the 21st Century," in Richard Landes and Steven T. Katz, eds.,

The Paranoid Apocalypse: A Hundred Year Retrospective on The Protocols of the Elders of Zion (New York: New York University Press, 2012), pp. 11–12.

46. Doris L. Bergen, "Antisemitism in the Nazi Era," in Albert S. Lindemann and Richard S. Levy, *Antisemitism: A History* (Oxford: Oxford University Press, 2010), pp. 196–211.
47. The Zionism-is-racism argument happens to be untrue. For an excellent discussion of this canard, see Gil Troy, *Moynihan's Moment: America's Fight Against Zionism as Racism* (New York and Oxford: Oxford University Press, 2012).
48. Taguieff, *Force of Prejudice*, p. 231.
49. Sarah Stern, "Campus Anti-Semitism," in *Briefing Report on Campus Anti-Semitism* (Washington, D.C.: U.S. Commission on Civil Rights, 2006), p. 25 (brackets added). Dabashi has contested this report, claiming that he did not use the term "Israeli Jews" and that this quotation misconstrues his views. See "Public Comments" in *Briefing Report*, p. 59. Stern argues that Dabashi had used the term "these people," referring to Israeli Jews when read in context. Ibid. at 69.
50. This notion is introduced in Kenneth L. Marcus, "Jurisprudence of the New Anti-Semitism," *Wake Forest Law Review* 44 (Summer 2009), p. 371.
51. For a discussion of the processes by which racial formation can be externally imposed, see Michael Omi and Howard Winant, *Racial Formation in the United States: From the 1960s to the 1980s* (New York: Routledge, 1986/1989), p. 66.
52. Jonathan Judaken, "So What's New? Rethinking the 'New Antisemitism' in a Global Age," *Patterns of Prejudice* 42 (2008), pp. 531–560, pp. 537–538.
53. See Charles R. Love, Program Manager, U.S. Department of Education, Office for Civil Rights, Region IX, In re University of California at Irvine, OCR Case No. 09-05-2013, Closure Letter to Susan Tuchman, Director, Center for Law and Justice, Zionist Organization of America, dated Nov. 30, 2007, p. 6 n.8 (quoting Amir Abdel Malik Ali).
54. Gabriel Schoenfeld, *The Return of Anti-Semitism* (San Francisco:Encounter Books, 2004), p. 19 (quoting B'Nai B'rith International, *Jihad, Jews, and Anti-Semitism in Syrian School Texts*, pp. 15–16 (2001)).
55. Marcus, *Jewish Identity and Civil Rights in America*, pp. 18–19.
56. See Michael Lerner, *The Socialism of Fools: Anti-Semitism on the Left* (Berkeley, CA: Inst. for Labor & Mental Health, 1992), p. 345.
57. Bachman v. St. Monica's Congregation, 902 F.2d 1259, 1260-1261 (7th Cir. 1990).
58. This creedal focus is implicit, for example, in Jacques Lacan's remark that Freud was forced to leave Nazi-occupied Austria "by

virtue of his tradition" (as opposed to his perceived race). Jacques Lacan, "The Freudian Thing, or the Meaning of the Return to Freud in Psychoanalysis," in *Écrits: A Selection*, trans. Alan Sheridan (New York: Norton, 1977), p. 118. Lacan's oddly euphemistic reference to Freud's "tradition" (as if the deeper sources of Freud's difference were potentially a source of embarrassment) may repress the deeper sources of Freud's mistreatment, but it also reveals another side of the same problem. The tradition to which Lacan refers—which Freud honored, ironically, more in the breach than in the observance—is the Jewish religion.

59. Léon Poliakov, *The History of Anti-Semitism*, vol. 1, *From the Time of Christ to the Court Jews*, trans. Richard Howard (New York: Vanguard, 1974), p. 23.
60. Wistrich, *Lethal Obsession*, p. 81.
61. Ibid.
62. Ibid.
63. Ibid.
64. Isaac, "Ancient Mediterranean and the Pre-Christian Era," p. 38.
65. Poliakov, *History of Anti-Semitism*, vol. 1, pp. 29–32.
66. Wistrich, *Lethal Obsession*, p. 79.
67. Bernard Lewis, "The New Anti-Semitism," *The American Scholar* 75:1 (Winter 2006), pp. 25–33.
68. Wistrich, *Lethal Obsession*, p. 85.
69. Gospel of John 8:39–47.
70. Wistrich, *Lethal Obsession*, p. 85.
71. Poliakov, *History of Anti-Semitism*, vol. 1, pp. 24–25.
72. Wistrich, *Lethal Obsession*, p. 86.
73. Ibid.
74. Poliakov, *History of Anti-Semitism*, vol. 1, p. 25.
75. "Homily I: Against the Jews," in Wayne A. Meeks and Robert L. Wilken, *Jews and Christians in Antioch in the First Four Centuries of the Common Era* (Missoula, MT: Scholars Press, 1978), p. 97, quoted in Wistrich, *Lethal Obsession*, p. 86.
76. Saint John Chrysostom, *The Fathers of the Church*, vol. 68, *Discourses Against Judaizing Christians*, trans. and ed. Paul W. Harkins (Washington, DC: Catholic University of America Press, 1979), excerpted in Marvin Perry and Frederick M. Schweitzer, *Antisemitic Myths: A Historical and Contemporary Anthology* (Bloomington: Indiana University Press, 2008), pp. 6–9.
77. Wistrich, *Lethal Obsession*, p. 90.
78. Ibid., p. 91.
79. Ibid., pp. 88–89.
80. Quoted in Alex Novikoff, "The Middle Ages," in Albert S. Lindemann and Richard S. Levy, *Antisemitism: A History* (Oxford: Oxford University Press, 2010), pp. 63–78.

81. Andrew Bostom, ed., *The Legacy of Islamic Antisemitism* (Amherst, NY: Prometheus Books, 2008).
82. Norman A. Stillman, "Anti-Judaism and Antisemitism in the Arab and Islamic World Prior to 1948," in Albert S. Lindemann and Richard S. Levy, *Antisemitism: A History* (Oxford: Oxford University Press, 2010), pp. 212–221.
83. Haggai Ben-Shammai, "Jew Hatred in the Islamic Tradition and the Koranic Exegesis," in Bostom, ed., *Legacy of Islamic Antisemitism*, p. 223.
84. Al-Jaubari, "To Disclose the Fraudulence of the Jewish Men of Learning," in Bostom, ed., *Legacy of Islamic Antisemitism*, trans. Moshe Perlmann, p. 321.
85. See, e.g., Al-Jahiz, "Why the Muslims Prefer the Christians to the Jews," in Bostom, ed., *Legacy of Islamic Antisemitism*, trans. Joshua Finkel, pp. 317–318.
86. Wistrich, *Lethal Obsession*, p 439.
87. Ibid.
88. Quoted in Paul Berman, "Something's Changed," in Ron Rosenbaum, ed., *Those Who Forget the Past: The Question of Anti-Semitism* (New York: Random House, 2004), pp. 18–19.
89. Quoted in Wistrich, *Lethal Obsession*, p. 33.
90. Stillman, "Anti-Judaism and Antisemitism in the Arab and Islamic World Prior to 1948," pp. 212–221.
91. Meir Litvak and Esther Webman, "Israel and Antisemitism," in Albert S. Lindemann and Richard S. Levy, *Antisemitism: A History* (Oxford: Oxford University Press, 2010), pp. 237–249.
92. Ibid.
93. Leora Batnitzky, *How Judaism Became a Religion: An Introduction to Modern Jewish Thought* (Princeton, NJ: Princeton University Press, 2011), p. 13.
94. Eric L. Goldstein, *The Price of Whiteness: Jews, Race, and American Identity* (Princeton, NJ: Princeton University Press, 2007); Karen Bodkin, *How Jews Became White Folks and What That Says About the Rest of Us* (New Brunswick, NJ: Rutgers University Press, 1998).
95. Pew Research Center, *A Portrait of Jewish Americans* (October 1, 2013), http://www.pewforum.org/2013/10/01/jewish-american-beliefs-attitudes-culture-survey/.
96. Robert D. Putnam, *Bowling Alone: The Collapse and Revival of American Community* (New York: Touchstone Books, 2001).
97. James Baldwin, "Negroes Are Anti-Semitic Because They're Anti-White," in Nat Hentoff, ed., *Anti-Semitism and Jewish Racism* (New York: Richard W. Baron, 1969), p. 9.
98. Marcus, *Jewish Identity and Civil Rights in America*.
99. Kenneth L. Marcus, "Three Conceptions of Religious Freedom," in Yedidia Stern, Hanoch Dagan, and Shahar Lifshitz, *Religion and Human Rights Discourse* (Jerusalem: Israel Democracy Institute, 2014).

100. Erving Goffman, *Stigma: Notes on the Management of Spoiled Identity* (New York: Touchstone, 1986). Kenji Yoshino develops Goffman's concept in *Covering: The Hidden Assault on Our Civil Rights* (New York: Random House, 2006).
101. See Leora Batnitzky, "From Collectivity to Individuality: The Shared Trajectories of Modern Concepts of 'Religion' and 'Human Rights,'" in Stern, et al., *Religion and Human Rights Discourse*.
102. 481 U.S. 604 (1987). This argument is developed in Kenneth L. Marcus, "Anti-Zionism as Racism: Campus Anti-Semitism and the Civil Rights Act of 1964," *William & Mary Bill of Rights Journal* 15 (Apr. 2007), pp. 837–891.
103. Quoted in David Nirenberg, *Anti-Judaism: The Western Tradition* (New York: W.W. Norton, 2013), p. 113.
104. Aluma Solnick, "Based on Qur'anic Verses, Interpretations, and Traditions, Muslims State: The Jews Are the Descendants of Apes, Pigs, and Other Animals," in Bostom, ed., *Legacy of Islamic Antisemitism*, pp. 633–640.
105. S'ad Al-Bawardi, quoted in B. Chernitsky and E. Glass, *Antisemitic Statements in Wake of Gaza War,* Inquiry and Analysis Series Report No. 507 (Washington, DC: MEMRI, March 30, 2009).
106. Neil J. Kressel, *"The Sons of Pigs and Apes": Muslim Antisemitism and the Conspiracy of Silence* (Washington, DC: Potomac Books, 2012), p. 26.
107. Anti-Defamation League, *Middle East Press Review: Anti-Semitism and Other Trends, July–December 2012* (New York: Anti-Defamation League, 2013), p. 7.
108. Elisabeth Young-Bruehl, *The Anatomy of Prejudices* (Cambridge, MA: Harvard University Press, 1996), pp. 33–34.
109. Ibid., pp. 34–35.
110. Ibid.
111. European Jewish Press, *Dutch University Cancels Conference with Islamic Scholar for His Anti-Semitic Remarks* (Feb. 18, 2012), www.ejpress.org/article/56275.
112. Jacques Derrida, *The Beast & the Sovereign,* Vol. 1 (Chicago: University of Chicago Press, 2009, pp. 126, 127.
113. Aristotle, *Politics* I.I253a, 4.
114. Derrida, *The Beast & the Sovereign*, p. 26.
115. See, generally, Daniel Jonah Goldhagen, *Worse Than War: Genocide, Eliminationism, and the Ongoing Assault on Humanity* (New York: Public Affairs, 2009), pp. 319–341.
116. Kenneth L. Marcus, "Accusation in a Mirror," *Loyola University Chicago Law Journal* 43:2 (Winter 2012), pp. 357–393.
117. Sigmund Freud, *Civilization and Its Discontents*, trans. James Strachey (New York: Norton, 1961), pp. 80–82.
118. Ibid., pp. 68–74, 81.

119. Ibid., pp. 56–61.
120. Max Horkheimer and Theodor W. Adorno, *Dialectic of Enlightenment: Philosophical Fragments*, trans. Edmund Jephcott, ed. Gunzelin Schmid Noerr (Stanford: Stanford University Press, 2002), p. 154.
121. Michel Foucault, *The History of Sexuality*, vol. 1, *An Introduction*, trans. Robert Hurley (New York: Random House, 1990), p. 143.
122. Giorgio Agamben, *Homo Sacer: Sovereign Power and Bare Life*, trans. Daniel Heller-Roazen, (Stanford: Stanford University Press, 1998), p. 7.
123. Ibid., p. 11.
124. Nirenberg, *Anti-Judaism*, p. 187.
125. Novikoff, "Middle Ages," pp. 63–78.
126. Nirenberg, *Anti-Judaism*, p. 191.
127. Didi Herman, *An Unfortunate Coincidence: Jews, Jewishness and English Law* (Oxford: Oxford University Press, 2011), p. 10.
128. Anthony Julius, *Trials of the Diaspora: A History of Anti-Semitism in England* (Oxford: Oxford University Press, 2010), p. 106.
129. Pascal Bruckner, *The Tyranny of Guilt: An Essay on Western Masochism*, trans. Steven Rendall (Princeton, NJ: Princeton University Press, 2010), pp. 68–70.
130. Sander Gilman, *Jewish Self-Hatred: Anti-Semitism and the Hidden Language of the Jews* (Baltimore, MD: Johns Hopkins University Press, 1986), p. 2.

Chapter 3

1. *The Jewish Encyclopedia*, vol. 1 (1901), http://www.jewishencyclopedia.com/articles/1603-anti-semitism.
2. Leon Wieseltier, "Against Ethnic Panic: Hitler is Dead," *The New Republic* (May 27, 2002), reprinted in Ron Rosenbaum, ed., *Those Who Forget the Past: The Question of Anti-Semitism* (New York: Random House, 2004), pp. 178, 181.
3. *Sifrei* to Numbers parashat Beha-alotecha 69, Bar Ilan University Online Response Project, www.rcsponsa.co.il.default.aspx.
4. Genesis 36:12.
5. Exodus 17:16.
6. Midrash Rabbah Esther 7:10.
7. Leon Wieseltier, "Against Ethnic Panic," pp. 178, 181.
8. Numbers 21:1.
9. Midrash Tanhuma (Wasaw) Parashat Hukkat 18, Bar Ilan University Online Response Project, www.responsa.co.il.default.aspx.
10. *Rashi* to Numbers 21:1.
11. Paul Johnson, "The Anti-Semitic Disease," *Commentary* (June 2005), http://www.commentarymagazine.com/viewarticle.cfm/the-anti-semitic-disease-9904.

12. Dennis Prager and Joseph Telushkin, *Why the Jews? The Reason for Antisemitism* (New York: Touchstone, 1983), p. 6 (emphasis original).
13. Robert S. Wistrich, *Antisemitism: The Longest Hatred* (New York: Schocken Books 1991), p. xvi–xvii.
14. Ibid.
15. Gavin Langmuir, "Toward a Definition of Antisemitism," in *Toward a Definition of Antisemitism* (Berkeley: University of California Press, 1990), p. 315.
16. Albert S. Lindemann and Richard S. Levy, "Introduction," to *Antisemitism: A History* (Oxford: Oxford University Press, 2010), p. 2.
17. Emanual Levinas, *Difficult Freedom: Essays on Judaism* (Baltimore, MD: Johns Hopkins University Press, 1997), p. 225.
18. Hannah Arendt, *The Origins of Totalitarianism* (New York: Schocken Books, 2004), p. 17.
19. Wieseltier, "Against Ethnic Panic," pp. 178, 183.
20. David Nirenberg, *Anti-Judaism: The Western Tradition* (New York: W.W. Norton, 2013), p. 9.
21. Wistrich, *Antisemitism*, p. xvii.
22. Shaye J. D. Cohen, "'Anti-Semitism' in Antiquity: The Problem of Definition," in David Berger, ed., *History and Hate: The Dimensions of Anti-Semitism* (New York: The Jewish Publication Society, 1986), pp. 43–47, 45.
23. Walter Laqueur, *The Changing Face of Anti-Semitism: From Ancient Times to the Present Day* (Oxford: Oxford University Press 2006), p. 33.
24. Walter Benjamin, "Theses on the Philosophy of History," in *Illuminations*, ed. Hannah Arendt, trans. Harry Zohn (New York: Schocken Books, 1968), p. 257.
25. Arendt, *Origins of Totalitarianism*, p. 3.
26. Langmuir, *Toward a Definition of Antisemitism*, p. 315.
27. Benjamin, "Theses on the Philosophy of History," p. 257.
28. Steven Beller, *Antisemitism: A Very Short Introduction* (Oxford: Oxford University Press, 2007), p. 4.
29. Wieseltier, "Against Ethnic Panic," pp. 178, 181.
30. Ruth Wisse, "The Anti-Semite's Pointed Finger," COMMENTARY (Nov. 2010), p. 24.
31. Hannah Arendt, "Antisemitism," in *The Jewish Writings*, ed. Jerome Kohn and Ron H. Feldman (New York: Schocken, 2007), pp. 47–48.
32. Arendt, *Origins of Totalitarianism*, p. 16.
33. Ibid., p. 17.
34. Anthony Julius, *Trials of the Diaspora: A History of Antisemitism in England* (Oxford: Oxford University Press, 2010), p. xliii.
35. Ibid.
36. Labels can be confusing. For example, Walter Benjamin used the term "historicism" in precisely the opposite of the sense used here. See Benjamin, "Theses on the Philosophy of History," pp. 253–264.

37. Langmuir, *Toward a Definition of Antisemitism*, p. 2.
38. Richard S. Levy, "Political Antisemitism in Germany and Austria, 1848–1914," in Albert S. Lindemann and Richard S. Levy, *Antisemitism: A History* (Oxford: Oxford University Press, 2010), pp. 63–78.
39. Dina Porat, "Historical Perspective," in Dina Porat and Kenneth Stern, *Defining Antisemitism*, 2005, www.tau.ac.il/Anti-Semitism/asw2003-4/porat.htm (quoting *Everyman's Encyclopedia* [UK, 1949, NY, 1951; 3rd ed.], Vol. 7, p. 373).
40. Ibid.
41. Ibid.
42. Arendt, "Antisemitism," p. 49.
43. Arendt, *Origins of Totalitarianism*, p. 4.
44. Ibid.
45. Ibid.
46. Zygmunt Bauman, *Modernity and the Holocaust* (Ithaca, NY: Cornell University Press, 1989), pp. 61–62.
47. David M. Seymour, *Law, Antisemitism and the Holocaust* (New York: Routledge, 2007), p. xix.
48. Arendt, *Origins of Totalitarianism*.
49. Michel Foucault, *"Society Must be Defended": Lectures at the Collège de France 1975–1976* (New York: Picador, 1997), pp. 88–89.
50. Albert S. Lindemann, *Esau's Tears: Modern Anti-Semitism and the Rise of the Jews* (Cambridge: Cambridge University Press, 1997).
51. Levy, "Political Antisemitism in Germany and Austria," pp. 63–78.
52. Alex Novikoff, "The Middle Ages," in Lindemann and Levy, *Antisemitism: A History*, pp. 63–78.
53. David Nirenberg, "Anti-Judaism as a Critical Theory," *The Chronicle Review*, B11–B13, B11 (Feb. 1, 2013).
54. Georg Christoph Berger Waldenegg, *Antisemitismus: "Eine gefährliche Vokabel"? Diagnose eines Wortes* (Vienna: Böhlau, 2003).
55. Cf. Léon Poliakov, *The History of Anti-Semitism*, vol. 1, *From the Time of Christ to the Court Jews*, trans. Richard Howard (New York: Vanguard, 1974), pp. 29–35 (painting a more benign portrait of ninth-century Christian attitudes toward Jews, especially in Carolingian Europe).
56. Nirenberg, *Anti-Judaism*, p. 9.
57. Florette Cohen, Lee Jussim, Gautam Bhasin, and Elizabeth Salib, "The Modern Anti-Semitism Israel Model: An Empirical Relationship Between Modern Anti-Semitism and Opposition to Israel," *Conflict & Communication Online* 10:1 (2011).
58. The origins of the blood libel are traced in Poliakov, *History of Anti-Semitism*, vol. 1, pp. 56–64.
59. Robert Wistrich, *A Lethal Obsession: Anti-Semitism from Antiquity to the Global Jihad* (New York: Random House, 2010), pp. 94–95.
60. Ibid., p. 95.

61. Marvin Perry and Frederick M. Schweitzer, *Antisemitism: Myth and Hate from Antiquity to the Present* (New York: Palgrave Macmillan, 2002), pp. 43–72; Novikoff, "The Middle Ages," pp. 63–78.
62. Perry and Schweitzer, *Antisemitism*, pp. 43–72.
63. Ibid., pp. 56–58.
64. Ibid.
65. Wistrich, *Lethal Obsession*, p. 95.
66. Perry and Schweitzer, *Antisemitism*, p. 60.
67. Norman A. Stillman, "Anti-Judaism and Antisemitism in the Arab and Islamic World Prior to 1948," in Lindemann and Levy, *Antisemitism: A History*, pp. 212–221.
68. Perry and Schweitzer, *Antisemitism*, p. 45.
69. Laurence Loeb, "'Outcast': Shi'a Intolerance," in Andrew Bostom, ed., *The Legacy of Islamic Antisemitism* (Amherst, NY: Prometheus Books, 2008), p. 564.
70. Perry and Schweitzer, *Antisemitism*, p. 69.
71. Ibid.
72. Wistrich, *Lethal Obsession*, p. 497.
73. Richard Landes, "Jewish Self-Criticism, Progressive Moral *Schadenfrude*, and the Suicide of Reason," in Richard Landes and Steven T. Katz, eds., *The Paranoid Apocalypse: A Hundred Year Retrospective on The Protocols of the Elders of Zion* (New York: New York University Press, 2012), pp. 229–250.
74. Jeffrey R. Woolf, "The Medieval Roots of *The Protocols of the Elders of Zion*," in Landes and Katz, eds., *Paranoid Apocalypse*, pp. 49–55; Norman Cohn, *Warrant for Genocide: The Myth of the Jewish World Conspiracy and the Protocols of the Elders of Zion* (London: Serif, 1967).
75. Richard Landes and Steven T. Katz, "Introduction: The Protocols at the Dawn of the 21st Century," in Landes and Katz, eds., *Paranoid Apocalypse*, p. 1.
76. Ibid., p. 1.
77. Slavoj Žižek, *Enjoy Your Symptom: Jacques Lacan in Hollywood and Out* (New York: Routledge, 2008), p. 92.
78. Ibid., p. 94.
79. Elisabeth Young-Bruehl, *The Anatomy of Prejudices* (Cambridge, MA: Harvard University Press, 1996), p. 53.
80. Max Horkheimer and Theodor W. Adorno, *Dialectic of Enlightenment: Philosophical Fragments*, trans. Edmund Jephcott, ed. Gunzelin Schmid Noerr (Stanford: Stanford University Press, 2002), p. 154.
81. Ibid., p. 52.
82. Ibid., p. 53.
83. Bruno Bettelheim and Morris Janowitz, *Dynamics of Prejudice: A Psychological and Sociological Study of Veterans* (New York: Harper, 1950), pp. 58–61, 76–85.

84. Stuart Svonkin, *Jews Against Prejudice: American Jews and the Fight for Civil Liberties* (New York: Columbia University Press, 1997), pp. 38–39, quoting Nathan Ackerman and Marie Jahoda, *Anti-Semitism and Emotional Disorder* (New York: Harper, 1950), pp. 8–9.
85. Slavoj Žižek, *The Year of Living Dangerously* (London: Verso, 2012), p. 23.
86. Benjamin, "Theses on the Philosophy of History."
87. Žižek, *Enjoy Your Symptom*, p. 94.
88. Ibid.
89. Robert Fine, "On Doing the Sociology of Antisemitism," *European Sociologist* 33, (Winter 2012), p. 4, http://www.europeansociology.org/docs/ESA_Newsletter_Winter2012_HR.pdf.
90. Ibid.

Chapter 4

1. Pierre-André Taguieff, *The Force of Prejudice: On Racism and Its Doubles*, trans. and ed. Hassan Melehy (Minneapolis: University of Minnesota Press, 2001), p. 21.
2. Zygmunt Bauman, *Modernity and the Holocaust* (Ithaca, NY: Cornell University Press, 1989), p. 62.
3. Robert Wistrich, *A Lethal Obsession: Anti-Semitism from Antiquity to the Global Jihad* (New York: Random House, 2010), pp. 13–14.
4. Ibid., p. 15.
5. Quoted in Stuart Svonkin, *Jews Against Prejudice: American Jews and the Fight for Civil Liberties* (New York: Columbia University Press, 1997), p. 155.
6. Ibid., p. 18.
7. Ibid., p. 21.
8. Ibid., p. 22.
9. Theodor W. Adorno, Else Frenkel-Brunswik, Daniel Levinson, and Nevitt Sanford, *The Authoritarian Personality* (New York: Harper and Row, 1950).
10. Gordon Allport, *The Nature of Prejudice* (Reading, MA: Addison-Wesley, 1954; New York: Anchor, 1958).
11. Salo W. Baron, "Changing Patterns of Antisemitism," *Jewish Social Studies* 38:1 (1976), pp. 5–38.
12. Joint Committees I (on Constitutional, Presidency of the Council of Ministers and Interior Affairs) and III (on Foreign and European Union Affairs), *Final Report of the Fact-Finding Inquiry on Anti-Semitism* (Oct. 14, 2011), p. 18.
13. Wistrich, *Lethal Obsession*, p. 10.
14. Slavoj Žižek, *The Sublime Object of Ideology* (London: Verso, 1989), p. xxvi.
15. Clark Freshman, "Whatever Happened to Anti-Semitism? How Social Science Theories Identify Discrimination and Promote Coalitions Between 'Different' Minorities," *Cornell Law Review* 85 (2000), pp. 313, 317–319.

16. Quoted in Svonkin, *Jews Against Prejudice*, p. 18.
17. Bernard Harrison, "Anti-Zionism, Antisemitism, and the Rhetorical Manipulation of Reality," in Alvin H. Rosenfeld, *Resurgent Antisemitism: Global Perspectives* (Bloomington: Indiana University Press, 2013), p. 11.
18. Elisabeth Young-Bruehl, *The Anatomy of Prejudices* (Cambridge, MA: Harvard University Press, 1996), p. 18.
19. Ruth Wisse, "The Suicidal Passion: Who Is Damaged More by Anti-Semitism—Jews, or Those who Organize Politics against Them?," *The Weekly Standard* 17:10 (Nov. 21, 2011).
20. Ibid.
21. Harrison, "Anti-Zionism, Antisemitism," pp. 11–13.
22. Freshman, "Whatever Happened to Anti-Semitism?," p. 313.
23. Ibid., p. 409.
24. Wistrich, *Lethal Obsession*, p. 8.
25. Ben-Zion Netanyahu, "Antisemitism," in *The Hebrew Encyclopedia* (Jerusalem/Tel Aviv, 1959; in Hebrew), vol. 4, pp. 493–508, quoted, pp. 496–497, quoted in Dina Porat, "Historical Perspective," in Dina Porat and Kenneth Stern, *Defining Antisemitism* (Tel Aviv University, 2005), www.tau.ac.il/Anti-Semitism/asw2003-4/porat.htm.
26. Wistrich, *Lethal Obsession*, p. 8.
27. Léon Poliakov, *The History of Anti-Semitism,* vol. 1, *From the Time of Christ to the Court Jews*, trans. Richard Howard (Philadelphia: University of Pennsylvania Press, 2003), p. 4.
28. Gavin I. Langmuir, *Toward a Definition of Antisemitism* (Berkeley: University of California Press, 1990), p. 317.
29. Steven Beller, *Antisemitism: A Very Short Introduction* (Oxford: Oxford University Press, 2007), p. 2.
30. Žižek, *Sublime Object of Ideology*, p. xxvii.
31. Helen Fein, "Dimensions of Antisemitism: Attitudes, Collective Accusations, and Actions," in Helen Fein, *The Persisting Question: Sociological Perspectives and Social Contexts of Modern Antisemitism* (Berlin: Walter de Gruyter, 1987), p. 68.
32. Quoted in Anthony Julius, Claimant's skeletal argument, Fraser v. University and College Union (for hearing on 29 October, 2012), p. 11.
33. Alvin H. Roseneld, *The End of the Holocaust* (Bloomington: Indiana University Press, 2011), pp. 238–270.
34. Wistrich, *Lethal Obsession*, pp. 427–428.
35. Gabriel Noah Brahm, Jr., "Holocaust Envy: The Libidinal Economy of the New Antisemitism," *Journal for the Study of Antisemitism* 3:2 (2011), pp. 489–505.
36. Bruno Chaouat expands on these points in "Antisemitism Redux: On Literary and Theoretical Perversions," in Alvin H. Rosenfeld, *Resurgent Antisemitism: Global Perspectives* (Bloomington: Indiana University Press, 2013), p. 120.

37. Roseneld, *End of the Holocaust*, pp. 250–254.
38. Alain Badiou, "Uses of the Word Jew," in *Polemics* (London: Verso, 2006), pp. 157–158.
39. Alain Badiou, *Ethics: An Essay on the Understanding of Evil* (Peter Hallward, translator) (London: Verso, 2013), pp. 75–76; Alain Badiou, "Israel: The Country in the World Where There are the Fewest Jews?" in *Polemics*, pp. 167–171.
40. Badiou, "Israel," in *Polemics*, pp. 169–170.
41. Badiou has repeatedly returned to these questions, e.g., in "Against Negationism," In *Polemics*, pp. 195–201.
42. Cécile Winter, "The Master-Signifier of the New Aryans: What Made the Word 'Jew' into an Arm Brandished Against the Multitude of 'Unpronounceable Names,'" in *Polemics*, pp. 217–229.
43. Ibid., p. 226.
44. Žižek, *Sublime Object of Ideology*, p. 95.
45. Ernesto Laclau and Chantal Mouffe, *Hegemony and Socialist Strategy: Towards a Radical Democratic Politcs* (London: Verso, 2nd ed., 2001), p. 112.
46. Žižek, *Sublime Object of Ideology*, pp. 95–96.
47. András Kovács, "Antisemitic Prejudice and Political Antisemitism in Present-Day Hungary," *Journal for the Study of Antisemitism* 4:2 (2013), pp. 443, 464.
48. Ernest Sternberg, "Purifying the World: What the New Radical Ideology Stands For," *Orbis* (Winter 2010), p. 61.
49. Quoted in Wistrich, *Lethal Obsession*, p. 6.
50. Slavoj Žižek, *For They Know Not What They Do: Enjoyment as a Political Factor* (London: Verso, 2008), pp. 17–18.
51. Wistrich, *Lethal Obsession*, p. 6.
52. Quoted in Matthias Küntzel, "The Roots of Antisemitism in the Middle East: New Debates," in Rosenfeld, *Resurgent Antisemitism*, p. 283.
53. Alvin H. Rosenfeld, "Responding to Campus-Based Anti-Zionism: Two Models," in Eunice G. Pollack, *Antisemitism on the Campus: Past & Present* (Boston: Academic Studies Press, 2011), pp. 414, 416.
54. Ibid., pp. 414, 417.
55. Sternberg, "Purifying the World," p. 81.

Chapter 5

1. European Union Monitoring Center, "Manifestations of Antisemitism in the EU 2002–2003" (Vienna, 2004), p. 12, http://fra.europa.eu/sites/default/files/fra_uploads/184-AS-Main-report.pdf.
2. Charles Y. Glock and Rodney Stark, *Christian Beliefs and Anti-Semitism* (New York: Harper & Row, 1966), p. 102.
3. Daniel A. Farber and Suzana Sherry, *Beyond All Reason: The Radical Assault on Truth in American Law* (New York: Oxford University Press, 1997), pp. 52–71.

4. Ibid., p. 9.
5. Edward L. Rubin, "Jews, Truth, and Critical Race Theory," *Northwestern University Law Review* 93 (Winter 1999), pp. 525, 528 (reviewing Farber and Sherry, *Beyond All Reason*).
6. Helen Fein, "Dimensions of Antisemitism: Attitudes, Collective Accusations, and Actions," in *The Persisting Question: Sociological Perspectives and Social Contexts of Modern Antisemitism* (Berlin: Walter De Gruyter, 1987), pp. 67, 69 note 6.
7. Robert Wistrich, *A Lethal Obsession: Anti-Semitism from Antiquity to the Global Jihad* (New York: Random House, 2010), p. 114.
8. Ibid., pp. 130–153. This ruse often wore thin, as when one Soviet propagandist wrote that Zionist "gangsterism" had "its ideological roots in the scrolls of the 'holy' Torah and the precepts of the Talmud."
9. This does not even count resolutions of Human Rights Council or Commission on Human Rights.
10. These include the Special Committee to Investigate Israeli Practices Affecting the Human Rights of the Palestinian People and Other Arabs of the Occupied Territories (established in 1968), the Committee on the Exercise of the Inalienable Rights of the Palestinian People (1975), and the Division for Palestinian Rights (1981).
11. U.S. Department of State, *Contemporary Global Anti-Semitism: A Report Provided to the United States Congress* (2008).
12. Ibid.
13. Kofi Annan, Then-Secretary General of the United Nations, "Seminar on Anti-Semitism" (June 2004), quoted in U.S. Department of State, *Contemporary Global Anti-Semitism: A Report Provided to the United States Congress* (2008).
14. Imre Kertész, "The Language of Exile," *Guardian* (Oct. 19, 2002), available at http://books.guardian.co.uk/review/story/0,12084,814056,00.html.
15. For the author's take on this question, see Kenneth L. Marcus, *Jewish Identity and Civil Rights in America* (New York: Cambridge University Press, 2010).
16. Alain Badiou, "The Word 'Jew' and the Sycophant," in *Polemics* (London: Verso, 2006), pp. 230–231. The particular standards Badiou has in mind are not those of Orthodox Judaism but of the particular brand of progressive, or "universalist and egalitarian," politics to which he subscribes. As a Marxist critic of the Soviet Union, he similarly argues that Brezhnev's Russia should not be considered communist. The problem with the latter claim is that the Soviet Union provides the most significant actual example of what it means for a state to adopt communist ideology, just as Israel is the only example of a state explicitly established for the Jewish people.
17. Melanie Phillips, "The Chosen Person," *Haaretz* (Nov. 7, 2003), http://www.haaretz.com/the-chosen-person-1.104861.

18. Wistrich, *Lethal Obsession*, p. 396.
19. Alain Badiou, "Israel: the Country in the World Where There Are the Fewest Jews," in *Polemics* (London: Verso, 2006), pp. 167–171.
20. Revital Blumenfeld, "A. B. Yehoshua: Americans, Unlike Israelis, Are Only Partial Jews," *Haaretz* (Mar. 18, 2012), http://www.haaretz.com/print-edition/news/a-b-yehoshua-americans-unlike-israelis-are-only-partial-jews-1.419240.
21. Wistrich, *Lethal Obsession*, p. 521.
22. Judith Butler, *Precarious Life: The Powers of Mourning and Violence* (London: Verso, 2004), p. 15.
23. Butler surely overstates her case in arguing that Zionism has gained hegemony over Jewishness in recent years. Organized Jewish cultural life, if one may forgive the oxymoron, has nurtured far too many conflicting voices, not to mention too many apathetic or withdrawn individuals, to speak of such hegemony.
24. Emanuele Ottolenghi, "Present-day Antisemitism and the Centrality of the Jewish Alibi," in Alvin H. Rosenfeld, *Resurgent Antisemitism: Global Perspectives* (Bloomington: Indiana University Press, 2013), pp. 427–428.
25. Butler, *Precarious Life*, pp. 113–114.
26. Judith Butler, *Parting Ways: Jewishness and the Critique of Zionism* (New York: Columbia University Press, 2012), p. 20.
27. *Fraser v. University College Union*, U.K. Employment Tribunal (London) (Case No. 2203290/2011) (March 22, 2013). Sadly, the tribunal failed to grasp Julius's logic, as the next chapter will explain.
28. Ibid., (closing statement).
29. Butler, *Parting Ways*, p. 20.
30. Anthony Julius, *Trials of the Diaspora: A History of Anti-Semitism in England* (Oxford: Oxford University Press, 2010), p. 65.
31. Ibid., p. 502.
32. Terry Eagleton, *Ideology: An Introduction* (London: Verso, 1001), p. 25; Raymond Geuss, *The Idea of a Critical Theory: Habermas and the Frankfurt School* (Cambridge: Cambridge University Press, 1981).
33. Slavoj Žižek, *The Year of Living Dangerously* (London: Verso, 2012), p. 13 note 6.
34. Adolf Hitler, *Mein Kampf*, trans. Ralph Manheim (Boston: Mariner, 1999), p. 59.
35. Ani DiFranco, song, "My IQ," *Puddle Dive* (Righteous Babe Records, 1993), quoted as motto to Michael Hardt and Antonio Negri, *Empire* (Cambridge, MA: Harvard University Press, 2000).
36. See Hitler, *Mein Kampf*, p. 52 (expressing contempt for religious anti-Semitism).
37. Gavin Langmuir, "Toward a Definition of Antisemitism," in *Toward a Definition of Antisemitism* (Berkeley: University of California Press, 1990), p. 328.
38. I am indebted to the late Gary Tobin and Aryeh Weinberg for this example.

39. Query whether the movie industry question could serve as a useful indicator of anti-Semitism, despite its evident truth, if those who are not anti-Semites invariably deny it out of politeness.
40. Hannah Arendt, *The Origins of Totalitarianism* (New York: Schocken Books, 2004), p. 83.
41. Brian Klug, "The Collective Jew: Israel and the New Antisemitism," *Patterns of Prejudice* 37:2 (2003), pp. 123–124 (emphasis added).
42. Jean-Paul Sartre, *Anti-Semite and Jew*, trans. George C. Becker (New York: Schocken Books, 1995), p. 16.
43. *Encyclopedia of the Holocaust*, editor-in-chief: Israel Gutman (Yad Vashem / Sifriat Poalim, 1990; in Hebrew), vol. 1, pp. 98–116, quoting Porat, "Historical Perspective."
44. Gordon Allport, *The Nature of Prejudice* (New York: Basic Books, 1954) (emphasis added).
45. Julius, *Trials of the Diaspora*, p. 47.
46. Langmuir, *Toward a Definition of Antisemitism*, p. 315.
47. David Berger, "Anti-Semitism: An Overview," in *History and Hate: The Dimensions of Anti-Semitism* (New York: The Jewish Publication Society, 1986), pp. 3–14.
48. Klug, "Collective Jew," pp. 123–124.
49. Dina Porat, "Historical Perspective," in Dina Porat and Kenneth Stern, *Defining Antisemitism*, 2005, www.tau.ac.il/Anti-Semitism/asw2003-4/porat.htm.
50. Ibid.
51. Julius, *Trials of the Diaspora*, pp. 3–4.
52. Ibid., p. 24.
53. Frederick Weil, "The Extent and Structure of Anti-Semitism in Western Populations Since the Holocaust," in Fein, *The Persisting Question: Sociological Perspectives and Social Contexts of Modern Antisemitism* (Berlin: Walter De Gruyter, 1987), p. 164.
54. Melvin M. Tumin, "Anti-Semitism and Status Anxiety: A Hypothesis," *Jewish Social Studies* 4 (1971), p. 309.
55. The hypothetical would be difficult if the activist held individual Jews collectively responsible for the actions of other Jews or if the activist resorted to anti-Semitic stereotypes and defamations.
56. See, generally, Matthias Küntzel, "The Roots of Antisemitism in the Middle East: New Debates," in Rosenfeld, *Resurgent Antisemitism*, pp. 384–385.
57. Anti-Defamation League, "Attitudes Toward Jews and the Middle East in Six European Countries" (2007), p. 14, http://archive.adl.org/anti_semitism/European_Attitudes_Survey_July_2007.pdf.
58. Wistrich, *Lethal Obsession*, pp. 346, 357.
59. Alain Badiou and Eric Hazan, "'Anti-Semitism Everywhere' in France Today," in Alain Badou, Eric Hazan, and Ivan Segré, *Reflections on Anti-Semitism*, trans. David Fernbach (London: Verso, 2013), p. 14.
60. Küntzel, "Roots of Antisemitism in the Middle East," p. 385.

61. David Nirenberg, *Anti-Judaism: The Western Tradition* (New York: W.W. Norton, 2013), p. 197.
62. Bernard Lewis, *Semites and Anti-Semites: An Inquiry into Conflict and Prejudice* (New York: W.W. Norton & Co., 1986), p. 11.
63. Ibid.
64. Quoted in Wistrich, *Lethal Obsession*, p. 283.
65. Paula E. Hyman, *The Jews of Modern France* (Berkeley: University of California Press, 1998), p. 211.
66. Günther Jikeli, "Antisemitism among Young European Males," in Rosenfeld, *Resurgent Antisemitism*, p. 282.
67. Ibid., pp. 282–283.
68. Quoted in Alvin H. Rosenfeld, "The End of the Holocaust and the Beginning of a New Antisemitism," in Rosenfeld, *Resurgent Antisemitism*, p. 525.
69. Günther Jikeli, "Antisemitism among Young European Males," in Rosenfeld, *Resurgent Antisemitism*, p. 283.
70. Wistrich, *Lethal Obsession*, p. 363.
71. Itamar Marcus and Barbara Crook, "The Protocols of the Elders of Zion: An Authentic Document in Palestinian Authority Ideology," in Richard Landes and Steven T. Katz, eds., *The Paranoid Apocalypse: A Hundred Year Retrospective on The Protocols of the Elders of Zion* (New York: New York University Press, 2012), pp. 152–160.
72. Klug, "Collective Jew," p. 14.
73. Michel Wieviorka, *The Lure of Anti-Semitism: Hatred of Jews in Present-Day France* (Leiden: Brill, 2007).
74. Jikeli, "Antisemitism among Young European Males," in Rosenfeld, *Resurgent Antisemitism*, p. 275; Günther Jikeli, "Anti-Semitism in Youth Language: The Pejorative Use of the Terms of 'Jew' in German and French Today," *Conflict & Communication Online* 9:1 (2010), pp. 1–13.
75. Günther Jikeli, "Antisemitism among Young European Males," in Rosenfeld, *Resurgent Antisemitism*, p. 282.
76. Al-Aksa TV, Music Video, "Killing Jews Is Worship that Draws Us Close to Allah," translation by Palestinian Media Watch, http://palwatch.org/pages/news_archive.aspx?doc_id=8087. It was chosen from the countless expressions of similar sentiment on the arbitrary ground that its translation appeared on the day that this paragraph was written.
77. Wistrich, *Lethal Obsession*, p. 5.
78. Catherine Chatterley elegantly expresses this point for a conference paper delivered at the Indiana University conference on "Ideological Sources of Campus Anti-Semitism," which Tammi Rossman-Benjamin and I co-convened in 2012 under the aegis of Alvin Rosenfeld's Institute for the Study of Contemporary Antisemitism.
79. European Union Monitoring Centre, "Manifestations of Antisemitism in the EU 2002–2003" (Vienna, 2004), p. 12, http://fra.europa.eu/sites/default/files/fra_uploads/184-AS-Main-report.pdf.

80. Alvin H. Rosenfeld, *The End of the Holocaust* (Bloomington: Indiana University Press, 2011), pp. 238–270.
81. Deborah Lipstadt, *Denying the Holocaust: The Growing Assault on Truth and Memory* (New York: Free Press, 1993), p. 3.
82. Ibid.
83. Dina Porat, "Holocaust Denial and the Image of the Jew, or: 'They Boycott Auschwitz as an Israeli Product,'" in Rosenfeld, *Resurgent Antisemitism*, pp. 467–481.
84. Ibid., pp. 469–472.
85. Linda Maizels, "On Whiteness and Jews," *Journal for the Study of Antisemitism* 3:2 (2011), p. 464.
86. Wistrich, *Lethal Obsession*, p. 632.
87. Lipstadt, *Denying the Holocaust*, p. 23.
88. Rosenfeld, *End of the Holocaust*, pp. 244, 247.
89. Kenneth Lasson, "In an Academic Voice: Antisemitism and Academic Bias," *Journal for the Study of Antisemitism* 3:2 (2011), p. 385.
90. These binaries somewhat resemble the old distinction between "sex" as a natural or biological and "gender" as a cultural production. In terms of Claude Lévy-Strauss's structural anthropology, they could be analogized to the "raw" and the "cooked." Some feminist theorists have argued that the natural or biological female is to the "raw" as the socially subordinate "woman" is to the "cooked." In the same way, and with an obscene literalness, the conceptual Jew can be seen to be cooked, while the actual Jew remains raw. The problem, as Judith Butler has shown, is that such identities are "always already 'cooked,'" in the sense that the very idea of nature is historically situated. *See* Judith Butler, *Gender Trouble* (London: Routledge, 1990), Kindle location 859 of 2876.
91. Benjamin Isaac, "The Ancient Mediterranean and the Pre-Christian Era," in Albert S. Lindemann and Richard S. Levy, *Antisemitism: A History* (Oxford: Oxford University Press, 2010), p. 45.
92. Ibid., p. 46.
93. Florette Cohen, Lee Jussim, Kent D. Harber, and Gautam Bhasin, "Modern Anti-Semitism and Anti-Israel Attitudes," *Journal of Personality and Social Psychology* 97 (2009), pp. 290–306.
94. Slavoj Žižek, *The Sublime Object of Ideology* (London: Verso, 1989), p. 3 (emphasis original).
95. Ibid., pp. 3–7.
96. Sigmund Freud, *The Interpretation of Dreams* (Harmondsworth: Penguin, 1977), p. 650.
97. Žižek, *Sublime Object of Ideology*, p. 7.
98. Freud, *Interpretation of Dreams*, p. 650.
99. Žižek, *Sublime Object of Ideology*, p. 7.
100. Ibid., p. 106.
101. Ibid., pp. 106–107 (emphasis original).

102. Ibid., p. 107.
103. Zygmunt Bauman, *Modernity and the Holocaust* (Ithaca, NY: Cornell University Press, 1989), p. 39.
104. Paul Johnson, "The Anti-Semitic Disease," *Commentary* (June 2005), pp. 33-38, http://www.commentarymagazine.com/viewarticle.cfm/the-anti-semitic-disease-9904.
105. Ibid.
106. Jonathan Sacks, "Lecture to Inter-Parliamentary Committee Against Antisemitism on February 28, 2002," *A New Antisemitism* (London: Profile Books, 2003), p. 40, quoted in Edward Alexander, *The State of the Jews* (New Brunswick, NJ: Transaction Books, 2012), p. 109.
107. Julius, *Trials of the Diaspora*, p. 47.
108. Bauman, *Modernity and the Holocaust*, p. 40. Bauman uses the term "conceptual Jew."
109. Ibid., p. 39.
110. Ibid.
111. Žižek, *Sublime Object of Ideology*, p. 109.
112. Ibid., p. 110.

Chapter 6

1. *Webster's Third New International Dictionary* (1966), p. 96.
2. Heinrich Broder, "Open Letter: You Are No Less Antisemites Than Your Nazi Parents," *Forum* (Winter 1981), pp. 42–43, 109–117, quoted in Robert S. Wistrich, *A Lethal Obsession: Anti-Semitism from Antiquity to the Global Jihad* (New York: Random House, 2010), p. 253.
3. Wistrich, *Lethal Obsession*, p. 59.
4. R. D. Eagleson, "Webster's Third: A Lexicographical Battleplace," *Australian Journal of Education* 9:3 (Oct. 1965), pp. 202–214. Even apart from its definition of anti-Semitism, the publication of *Webster's Third* has been described, without irony or exaggeration, as the "most shocking event in American lexicographical history." Allan Metcalf, "Unabridged," *Chronicle of Higher Education* (June 3, 2013), http://chronicle.com/blogs/linguafranca/2013/06/03/unabridged/.
5. While the term had been included in the dictionary's 1934 edition as well, the *Third* neglected to characterize the term as "Dialect or Illiterate."
6. Dina Porat, "Historical Perspective," in Dina Porat and Kenneth Stern, *Defining Antisemitism*, 2005, available at: www.tau.ac.il/Anti-Semitism/asw2003-4/porat.htm.
7. Wistrich, *Lethal Obsession*, pp. 323–324.
8. American Arab Anti-Discrimination Commission, Press Release, "ADC Demands Merriam Webster Correct Definition of 'anti-Semitism,'" (Mar. 16, 2004), http://www.adc.org/index.php?id=2172.

9. Geoffrey Nunberg, "Lexical Lessons; What the Good Book Says: Anti-Semitism, Loosely Defined," *New York Times*, (Apr. 11, 2004), http://www.nytimes.com/2004/04/11/weekinreview/lexical-lessons-what-the-good-book-says-anti-semitism-loosely-defined.html.
10. Ibid.
11. The concept thus clearly excludes those who oppose the pre-Messianic establishment of the State of Israel as theologically premature, such as the *Neturei Karta*, or who oppose the State of Israel on general antinationalist grounds, including some anarchists, or who merely criticize substantive policies of the State of Israel as they would those of any other government.
12. Abraham H. Foxman, *Never Again? The Threat of the New Anti-Semitism* (New York: Harper Collins, 2003), p. 17.
13. Wistrich, *Lethal Obsession*, p. 58.
14. David Hirsh, "Defining Antisemitism Down: The EUMC Working Definition and Its Disavowal By the University & College Union," *Fathom* (Summer 2013), p. 11.
15. Ibid.
16. Ibid.
17. Wistrich, *Lethal Obsession*, p. 406.
18. Steven K. Baum, *Antisemitism Explained* (Lanham, MD: University Press of America, 2012), pp. 188–189 (summarizing empirical research).
19. Edward H. Kaplan and Charles A. Small, "Anti-Israel Sentiment Predicts Anti-Semitism in Europe," *Journal of Conflict Resolution* 50 (2006): 548–561.
20. Ibid., p. 560.
21. Steven K. Baum and Masato Nakazaw, "Antisemitism and Anti-Israeli Senteiment," *Journal of Religion & Society* (2007) 1:9; Steven K. Baum, "Christian and Muslim Antisemitism," *Journal of Contemporary Religion* 23 (2009), pp. 77–86.
22. Baum, *Antisemitism Explained*, p. 188.
23. David Hirsh, "Defining Antisemitism Down: The EUMC Working Definition and Its Disavowal by the University & College Union," *Fathom* (Summer 2013), p. 6.
24. Quoted in Manfred Gerstenfeld, "The War of a Million Cuts: Delegitimizing Israel and the Jews" (unpublished manuscript in possession of the author).
25. Per Ahlmark, "Combating Old/New Antisemitism," Yad Vashem, April 11, 2002, speech at the International Conference on the "Legacy of Holocaust Survivors," in Vidal Sassoon International Center for the Study of Antisemitism, *Annual Report* (Jerusalem, Hebrew University, 2002), p. 8.
26. Hirsh, "Defining Antisemitism Down," p. 5.
27. Ibid., pp. 6–7.

28. Ibid., p. 7.
29. European Union Monitoring Centre for Racism and Xenophobia, "Manifestations of Antisemitism in the EU 2002–2003" (Vienna, Austria: European Monitoring Centre on Racism and Xenophobia, 2004), http://fra.europa.eu/sites/default/files/fra_uploads/184-AS-Main-report.pdf.
30. "EU Anti-Racism Body Publishes Antisemitism Reports," EUMC Media Release, March 31, 2004.
31. Kenneth Stern, "Proposal for a Redefinition of Antisemitism," in Dina Porat, "HIstorical Perspective," in Dina Porat and Kenneth Stern, *Defining Antisemitism*, 2005, www.tau.ac.il/Anti-Semitism/asw2003-4/porat.htm.
32. European Union Monitoring Centre, "Manifestations of Antisemitism in the EU 2002–2003," p. 13.
33. Ibid.
34. Ibid.
35. Ibid.
36. Ibid.
37. Stern, "Proposal for a Redefinition of Antisemitism." In fairness, the EUMC did assert that certain anti-Israeli incidents should be monitored, but they did not explain how they would do so.
38. Natan Sharansky, "Anti-Semitism in 3D," *Jerusalem Post* (February 23, 2004), http://www.foiwa.org.au/sites/default/files/pdf/Anti-Semitism-in-3D.pdf. Several months later, Sharansky published a slightly expanded version of this article as the foreword to an issue of the *Jewish Political Studies Review*. Natan Sharansky, "3D Test of Anti-Semitism: Demonization, Double Standards, Delegitimization," *Jewish Political Studies Review*, 16:3–4 (Fall 2004), http://jcpa.org/phas/phas-sharansky-f04.htm.
39. Sharansky, "Anti-Semitism in 3D."
40. Rahyab.news.com, April 20, 2013, quoted and translated by the Middle East Media Research Institute, "Iranian Official: The Jews Use Sorcery Against Iran" (April 28, 2013), http://www.memri.org/report/en/0/0/0/0/0/0/7154.htm.
41. Sharansky, "3D Test of Anti-Semitism."
42. Sina Arnold, "Antisemitism and the Contemporary American Left: An Uneasy Relationship," seminar paper delivered at "Deciphering the 'New' Antisemitism, April 2014, Institute for Contemporary Antisemitism, Indiana University at Bloomington.
43. Sharansky, "Anti-Semitism in 3D."
44. Ibid.
45. Organization for Security and Cooperation in Europe, Press Release, "OSCE 'Berlin Declaration' Sets Out Concrete Measures to Fight Anti-Semitism," April 29, 2004, http://www.osce.org/cio/56259.

46. Michael Whine, "Progress in the Struggle Against Anti-Semitism in Europe: The Berlin Declaration and the European Union Monitoring Centre on Racism and Xenophobia's Working Definition of Anti-Semitism," Jerusalem Center for Public Affairs, No. 41, February 1, 2006, http://jcpa.org/article/progress-in-the-struggle-against-anti-semitism-in-europe-the-berlin-declaration-and-the-european-union-monitoring-centre-on-racism-and-xenophobias-working-definition-of-anti-semitism/.
47. Berlin Declaration, Bulgarian Chairmanship, the Chairman-in-Office, www.osce.org/documents/cio/204/042828_euipdf.
48. Stern, "Proposal for a Redefinition of Antisemitism."
49. Ibid.
50. Dina Porat and Esther Webman, "Introduction," in Dina Porat and Esther Webman, compilers, *The Working Definition of Antisemitism—Six Years After: Unedited Proceedings of the 10th Biennial Seminar on Antisemitism* (Tel Aviv: Kantor Center for the Study of Contemporary European Jewry, 2012), p. 1, http://kantorcenter.tau.ac.il/sites/default/files/proceeding-all_6.pdf.
51. Office for Democratic Institutions and Human Rights, "Education on the Holocaust and on Anti-Semitism: An Overview and Analysis of Educational Approaches (Organization for Security and Cooperation in Europe, 2006)," pp. 19–20, http://www.osce.org/odihr/18818.
52. Working Definition.
53. Ibid.
54. Ibid.
55. Office for Democratic Institutions and Human Rights, "Education on the Holocaust and on Anti-Semitism," pp. 19–20.
56. Dina Porat, "The International Working Definition of Antisemitism and Its Detractors," *Israel Journal of Foreign Affairs* 5:3 (2011), p. 6.
57. Ibid.
58. Mike Whine, "Short History of the Definition," in Porat and Webman, compilers, *Working Definition of Antisemitism—Six Years After*.
59. Stern, "Proposal for a Redefinition of Antisemitism," citing Decision, Vilnius City District 2 Court judge A. Cininas, #A11-01087-497/2005, 7 July 2005.
60. Inter-parliamentary Coalition for Combating Antisemitism, The Ottawa Protocol on Combating Antisemitism, http://www.antisem.org/archive/ottawa-protocol-on-combating-antisemitism/.
61. U.S. Department of State, Office to Monitor & Combat Anti-Semitism, Fact Sheet: "'Working Definition' of Anti-Semitism" (2007), http://web.archive.org/web/20070429125033/http://www.state.gov/g/drl/rls/56589.htm.
62. At that time, I served as the Commission's staff director.
63. See, generally, Hirsh, "Defining Antisemitism Down," p. 9.

64. Ronnie Fraser, Speech to UCU Congress, reprinted as David Hirsh, "Ronnie Fraser's (Academic Friends of Israel) Speech to UCU Congress," Engage, May 31, 2011, http://engageonline.wordpress.com/2011/05/31/ronnie-frasers-speech-to-ucu-congress/.
65. Hirsh, "Defining Antisemitism Down," p. 9.
66. Frederic Jameson, *The Ideologies of Theory*, vol. 1 (Minneapolis: University of Minnesota Press, 1988), p. 7.
67. Slavoj Žižek, *For They Know Not What They Do: Enjoyment as a Political Factor* (London: Verso, 2008), p. 18.
68. Dina Porat, ed., *Anti-Semitism Worldwide 2013: General Analysis* (Tel Aviv: Kantor Center for the Study of European Jewry at Tel Aviv University, 2014), http://kantorcenter.tau.ac.il/sites/default/files/Doch_2013.pdf.
69. Amy Elman, "The EU's Responses to Contemporary Antisemitism: A Shell Game," seminar paper delivered at "Deciphering the 'New' Antisemitism, April 2014, Institute for Contemporary Antisemitism, Indiana University at Bloomington, p. 13.
70. U.S. Department of State, Special Envoy to Monitor and Combat Anti-Semitism, Fact Sheet, "Defining Anti-Semitism" (June 8, 2010), http://www.state.gov/j/drl/rls/fs/2010/122352.htm.
71. Ibid.
72. Ibid.
73. Ibid. (emphasis contained in original).
74. Ibid.
75. Letter from Charles R. Love, Program Manager, U.S. Department of Education, Office for Civil Rights, Region IX, to Dr. Michael V. Drake, Chancellor, University of California, Irvine, In re OCR Case No. 09-05-2013 (Nov. 30, 2007) [hereinafter *In re University of California at Irvine*, OCR Case No. 09-05-2013], available at http://www.ocregister.com/newsimages/news/2007/12/OCR_Report_120507-Z05145157-0001.pdf, p. 2.
76. In 2010, OCR finally announced that it would revert to the policy of protecting Jewish students that I had adopted late in the first George W. Bush administration. In 2013, OCR affirmed the dismissal of ZOA's Irvine complaint. Since OCR provided no explicit basis for its decision, it appeared that OCR might be backsliding to its previous position.
77. In this second case, OCR notified ZOA on April 25, 2008, that it was opening for investigation ZOA's "complaint" against Irvine. OCR Case No. 09-07-2205. This was something of a fiction, since ZOA had not filed a second complaint against Irvine. Rather, it had updated OCR of new incidents at Irvine since it filed its first complaint. OCR simply chose to treat these later incidents as if they were contained in a separate complaint and investigated them separately.

78. Zachary Pelchat, Team Leader, U.S. Department of Education, Office for Civil Rights, Decision Letter to Susan Tuchman, Zionist Organization of America, August 19, 2013, Case No. 09-07-2205 (*In re University of California at Irvine*).
79. *In re University of California at Irvine*, p. 6.
80. This does not mean however that the Muslim student's right to engage in such speech abrogated Irvine's duty to mitigate a hostile environment for Jewish students. That is to say, if the speech contributed to a hostile environment for Jewish students, then the university was obligated to address it in some manner. There are many effective responses that administrators may take to hurtful and uncivil campus discourse short of punishing speech that is protected under the Constitution. See Kenneth L. Marcus, "The LDB Best Practices Guide for Combating Campus Anti-Semitism and Anti-Israelism," Louis D. Brandeis Center website, http://brandeiscenter.com/index.php?/publications/factsheets/best_practices_guide_for_combating_campus_anti_semitism_and_anti_israelism.
81. *In re University of California at Irvine*, p. 4.
82. U.S. Department of Education, Office for Civil Rights presentation, "Bullying, Peer Harassment, and Civil Rights," 2012 ADC National Convention, June 23, 2012, p. 25 (PowerPoint slide, "Racial Harassment: Example 4").
83. Ibid.
84. Ibid., p. 25. Galanter acknowledges that the First Amendment may protect some of the hecklers' conduct but that direct physical harassment such as rock-throwing would not be and threats of physical harm are also generally not protected.
85. Ibid.
86. Richard Cravatts, "Antisemitism and the Academic Left," *Journal for the Study of Antisemitism* 3:2 (2011), pp. 435–436.
87. Susan B. Tuchman, "Statement Submitted to the U.S. Commission on Civil Rights Briefing on Campus Anti-Semitism," *Briefing Report on Campus Antisemitism* (Washington, D.C.: U.S. Commission on Civil Rights, 2006), pp. 13–21.
88. Ibid., p. 17.
89. Leila Beckwith, "Antisemitism at the University of California," *Journal for the Study of Antisemitism* 3:2 (2011), p. 451.
90. Ibid., p. 448.
91. Walter Laqueur, *The Changing Face of Antisemitism* (Oxford: Oxford University Press).
92. Kenneth Lasson, "In an Academic Voice: Antisemitism and Academic Bias," *Journal for the Study of Antisemitism* 3:2 (2011), p. 358. As tensions mounted, university and city police hurried the Jewish students off of the public plaza to avoid a potentially violent confrontation. See U.S.C.C.R.,

Briefing Report on Campus Antisemitism (Washington, D.C.: U.S. Commission on Civil Rights, 2006), p. 24.
93. Naftali Bendavid, "Poll Says Anti-Semitism Is Global Matter," *Wall Street Journal,* (May 13, 2014), http://online.wsj.com/news/articles/SB10001424052702304655304579551974194329920?mg=reno64wsj&url=http%3A%2F%2Fonline.wsj.com%2Farticle%2FSB10001424052702304655304579551974194329920.html.
94. These figures may be found in the Anti-Defamation League's interactive web site, "The ADL Global 100" at http://global100.adl.org/#country/netherlands.
95. Baum, *Antisemitism Explained*, pp. 160–161.
96. Ibid.
97. Florette Cohen, Lee Jussim, Gautam Bhasin, and Elizabeth Salib, "The Modern Anti-Semitism Israel Model: An Empirical Relationship Between Modern Anti-Semitism and Opposition to Israel," *Conflict & Communication Online* 10:1 (2011), http://www.cco.regener-online.de/2011_1/pdf/cohen.pdf; Florette Cohen, Lee Jussim, Kent D. Harber, and Gautam Bhasin, "Modern Anti-Semitism and Anti-Israel Attitudes," *Journal of Personality and Social Psychology* 97 (2009): 290–306.
98. The theory is that we fall back on our own worldviews, including our prejudices, when we feel threatened.
99. Cohen et al., "Modern Anti-Semitism and Anti-Israel Attitudes," p. 303.
100. Ben [Haggerty] a/k/a Macklemore, blog posting, Macklemore and Ryan Lewis blog, Macklemore.com website, May 19, 2014, http://macklemore.com/post/86276707372/family-friends-and-fans-alike-who-know-me-well.
101. Alan Duke, "Macklemore Apologizes for Wig, Beard and Nose but Defends 'Random' Disguise," CNN.com website, May 20, 2014, http://www.cnn.com/2014/05/20/showbiz/macklemore-costume-apology/.
102. Bernard Harrison, *The Resurgence of Antisemitism* (Lanham, MD: Rowman & Littlefield, 2006), p. 108.
103. Ibid.
104. U.S. Commission on Civil Rights, "Findings and Recommendations of the United States Commission on Civil Rights Regarding Campus Antisemitism," in *Briefing Report on Campus Antisemitism* (Washington, D.C.: U.S. Commission on Civil Rights, 2006), p. 72. The author was the principal draftsman of the Commission's "Findings and Recommendations."
105. Ibid.
106. Judith Butler, *Parting Ways: Jewishness and the Critique of Zionism* (New York: Columbia University Press, 2012), p. 116.
107. Cohen et al., "Modern Anti-Semitism and Anti-Israel Attitudes," p. 303.

108. András Kovács, "Antisemitic Prejudice and Political Antisemitism in Present-Day Hungary," *Journal for the Study of Antisemitism* 4:2 (2013), pp. 443, 465.
109. Alvin H. Rosenfeld, "Responding to Campus-Based Anti-Zionism: Two Models," in Eunice G. Pollack, *Antisemitism on the Campus: Past and Present* (Boston: Academic Studies Press, 2011), pp. 414, 417.
110. *Fraser v. University College Union*, U.K. Employment Tribunal (London) (Case No. 2203290/2011) (March 22, 2013).
111. The tribunal actually berated Fraser for bringing his action and denounced the impressive array of scholars and parliamentarians who had testified in his favor. Although the tribunal is a relatively obscure and inferior body, and its decisions have no binding precedential affect, the *Fraser* case has generated considerable discussion, especially within England's Jewish community, about the place of anti-Israel hostility in a proper definition of anti-Semitism.
112. *Fraser v. University College Union*, U.K. Employment Tribunal (London) (Case No. 2203290/2011) (March 22, 2013), Paragraph 153.
113. Psalm 137. These lines are customarily recited by observant Jews, among other times, before grace after certain meals, during weddings, and on the holiday of Tisha B'Av.
114. Simon Sebag Montegiore, *Jerusalem: The Biography* (New York: Vintage Books, 2011), p. 145.
115. Kimberly A. Yuracko, "Trait Discrimination as Race Discrimination: An Argument about Assimilation," *George Washington Law Review* 74:3 (Apr. 2996), pp. 365, 374.
116. Frontiero v. Richardson, 411 U.S. 677, 686 (1973).
117. Rogers v. Am. Airlines, Inc., 527 F. Supp. 229, 232 (S.D.N.Y. 1981).
118. Earwood v. Cont'l Se. Lines, Inc., 539 F.2d 1349, 1351 (4th Cir. 1976).
119. Garcia v. Spun Steak Co., 998 F.2d 1480, 1487-89 (9th Cir. 1993).
120. Wofford v. Safeway Stores, Inc., 78 F.R.D. 460, 469 (N.D. Cal. 1978).
121. Samuel A. Marcosson, "Constructive Immutability," 3 *U. Pa. J. Const. L.* 646, 647 (2001); Marc R. Shapiro, "Treading the Supreme Court's Murky Immutability Waters," 38 Gonz. L. Rev. 409, 412 (2002-2003)
122. See, e.g., Kenji Yoshino, "Assimilationist Bias in Equal Protection: The Visibility Presumption and the Case of 'Don't Ask, Don't Tell,'" 108 Yale L.J. 485, 490-91 (1998) (criticizing the concept of immutability and arguing for its elimination).
123. Hernandez-Montiel v. INS, 225 F.3d 1084, 1093 (9th Cir. 2000).
124. Zavaleta-Lopez v. Att'y Gen., 360 F. App'x 331, 333 (3d Cir. 2010).
125. Sharona Hoffman, "The Importance of Immutability in Employment Discrimination Law," 52 *William & Mary Law Review*. 1483, 1513 (April 2011).
126. Ibid., p. 1518; 42 U.S.C.A. § 12102(4)(E)(i)(I)-(IV) (stating that determinations regarding disabilities shall be made without regard to mitigating measures and describing such measures).

127. Michael W. McConnell, "Religious Freedoms at a Crossroads," 59 *University of Chicago Law Review* 115, 125 (1992).
128. Butler, *Parting Ways*.
129. Ibid., p. 4.
130. Ibid.
131. Others take the opposite approach, charging the Jewish community with a failure to engage in self-criticism.
132. Emanuele Ottolenghi, "Present-day Antisemitism and the Centrality of the Jewish Alibi," in Alvin H. Rosenfeld, *Resurgent Antisemitism: Global Perspectives* (Bloomington: Indiana University Press, 2013), p. 425.
133. Sander Gilman, *Jewish Self-Hatred: Anti-Semitism and the Hidden Language of the Jews* (Baltimore, MD: Johns Hopkins University Press, 1986), p. 1.
134. Arye L. Hillman, "Economic and Behavioral Foundations of Prejudice," in Charles Asher Small, ed., *Global Antisemitism: A Crisis of Modernity* (Leiden: Brill, 2013), p. 62.
135. Shulamit Volkov, "Readjusting Cultural Codes: Reflections on Anti-Semitism and Anti-Zionism," *Journal of Israeli History: Politics, Society, Culture* 25:1 (2006).
136. Arnold, "Antisemitism and the Contemporary American Left."
137. Anthony Julius, *Trials of the Diaspora: A History of Antisemitism in England* (Oxford: Oxford University Press, 2010), p. 67.
138. Niza Yanay, *The Ideology of Hatred: The Psychic Power of Discourse* (New York: Fordham University Press, 2013), p. 12.
139. Gilman, *Jewish Self-Hatred*, p. 2.
140. Mari J. Matsuda, "Public Response to Racist Speech: Considering the Victim's Story," in Mari J. Matsuda, Charles R. Lawrence III, Richard Delgado, and Kimberlè Williams Crenshaw, *Words That Wound: Critical Race Theory, Assaultive Speech, and the First Amendment* (Boulder: Westview 1993), p. 26.
141. Gordon Allport, *The Nature of Prejudice* (New York: Doubleday, 1958), p. 147.
142. Wistrich, *Lethal Obsession*, p. 515.
143. Ibid.
144. Ibid., p. 516.
145. Gilman, *Jewish Self-Hatred*, p. 391.
146. Tammi Rossman-Benjamin, "The Academic Legitimization of Anti-Zionism and Efforts to Combat it: A Case Study," in Eunice G. Pollack, ed., *Antisemitism on the Campus: Past and Present* (Boston: Academic Studies Press, 2011), pp. 393, 394–397.
147. Rosenfeld, "Responding to Campus-Based Anti-Zionism," p. 414.
148. Dalia Karpel, "History Professor Yehuda Bauer: 'Netanyahu Doesn't Know History,'" *Ha'aretz*, (Feb. 21, 2013), http://www.haaretz.com/weekend/magazine/history-professor-yehuda-bauer-netanyahu-doesn-t-know-history.premium-1.504937.

149. David Nirenberg, *Anti-Judaism: The Western Tradition* (New York: W.W. Norton, 2013), p. 176.
150. Psalms 78:36–37.
151. Nirenberg, *Anti-Judaism*, p. 176.
152. Acts 7:51–53, quoted in Nirenberg, *Anti-Judaism*, pp. 83–84.
153. Gilman, *Jewish Self-Hatred*, p. 2.
154. Julius, *Trials of the Diaspora*, p. 34.
155. Ibid., pp. 34–37. Indeed, many of the Jewish people's greatest persecutors throughout history have been rumored to be converted Jews, although historians have cast doubt on some of these rumors. *See* Léon Poliakov, *The History of Anti-Semitism*, vol. 1, *From the Time of Christ to the Court Jews,* trans. Richard Howard (New York: Vanguard, 1974), p. 52 text and n. 9.
156. Wistrich, *Lethal Obsession*, p. 320.

Conclusion

1. European Forum on Antisemitism, Working Definition of Antisemitism, http://www.european-forum-on-antisemitism.org/working-definition-of-antisemitism/english.
2. U.S. Department of State, Special Envoy to Monitor and Combat Anti-Semitism, Fact Sheet, "Defining Anti-Semitism" (June 8, 2010), http://www.state.gov/j/drl/rls/fs/2010/122352.htm (emphases added).
3. Caroline B. Glick, *The Israel Solution: A One-State Plan for Peace in the Middle East* (New York: Crown Books, 2014).
4. European Forum on Antisemitism, Working Definition of Antisemitism.
5. U.S. Dept. of State, "Defining Anti-Semitism." http://www.state.gov/j/drl/rls/fs/2010/122352.htm (emphases added).
6. Ibid. (emphases added).
7. Scott Sayare, "Suspect Held in Jewish Museum Killings," *New York Times* (June 1, 2014), http://www.nytimes.com/2014/06/02/world/europe/suspect-arrested-in-jewish-museum-killings-in-belgium.html?module=Search&mabReward=relbias%3Ar%2C%5B%22RI%3A8%22%2C%22RI%3A13%22%5D.
8. Robert Mackey, "Chilling Images of Gunman at Brussels Jewish Museum," *New York Times* (May 27, 2014), http://www.nytimes.com/2014/05/27/world/europe/chilling-images-of-gunman-at-brussels-jewish-museum.html?module=Search&mabReward=relbias%3Ar%2C%5B%22RI%3A8%22%2C%22RI%3A13%22%5D.
9. Letter from Charles R. Love, Program Manager, U.S. Department of Education, Office for Civil Rights, Region IX, to Dr. Michael V. Drake, Chancellor, University of California, Irvine, In re OCR Case No. 09-05-2013 (Nov. 30, 2007) [hereinafter In re University of California at Irvine, OCR Case No. 09-05-2013], available at http://www.ocregister.com/newsimages/news/2007/12/OCR_Report_120507-Z05145157-0001.pdf, p. 6.

10. Ibid.
11. Abraham H. Foxman, "An Open Letter on Academic Freedom and University Responsibility," http://www.commentarymagazine.com/wp-content/uploads/2013/02/adlletterbds.pdf.
12. Statement of Jewish Organizations on Boycott, Divestment and Sanctions (BDS) Campaigns Against Israel (Feb. 2011), http://www.jewishvirtuallibrary.org/jsource/IsraelonCampusReport2012.pdf.
13. Harold Brackman, *Boycott Divestment Sanctions (BDS) Against Israel: An Anti-Semitic, Anti-Peace Poison Pill* (Los Angeles: Simon Wiesenthal Center, 2013), p. 9, http://www.wiesenthal.com/atf/cf/%7B54d385e6-f1b9-4e9f-8e94-890c3e6dd277%7D/REPORT_313.PDF.
14. Palestinian Civil Society Calls for Boycott, Divestment and Sanctions against Israel Until It Complies with International Law and Universal Principles of Human Rights (Jul. 9, 2005), http://www.bdsmovement.net/call.
15. Brackman, *Boycott Divestment Sanctions*, p. 9.
16. Mitchell G. Bard and Jeff Dawson, *Israel and the Campus: The Real Story* (Chevy Chase, MD: The American-Israeli Cooperative Enterprise, 2012), p. 16.
17. Alan Baker, "Manipulation and Deception: The Anti-Israel 'BDS' Campaign (Boycott, Divestment, and Sanctions)," *Jerusalem Issue Brief*, 12:2 (Mar. 19, 2012), http://ambassadoralanbaker.com/manipulation-and-deception-the-anti-israel-bds-campaign-boycott-divestment-and-sanctions/.
18. Elisabeth Kuebler and Matthias Falter, "Durban Reviewed: The Transformation of Antisemitism in a Cosmopolitanizing Environment," in Charles Asher Small, ed., *Global Antisemitism: A Crisis of Modernity* (Leiden: Brill, 2013), pp. 203–221.
19. Robert S. Wistrich, *A Lethal Obsession: Anti-Semitism from Antiquity to the Global Jihad* (New York: Random House, 2010), p. 486.
20. Joëlle Fiss, *Durban Diaries: What Really Happened at the UN Conference Against Racism in Durban* (New York: American Jewish Committee, 2001), http://www.ajc.org/atf/cf/{42d75369-d582-4380-8395-d25925b85eaf}/THEDURBANDIARIES.PDF, p. 8.
21. Fiss, *Durban Diaries*, p. 9.
22. Kuebler and Falter, "Reviewed: The Transformation of Antisemitism in a Cosmopolitanizing Environment," pp. 208–209.
23. Mitchell Bard, *Arab League Boycott: Background and Overview*, Jewish Virtual Library (2007), http://www.jewishvirtuallibrary.org/jsource/History/Arab_boycott.html.
24. Ibid.
25. Martin A. Weiss, *Arab League Boycott of Israel* (Washington, D.C.: Congressional Research Service, 2013), http://www.fas.org/sgp/crs/mideast/RL33961.pdf, p. 1.
26. Weiss, *Arab League Boycott*, p. 3.

27. On the connections between Nazis propaganda and the modern ideologies of the Middle East, see Matthias Küntzel, *Jihad and Jew-Hatred: Islamism, Nazism, and the Roots of 9/11*, trans. Colin Meade (New York: Telos, 2009); Paul Berman, *The Flight of the Intellectuals* (New York: Melville House, 2011).
28. Jeffrey Herf, *Nazi Propaganda for the Arab World* (New Haven, CT: Yale University Press, 2009).
29. Ibid., p. 13.
30. Barry Rubin and Wolfgang G. Schwanitz, *Nazis, Islamists, and the Making of the Modern Middle East* (New Haven, CT: Yale University Press, 2014). New research indicates that German foreign policy toward the Middle East continued to bear the imprint of Nazi ideology during the Cold War era. Ulrike Becker, "Post War Antisemitism: Germany's Foreign Policy Toward Egypt," in Charles Asher Small, ed., *Global Antisemitism: A Crisis of Modernity* (Leiden: Brill, 2013), pp. 283–296.
31. Rubin and Schwanitz, *Nazis, Islamists*, p. 246.
32. Klaus-Michael Mallmann and Martin Cüppers, *Nazi Palestine: The Plans for the Extermination of the Jews in Palestine*, trans. Krista Smith (New York: Enigma Books, 2005), p. 211.
33. "Boycott of Jewish Businesses," *Holocaust Encyclopedia,* http://www.ushmm.org/wlc/en/article.php?ModuleId=10005678. Although the boycott was officially called for three days, April 1–3, 1933, the boycott is generally associated with the events of April 1.
34. Lucy S. Dawidowicz, *The War Against the Jews: 1933–1945* (New York: Bantam, 1986), p. 52.
35. "Boycott of Jewish Businesses," *Holocaust Encyclopedia*.
36. Brackman, *Boycott Divestment Sanctions*, p. 7.
37. "Boycott of Jewish Businesses," *Holocaust Encyclopedia*.
38. Ibid.
39. Bernard Lewis, *Semites & Anti-Semites* (New York: W.W. Norton, 1986), pp. 223–224.
40. Ibid., pp. 224–226.
41. Baker, "Manipulation and Deception."
42. These examples are drawn from reports that Jewish university students have recently made to attorneys at the Louis D. Brandeis Center for Human Rights Under Law (www.brandeiscenter.com).
43. Hannah Weisfeld, "When BDS and Anti-Semitism Meet," *The Daily Beast* (Dec. 14, 2012), http://www.thedailybeast.com/articles/2012/12/14/when-bds-and-anti-semitism-meet.html. It should be noted that the Palestine Solidarity Campaign issued a statement in opposition to the incident that Weisfeld reported.
44. Nora Gold, "Fighting Anti-Semitism in the Feminist Community," in Charles Asher Small, ed., *Global Antisemitism: A Crisis of Modernity* (Leiden: Brill, 2013), p. 144.

45. Mikis Theodorakis, "Letter to the Central Board of the Jewish Communities in Greece," (May 16, 2011), http://www.kis.gr/en/index.php?option=com_content&view=article&id=421:mikis-theodorakis-letter-to-the-central-board-of-jewish-communities-in-greece&catid=12:2009&Itemid=41.
46. NGO Monitor, "Antisemitic Theology," http://www.ngo-monitor.org/article/antisemitic_theology.
47. The resolution, which was widely interpreted as part of the BDS campaign even though it did not explicitly seek a boycott, divestment, or sanctions, ultimately garnered a majority of votes cast but failed to achieve the minimum vote required. This story was broken by Adam Kredo, "Professors Engage in Anti-Semitic Rhetoric on Secret Listserv," *Washington Free Beacon* (May 27, 2014), http://freebeacon.com/issues/professors-engage-in-anti-semitic-rhetoric-on-secret-listserv/. The ListServ may be found at "MLA Resolution 2014-1 Comments" at Pastebin, http://pastebin.com/HyJtnBeC.
48. MLA Resolution 2014-1 Comments at lines 523–526.
49. U.S. Dept. of State, "Defining Anti-Semitism," http://www.state.gov/j/drl/rls/fs/2010/122352.htm
50. Quoted in Don Giordano, "Does Temple University Deny the Holocaust Happened?," CBSPhilly (May 30, 2014), http://philadelphia.cbslocal.com/2014/05/30/dom-giordano-does-temple-university-deny-the-holocaust-happened/.
51. Giordano, "Does Temple University Deny the Holocaust Happened?"
52. MLA Resolution 2014-1 Comments at lines 790–792.
53. MLA Resolution 2014-1 Comments at lines 823–825. Ra'ad is unquestionably right that Ordóñez uses the term "Zionist attack dogs" metaphorically. Few readers would infer that Ordóñez literally had Israeli canines in mind.
54. Omar Barghouti, "Why Israel Fears the Boycott," *New York Times* (Jan. 31, 2014).
55. Judith Butler, "Remarks to Brooklyn College on BDS," *The Nation* (Feb. 7, 2013). For a more detailed response to Butler, see Cary Nelson, "The Problem with Judith Butler: The Political Philosophy of the Movement to Boycott Israel," *Los Angeles Review of Books* (Mar. 16, 2014), https://lareviewofbooks.org/essay/problem-judith-butler-political-philosophy-movement-boycott-israel.
56. Hernandez-Montiel v. INS, 225 F.3d 1084, 1093 (9th Cir. 2000).
57. U.S. Campaign for the Academic Boycott of Israel (USACBI), "FAQ's," USACBI website, http://www.usacbi.org.
58. The story of Jacqueline Kober is told in Chapter One.

INDEX

AAUP (American Association of University Professors), 21
Abu Ghraib, 134
Abū Muḥammad ʿAlī ibn Aḥmad ibn Saʿīd ibn Ḥazm, 44
academic boycotts of Israel. *See* boycott, divest from, and sanction (BDS) Israel movement
academic studies of anti-Semitism, 107–111
Ackerman, Nathan, 104
ADC (American Arab Anti-Discrimination Commission), 147–148, 150–151
ADL. *See* Anti-Defamation League
Adorno, Theodor, 34
  The Authoritarian Personality (with Horkheimer), 47, 82, 103, 107–108
adverse impact, as anti-Semitism, 121–122
adverse treatment, concept of, 158
African Americans. *See* anti-black racism

Agamben, Giorgio, 82, 83
aggression-resentment theory, 103
Agobard (Carolingian archbishop), 71
Ahlmark, Per, 151
Ahmadinejad, Mahmoud, 37, 204
AJC. *See* American Jewish Committee
Al-Gumhouriyya, 119
Al-Jazirah, 80
Allport, Gordon, 131, 188
  The Nature of Prejudice, 108
Al-Rahma TV, 135
Amalek (biblical figure), 86, 87, 92
American Arab Anti-Discrimination Commission (ADC), 147–148, 150–151
American Association of University Professors (AAUP), 21
American Jewish Committee (AJC), 20–21, 107, 162
  Studies in Prejudice, 107–108
American Jewish Congress, 107, 162
American Psychological Association (APA), 10–11
American Studies Association (ASA), 29

anti-Arab discrimination,
  anti-Semitism viewed as
  including, 59–61
anti-black racism
  anti-Semitism compared,
    10–11, 154
  homogenism and, 110
  people of color versus white, Jews
    as, 68–69, 77m111
  poll taxes and, 214
  tacitness principle and, 176
  unconscious or coded, 39–40
Anti-Defamation League (ADL)
  defining anti-Semitism and, 7,
    8, 21, 27
  Dutch respondents to survey of,
    132–133, 176
  homogenist approach and, 109
  Macklemore, *Thrift Shop*
    incident, 179
  phenomenology of anti-Semitism
    and, 35, 37, 51–52
  West Bank and Gaza residents,
    anti-Semitic attitudes of, 203
anti-Israel/anti-Zionist sentiments,
    32, 146–190. *See also*
    boycott, divest from,
    and sanction (BDS)
    Israel movement;
    Palestinians
  ability to criticize Israel without
    being labeled anti-Semitic,
    126–127, 148, 168, 193
  American civil rights enforcement
    and, 25–27
  Arab anti-Semitism, sources of,
    132–137
  Berlin Declaration, 159–161
  blood libel analogues, 224n15
  categorical denial of anti-Semitism
    of, 148–150
  "collective Jew," Israel viewed as,
    36, 133–134, 144, 160, 161,
    163, 174–175

delegitimization of Israel,
    158–159, 168
demonization of Israel,
    156–157, 168
denial and exaggeration of
    anti-Semitism and, 10–16
disguising anti-Semitism as,
    11, 146
double standards, 157–158, 161,
    163, 168
ethnic traits principle and, 175,
    181–185, 209–210
EUMC, first anti-Semitism
    definition of, 152–155
fences and barriers, 145
Gaza conflict and, 2, 7, 136, 137,
    148, 203
historicist approach to
    anti-Semitism and, 66
Holocaust, denial of exceptional
    nature of, 114–115
ideological approach to
    anti-Semitism and, 46
intentionality principle and,
    175–176
international political treatment of
    Israel, 83–84
International Working Definition
    on, 19–23, 161–167, 173–174
Jewish anti-Zionism, 147, 185–190
Jewish identity of Israelis and,
    124–125
Jews *as Jews* argument and,
    122–123
memetics principle and, 175,
    178–181
Muslim anti-Semitism and,
    132–137, 170–174
Nazism, Israeli policy equated
    with, 19, 25, 68, 116–117,
    173–174, 202
as new anti-Semitism, 11, 19, 39,
    46, 68, 151
nodal point theory and, 119

OCR investigations of, 169–174
principles identifying
    anti-Semitism in, 32,
    174–175, 193
as racial prejudice, 66–69
resurgence of anti-Semitism in
    Europe and, 150–152
Sharansky's 3-D Test and, 155–159,
    161, 167, 174
State Department definition of
    anti-Semitism and, 164,
    166–169, 173–174
statistical correlation of negative
    attitudes toward Jews and, 30,
    149–150, 177, 180
tacitness principle and, 175, 176–178
UCU and *Fraser* litigation,
    164–166
U.N. declaration of Zionism as
    racism (1975), 67
Webster's Third definition of
    anti-Semitism including,
    146–150
anti-Judaism, as term, 61, 64–65, 95
Antiochus Epiphanes, 71
anti-Semitism, defining. *See*
    defining anti-Semitism
anti-Semitism accusations
    as disingenuous or as form of attack
        (*See* Livingstone Formulation)
    in two-stage process (incident and
        blaming the victim), 14–15
anusim, 65
APA (American Psychological
    Association), 10–11
apes, Jews associated with, 80–81
Apollonius Molon, 98
Arab League, 204–205, 207, 213
Arabs. *See also* Muslims and
    anti-Semitism;
    Palestinians
    ADC (American Arab
        Anti-Discrimination
        Commission), 147–148
    anti-Arab discrimination,
        anti-Semitism viewed as
        including, 59–61
    correlation between anti-Israel and
        anti-Semitic views, 150
    Nazi propaganda directed at, 205
    sources of Arab anti-Semitism,
        132–137
Arad (Canaanite king), 86–87
Arafat, Yasser, 74, 86
Arendt, Hannah, 6, 44–45, 88, 90,
    92–93, 95–96, 130
Aristotle, 81–82
    Politics, 82
Arnold, Sina, 157
ASA (American Studies
    Association), 29
Asi, Muhammad al-, 173
assimilation, Jewish, 76, 78, 95, 107,
    110, 125, 147, 190, 192
Association of University Teachers
    (AUT) Council, UK, 149, 151
attitude, defining anti-Semitism as,
    30, 35–40, 55, 192
Attur, Emanuela, 15
Augustine of Hippo, 72, 83
Austria-Hungary, blood libel in, 101
AUT (Association of University
    Teachers) Council, UK,
    149, 151

Bachman v. St. Monica's
    Congregation, 63, 70
Badiou, Alain, 9, 52, 115–117,
    124–125, 143, 242n16
    Polemics, 116
Baker, Andrew, 162
Barbarians incident, 12, 33–35, 42,
    43–44, 64, 194, 197–198
bare life, concept of, 82–83
Barghouti, Omar, 211
Barre, Raymond, 134
Barton, Richard D., 21
Batnitzky, Leora, 76, 78

Battle, Sandra, 27
Bauer, Yehuda, 161, 189–190
Bauman, Zygmunt, 144–145
BDS. *See* boycott, divest from, and sanction (BDS) Israel movement
Beck, Glenn, 198
Belgium, massacre at Jewish Museum in, 7, 199–200
Benbasa, Esther, 12
Ben-Gurion, David, 106
Benjamin, Jon, 165
Benjamin, Walter, 90, 91, 104, 236n36
Bennett, Naftali, 13
Berger, David, 131
Berlin Declaration, 159–161
Bernard, Daniel, 37
Berneri, Camillo, *Le juif antisemite*, 125–126
bestialization, demonization, and dehumanization of Jews, 54, 66, 71, 73, 79–84
Bettelheim, Bruno, 104
bicyclist joke, 110, 119
Block, Josh, 16
blood libel, 36, 73, 75, 100–101, 163, 178, 179, 224n15
Bordieu, Pierre, 63
boycott, divest from, and sanction (BDS) Israel movement, 27–29, 202–214
  analysis of anti-Semitic nature of, 206–210
  AUT denunciation of criticism of, 149
  as double standard, 158
  Edinburgh University Student Association vote on, 16
  origins of, 203–206
  rejection of anti-Semitic critique by BDS leaders, 210–213
  Statement of Jewish Organizations on, 202–203
Brahm, Gabriel Noah, Jr., 115

Broder, Henryk, 146
Bruckner, Pascal, 83–84
Brussels, massacre at Jewish Museum in, 7, 199–200
Buruma, Ian, 13
Bush, George W., 24, 134, 164
Butler, Judith, 38, 53–54, 125, 126–128, 177, 180, 185–186, 189, 190, 211–212, 243n23, 246n90

Cain, Jews associated with, 72, 83
Caldarola, Giuseppe, 15
Canada, firebombing of Montreal Jewish elementary school in, 18, 154–155
Cantor, Eric, 198
CAP (Center for American Progress), 16
Catholic Church and anti-Semitism, 65, 126
Center for American Progress (CAP), 16
Centre for Research on Anti-Semitism (ZfA), 152
chimerical hatred of Jews, 83, 98, 132, 135, 137–138, 140–142, 175, 188, 191, 197
Chmielmicki, Bogdan, 86
Chomsky, Noam, 189, 190
chosenness, doctrine of, 68, 71, 113, 116
Christianity and anti-Semitism
  in BDS movement, 208
  blood libel, 36, 73, 75, 100–101, 163, 178, 179, 224n15
  deicide charge, 71–72, 133, 138, 163, 208
  doctrinal rivalry or disagreement versus, 70–71, 132
  historicism and, 94
  Jewish converts to Christianity, 62, 65, 70, 73, 83, 126, 132, 188
  Jewish sources for polemics, 79
  Muslim anti-Semitism influenced by, 75–76

protection of Jews by political
    powers and, 83, 133
religious hatred of Jews, 71–73,
    74–75, 76
Spanish Catholicism, historical, racial
    animus against Jews in, 65
Churchill, Ward, 172
Civil Rights Act of 1964 (U.S.), Title
    VI, 21, 24, 170, 172
civil rights enforcement in United
    States, 21, 24–27, 30, 32, 77,
    169–174, 194, 200–202
Civiltà Cattolica, La, 101
cognitive dimension of
    anti-Semitism, 47
collective responsibility attributed to
    Jews, 36, 133–134, 144, 160,
    161, 163, 174–175
Commentary magazine, 5, 21
Commission on Civil Rights, U.S.,
    20, 164, 179–180
comparison of anti-Semitism to other
    forms of racism and prejudice,
    30–31, 106–119, 192–193
  anti-black racism, 10–11, 154
  exceptionalism and its problems,
    112–117
  Exceptional Signifier, "the Jew" as,
    115–117
  homogenist theory and its
    problems, 106–112
  nodal point, anti-Semitism viewed
    as, 117–119, 193
  two-stage process (incident and
    blaming the victim), 14–15
conduct, anti-Semitism viewed
    primarily as, 30, 40–43, 55
continuity, failure of historicism to
    grasp, 98
conversion of Jews to other faiths, 62,
    65, 70, 73, 83, 126, 132, 188
Cotler, Irwin, 151
crypto-Judaism, 65
cultural normalcy of
    anti-Semitism, 52–54

cultural transmission of anti-Semitism
    and memetics principle, 32,
    175, 178–181

Dabashi, Hamid, 67, 231n49
Damascus Affair (1840), 75, 101
Dawidowicz, Lucy S., 205
defining anti-Semitism, 1–32,
    191–194. *See also*
    International Working
    Definition; State
    Department definition
  alternative terms for, 35, 36, 44, 61
  American civil rights enforcement
    and, 24–27
  anti-Zionist/anti-Israel sentiments
    and, 32, 146–190 (*See also*
    anti-Israel/anti-Zionist
    sentiments)
  BDS movement and, 27–29,
    202–214 (*See also* boycott,
    divest from,
    and sanction (BDS)
    Israel movement)
  characteristics of effective
    definitions, 191–194
  compared to other forms of
    racism and prejudice, 30–31,
    106–119, 192–193
    (*See also* comparison of
    anti-Semitism to other
    forms of racism and
    prejudice)
  as conduct versus attitude,
    30, 33–55 (*See also*
    phenomenology
    of anti-Semitism)
  denial and exaggeration, 10–16,
    113–114
  EU definition, 9, 17–23, 30, 41,
    60, 138, 142–143, 152–155,
    160–164, 166, 168
    (*See also* International
    Working Definition)
  general definition, 193–194

defining anti-Semitism *(Cont)*
  historicist versus eternalist approaches to, 31, 85–105 *(See also* eternalism; historicism)
  hyphenation versus non-hyphenation of term, 61–62
  importance of, 5–10, 191–192
  Jewish identity and the figural Jew, 31–32, 120–145 *(See also* Jewish identity and the figural Jew)
  origins and etymology of term, 9–10, 56–59
  principles for, 32, 174–175
  as racial versus religious prejudice, 30, 56–84 *(See also* race; religion)
  rate of anti-Semitic incidents, 7–8
  reluctance of Western observers regarding, 2–5
  resurgence of anti-Semitism in Europe and, 150–152
  shared meaning, lack of, 4–5, 6
  3-D Definition/Test, 23, 155–159, 161, 167, 174, 202, 215
  UCU definition, 165–166
dehumanization of Jews, 54, 66, 71, 73, 79–84
deicide charge, 71–72, 133, 138, 163, 208
delegitimization of Israel, 158–159, 168
demonization
  racial/religious, 54, 66, 71, 73, 79–84
  in Sharansky's 3-D Test, 155–157
  U.S. State Department on, 168
Derrida, Jacques, 81
dhimmitude, 69, 74
diaspora, anti-Semitism viewed as related to, 106–107
DiFranco, Ani, 129
disease or pathology anti-Semitism primarily viewed as, 30, 47–54, 55
  Judaism compared to, 48–49
disparate impact, as anti-Semitism, 121–122
disparate treatment, concept of, 158
displacement theory, 103–104
doctrinal rivalry or disagreement, anti-Semitism distinguished from, 70–71
double standards
  anti-Israeli/anti-Zionist sentiments and, 157–158, 161, 163, 168
  BDS and, 203, 209, 210, 211
  in general definition of anti-Semitism, 193–194
  in International Working Definition, 19, 195
  Jewish identity and the figural Jew, 19, 128–129, 130, 134
  in Sharansky's 3-D Test, 155, 157–158, 159
  in State Department definition, 195
Drumont, Édouard, 118
Durban I (World Conference against Racism or WCAR), 151, 204, 206

Earnest, Joseph, 3
Economic and Social Council, U.N., 63
economics
  rise of Jews in late 19th century Germany, 75, 97
  trauma or failure and prejudice, 104
Edinburgh University Student Association, vote on academic boycott of Israel, 16
Edward the Confessor, 83
Egypt
  blood libel cases, 101
  Hellenistic period, racist animus against Jews in, 65
Elman, Amy, 167

Encyclopedia of the Holocaust, 130
Enlightenment/emancipation, Holocaust viewed as product of, 52, 96–97
environmentalism or ecologism, 109, 118
Eötvösz, Joseph, 131
Equality Act 2010 (UK), 182
Eros and *Thanatos,* 82
eruvim, 145
"Esau hates Jacob," 85–87
essentialism
   eternalism viewed as tending toward, 90–91
   Jews-as-not-Jews formulation leading to, 139
   racism as, 63–64
eternalism, 31, 85–105
   as absolving of anti-Semites, 92–93
   as ahistoric, 89–90
   critiques of, 89–93
   defined and described, 85–89
   "Esau hates Jacob," 85–87
   as essentializing, 90–91
   historicism versus (*See* historicism)
   as philosophically or politically incorrect, 91–92
   repetition, viewing anti-Semitism as, 99–105
   as self-defeating, 92
   value of, 93
ethnic or racial prejudice, anti-Semitism as. *See* race
ethnic traits principle, 32, 175, 181–186, 209–210
EUMC (European Monitoring Centre on Racism and Xenophobia), 9, 17–23, 30, 41, 60, 138, 142–143, 152–155, 160–164, 166, 168. *See also* International Working Definition
Europe, resurgence of anti-Semitism in, 150–152
European Jewish Congress, 152

European Monitoring Centre on Racism and Xenophobia (EUMC), 9, 17–23, 30, 41, 60, 138, 142–143, 152–155, 160–164, 166, 168. *See also* International Working Definition
European Parliament, extreme right parties in, 7
European Union Fundamental Rights Agency (FRA), 8, 18, 22–23, 166–167
Everyman's Encyclopedia, 95
evil, Jews viewed as
   by Nazis, 66
   as racial hatred, 66, 68
   as religious hatred, 70, 72, 75
evolution over time, failure of historicism to grasp, 98–99
exceptionalism and its problems, 112–117
Exceptional Signifier, "the Jew" as, 115–117
exclusionary Zionism, 126

false versus true statements, anti-Semitism of, 127–130
Farber, Daniel, 121–122
FCR (Swiss Federal Commission Against Racism), 62
Fein, Helen, 45–46, 122
feminism, 109, 118, 119, 246n90
Ferdinand and Isabella (king and queen of united Spain), 65
figural Jew. *See* Jewish identity and the figural Jew
Fine, Robert, 105
Finkelstein, Norman, 189, 190
First Amendment free speech protections, 22, 171, 252n80, 252n85
Fischer, Joschka, 159
Fofana, Youssuf, 33
Foucault, Michel, 82, 89, 96–97
Foxman, Abraham, 27, 51–53, 148

FRA (Fundamental Rights Agency), EU, 8, 18, 22–23, 166–167
France
  anti-Semitic incidents in, 2–3, 133–135, 147–148
  Barbarians incident, 12, 33–35, 42, 43–44, 64, 194, 197–198
  blood libel in, 101
  denial of anti-Semitism before WWII in, 11
  Hyper Cacher kosher deli shootings, 3
  Muslim immigrant population of, 1, 133–135, 199
  National Front party in, 7
  Rue Copernic synagogue bombing, Paris, 134
  Toulouse Massacre, 1–2, 7, 32, 33, 34, 133, 194, 198–200
Fraser v. University and College Union, 127, 164–166, 182–183, 254n111
Freud, Sigmund, and Freudianism, 82, 227n69, 231–232n58
  The Interpretation of Dreams, 39, 141, 142
Fundamental Rights Agency (FRA), EU, 8, 18, 22–23, 166–167

Galanter, Seth, 172–173
Gaza conflict and anti-Semitism, 2, 7, 136, 137, 148, 203
genocide, as term, 115
Germany. *See also* Holocaust; Nazis and Nazism
  academic position on Arab anti-Semitism, 133
  blood libel in, 101
  contemporary Muslim anti-Semitism in, 135–137
  economic rise of Jews in late 19th-century, 75, 97
  foreign policy toward Middle East, 258n30

Gibson, Mel, 39, 51–54
Gilman, Sander, 84
  Jewish Self-Hatred, 189
Glock, Charles, 120
Goffman, Erving, 77
Golden Dawn party, Greece, 7
grand theories and homogenist theory of prejudice, 108
Grass, Günter, "What Must Be Said," 4–5, 7, 32, 194–197
Guérin, Jules, 58
Gutman, Israel, 130–131

Ha'aretz, 189
Haddad, Sheikh Haitham al-, 81
Hadith, 74
Haghazi, 74
Halderman, Linda, 22
Halimi, Ilan, 12, 33–35, 42, 43–44, 64, 194, 197–198
Halimi, Ruth, 34
Haman (biblical figure), 86, 87
Hamas Charter, 44
Harris, David, 21
Harrison, Bernard, 179
Harvard Crimson, 3–4, 196–197
Hasselman, Wilhelm, 122
hate speech bans, 22
hatred of Jews, defining anti-Semitism as primarily an attitude of, 30, 35–40
Hegel, Georg Friedrich Wilhelm, 52
Hellenistic world, Judaism, and anti-Semitism, 65, 70–71, 96
heterophobia, 106, 108–109, 111–112
Hinckley, John, 48
Hirsh, David, 149
historicism, 31, 85–105
  anti-Israel/anti-Zionist sentiments and, 66
  continuity and evolution over time, failure to grasp, 98–99
  critiques of, 97–95
  defined and described, 93–94

emancipation/Enlightenment,
    Holocaust viewed as product
    of, 52, 96–97
eternalism versus (*See* eternalism)
ideological approaches to
    anti-Semitism and, 44–45
late nineteenth/early twentieth
    century phenomenon,
    anti-Semitism viewed as,
    94–96, 99
perspective, association with
    loss of, 99
racial bigotry regarding Jews,
    history of, 64–66
racialist origins of term and, 56–59
religious bigotry regarding Jews,
    history of, 66, 70–76
repetition, viewing anti-Semitism
    as, 99–105
stability of figural Jew throughout
    history, dangers of overstating,
    141–142
strengths of, 99
Hitler, Adolf, 39, 66, 80, 86, 102,
    128–129, 204, 205
Mein Kampf, 60
Hollywood, disproportionate
    representation of Jews in,
    128–129, 129–130,
    244n39
Holocaust. *See also* Nazis and Nazism
anti-Semites horrified by, 112
Badiou's "Exceptional Signifier"
    argument, 116–117
charges of Jewish obsession with,
    115, 138, 139, 162, 208–209
as culmination rather than
    deviation of Enlightenment/
    emancipation, 52, 96–97
defining anti-Semitism after, 6
exceptional nature, denials of,
    114–115
globalization and generalization of
    concept of, 115

historicism and, 93, 95
racial definition of anti-Semitism
    and, 57
religion, conception of
    Judaism as, 77
taboo against anti-Semitism after,
    8, 10, 39
Holocaust denial, 123, 138–139, 161,
    162, 207, 208–209
"Holocaust envy," 115
Holocaust minimization, 208–209
homogenist theory and its problems,
    106–112
Horkheimer, Max, and Theodor
    Adorno, *The Authoritarian
    Personality*, 47, 82, 103,
    107–108
Huffman, Alice, 21
Human Rights Council, U.N., 123
Hungary, anti-Semitism and Jobbik
    party in, 180, 181
Hyper Cacher kosher deli shootings,
    France, 3
hyphenation versus non-hyphenation
    of anti-Semitic, 61–62
hysterical prejudice, 80

ideology
    anti-Semitism primarily defined as,
        30, 43–47, 52–54, 55, 192
    nodal points in, 117–119
immutable traits, concept of,
    183–185, 212
individualist Protestant conception of
    faith, 76–78
Ingraham, Laura, 198
in-group/out-group theory, 80–82,
    89, 107–111, 129, 188
insularity, Jewish, accusations
    of, 145
intentionality principle, 32, 175–176
intergroup conflict, hostility based
    on, 132
International Red Cross, 157

International Working Definition on anti-Israel/anti-Zionist sentiments, 19–23, 161–167, 173–174
  applied to anti-Semitic incidents, 195, 197–198, 199, 201, 202
  BDS movement and, 209
  conduct, anti-Semitism viewed as, 30, 40–43
  development of, 19–23
  general definition and, 194
Inter-Parliamentary Coalition for Combating Antisemitism, 20, 164
irrationality as defining feature of anti-Semitism, 142–145, 166
irreducible plurality, 94
Irvine cases (University of California at Irvine), 25–27, 68, 170–174, 200–202, 222n96, 251n77, 252n80
Isaac, Benjamin, 65
Ischinger, Wolfgang, 49, 52, 53
Islam. *See* Muslims and anti-Semitism
Israel. *See also* anti-Israel/anti-Zionist sentiments; boycott, divest from, and sanction (BDS) Israel movement; Palestinians
  Jewishness defined in relationship to, 124–126
  right of return to, 27, 134, 202, 203
Italy
  Nirenstein incident, 15, 16
  parliamentary inquiry into anti-Semitism, 62, 108

Jahoda, Marie, 104
Jameson, Frederic, 166
Janowitz, Morris, 104
Jauhari, Al-, 74
Jerusalem Post, 155
Jewish anti-Zionism, 147, 185–190

Jewish Encyclopedia, 58, 85
Jewish identity and the figural Jew, 31–32, 120–145
  anti-Israel/anti-Zionist sentiments as source of Arab anti-Semitism, 132–137
  binaries paralleling sex/gender distinction, 246n90
  chimerical hatred of Jews, 83, 98, 132, 135, 137–138, 140–142, 175, 188, 191, 197
  collective responsibility attributed to, 36, 133–134, 144, 160, 161, 163, 174–175
  distance between actual Jew and figural Jew, trap of focusing on, 141–142
  distorted image of Jews (Jews as *not* Jews), anti-Semitism defined as directed against, 120–121, 130–132, 139–142
  essentialism, avoiding, 139
  ethnic traits principle and, 32, 175, 181–186, 209–210
  irrationality as defining feature of anti-Semitism and, 142–145, 166
  Israel, Jewishness defined in relationship to, 124–126
  Jews *as Jews,* anti-Semitism defined as directed against, 120–124, 130, 142
  naïve empiricism, problem of, 139–140
  negative statements about Israel/Jews and, 126–130
  normative category, Jewishness as, 123–126
  particular misperceptions associated with figural Jew, 137–139, 142
  self-criticism and self-hatred, Jewish, 124–126
  stability of, overstating, 140–141

white versus non-white status
    attributed to Jews, 68–69, 77,
    111, 117
Jewish Voices for Peace, 189
Jews, defining prejudice against. See
    defining anti-Semitism
Jikeli, Günther, 135, 199
Jobbik party, Hungary, 180, 181
Joffe, Josef, 5
John, Gospel of, 71–72, 190
John Chrysostom, 49, 72, 79
Johnson, Paul, 47, 48, 52, 53, 143–144
Judaism, defining prejudice against.
    See defining anti-Semitism
Judensau, 54
Julius, Anthony, 46, 93–94, 127

Kantor Center for the Study of
    Contemporary European
    Jewry, Tel
  Aviv University, 8
Kerry, Cameron, 13, 186
Kerry, John, 13, 186, 210
Kertész, Imre, 124
Kielce massacre, Poland, 101
Kierkegaard, Søren, 104
Kirschen, Yaakov, 14
Klein, Théo, 223n7
Klug, Brian, 130, 165, 166
Kober, Josef and Jacqueline, 49–51
Koran, 73–74, 80, 205
Kovács, András, 180

Lacan, Jacques, 52, 115, 117, 128,
    231–232n58
Laclau, Ernesto, 117
Lang, Berel, 40
Langmuir, Gavin, 63, 90–91, 94, 98,
    112–113, 131
Lanzmann, Claude, 117
Laqueur, Walter, *The Changing Face of
    Antisemitism,* 6
Lasalle, Ferdinand, 122
Lassen, Christian, 58

Lerner, Michael, 40
Lero, Alessio, 208–209
Lévy-Strauss, Claude, 246n90
Lewis, Bernard, 60, 71, 207
Liberation, 134
Lithuania
    blood libel in, 101
    Respublika case and International
        Working Definition, 164
Livingstone, Ken, 11
Livingstone Formulation
    ability to criticize Israel without
        being labeled anti-Semitic,
        126–127
    Badiou's "Exceptional Signifier"
        argument as form of, 116–117
    BDS movement and, 28
    defined and described, 11–12
    YIISA and, 14
London Declaration,
        Inter-Parliamentary Coalition
        for Combating Antisemitism,
        20, 164
London Review of Books, 126
Los Angeles Review of Books, 29

MacEoin, Denis, 16
Macklemore, *Thrift Shop,* 178–179
Madoff, Bernie, 196
Magen David Adom, 157
Malik Ali, Amir, 68, 174
Marcus, Kenneth L., *Jewish Identity
    and Civil Rights in America,*
    24, 26, 222n96
Marr, Wilhelm, 10, 44, 57–58,
    62, 94–96
Marx, Karl, and Marxism, 46,
    103, 104, 105, 109, 119,
    181, 242n16
  On the Jewish Question, 46
  Theses on Feuerbach, ix
MCB (Muslim Council of Britain), 114
McConnell, Michael, 184
memetics principle, 32, 175, 178–181

Mencken, H. L., 131
Merah, Mohamed, 1, 32, 194, 198–200
Merriam-Webster dictionaries, 56, 62, 69, 228n2. See also *Webster's Third New International Dictionary*
Midrash, 86
Modern Language Association (MLA), 208–209, 259n47
Montagu, Ashley, 63
Montaigne, Michel de, 98
Montreal Jewish elementary school, firebombing of, 18, 154–155
mortality salience, 177, 180, 253n98
Mouffe, Chantal, 117
movie industry, disproportionate representation of Jews in, 128–129, 129–130, 244n39
Muhammad the Prophet, 73
multiculturalism, 121
Muslim Council of Britain (MCB), 114
Muslims and anti-Semitism. *See also* Arabs
anti-Israel/anti-Zionist sentiments and, 132–137, 170–174
apes and pigs, Jews referred to as, 80–81
blood libel, 75, 101, 224n15
collective responsibility attributed to Jews, 133–134
correlation between anti-Israel and anti-Semitic views, 150
empirical evidence regarding modern attitudes, 135–137, 199
EUMC 2004 report and, 152–153
ideological anti-Semitism, medieval, 44
Irvine cases and, 170–174
nodal point, Jews as, 119
religious anti-Semitism, 73–74, 75–76

National Association of Teachers in Further and Higher Education (NATFHE), UK, 148–149, 151
National Security Administration (NSA), U.S., 134
National Union of Students, UK, 164
Nazis and Nazism. *See also* Holocaust
Arabs, anti-Semitic propaganda aimed at, 205
boycotts, anti-Jewish, 205–206, 213
contemporary German foreign policy toward Middle East and, 258n30
erroneous conceptions of omnipotent Jewish power, 131
Golden Dawn, Greece, neo-Nazi sentiments of, 7
historicist equation of anti-Semitism with, 99
influence on later anti-Semitism and anti-Zionism, 101–102
Israeli policy equated with, 19, 25, 68, 116–117, 173–174, 202
Judaism compared to disease by, 49
Kober case, 49–51
nodal point, Jews as, 119
racial and religious motivations of, 65–66
Semites other than Jews, attitudes toward, 40
true versus false statements, anti-Semitism of, 128–129
Nelson, Cary, 21
Nemmouche, Mehdi, 199–200
Netanyahu, Benjamin, 4, 13, 27
Netanyahu, Ben-Zion, 112
Netherlands, attitudes toward Jews in, 109, 132–133, 176
Neturei Karta, 248n11
new anti-Semitism, 11, 19, 39, 46, 68, 151. *See also* anti-Israel/anti-Zionist sentiments
Newmark, Jeremy, 165
new racism, 67, 68
Newsweek, 7
New York Times, 1, 29
Nicolson, Harold, 36, 41

Nirenberg, David, 54, 89, 98, 228n90
  Anti-Judaism, 46
Nirenstein, Fiamma, 15, 16
nodal point, anti-Semitism viewed as, 117–119, 193
normalization
  of anti-Semitism, 52–54
  of Israel, BDS movement opposing, 206
nostalgia and historical repetition, 105
NSA (National Security Administration), U.S., 134
Nuriel, Carole, 35

Obama, Barack, 3, 16, 24–25, 26, 134, 164, 167
obsessional prejudice, 80
OCR (Office for Civil Rights), U.S. Department of Education, 21, 24–27, 30, 32, 77, 169–174, 194, 200–202, 222n96, 251–252n76–77
ODIHR (Office for Democratic Institutions and Human Rights), OSCE, 160, 162, 163
Office for Civil Rights (OCR), U.S. Department of Education, 21, 24–27, 30, 32, 77, 169–174, 194, 200–202, 222n96, 251–252n76–77
Office for Democratic Institutions and Human Rights (ODIHR), OSCE, 160, 162, 163
Office to Monitor and Combat Global Antisemitism, U.S. State Department, 164
one-state solutions to Israeli-Palestinian conflict, 3, 196–197
Ordóñez, Elizabeth Jane, 209
Organization for Security and Co-operation in Europe (OSCE), 20, 151–152, 159–161, 163

orientalism, 58, 59
Origen, 72
Orwell, George, 131
OSCE (Organization for Security and Co-operation in Europe), 20, 151–152, 159–161, 163
Oslo Process, 151
Ottawa Protocol, Inter-Parliamentary Coalition for Combating Antisemitism, 20, 164
out-group/in-group theory, 80–82, 89, 107–111, 129, 188
Oxford English Dictionary, 37

PACBI (Palestinian Campaign for the Academic and Cultural Boycott of Israel), 206
Palestinian Call for BDS, 203–204, 206, 207, 213
Palestinian Campaign for the Academic and Cultural Boycott of Israel (PACBI), 206
Palestinians. *See also* anti-Israel/anti-Zionist sentiments; Arabs; boycott, divest from, and sanction (BDS) Israel movement; Muslims and anti-Semitism
  ADL finding of anti-Semitic attitudes of West Bank and Gaza residents, 203
  double standard of self determination for, 158
  Gaza conflict and anti-Semitism, 2, 7, 136, 137, 148, 203
  Ministry of Education textbook on *Protocols of the Elders of Zion,* 136
  one-state solutions to Israeli-Palestinian conflict, 3, 196–197
  right of return and, 27, 202, 203
  Second Intifada, 6, 19, 147, 151
Pappé, Ilan, 189
Passy, Solomon, 160

pathology or disease
  anti-Semitism primarily viewed as, 30, 47–54, 55
  Judaism compared to, 48–49
personal responsibility for anti-Semitism, 49, 51–54, 55
perspective, historicism associated with loss of, 99
Petegorsky, David W., 107
Peter the Venerable (abbot of Cluny), 73
Petlura, Symon, 86
phenomenology of anti-Semitism, 30, 33–55
  as attitude, 30, 35–40, 55, 192
  cognitive dimension of, 37
  as conduct, 30, 40–43, 55
  as ideology, 30, 43–47, 52–54, 55, 192
  as pathology or disease, 30, 47–54, 55
philosophical/political incorrectness
  of eternalism, 91–92
  in post-Marxism, 52
pigs, Jews associated with, 54, 80–81
Pipes, Daniel, 171
Poland, blood libel in, 101
Poliakov, Léon, 91, 112
political/philosophical incorrectness
  of eternalism, 91–92
  in post-Marxism, 52
poll taxes, 214
Porat, Dina, 19, 41, 95, 131, 161
Posner, Richard, 63, 70
post-Marxism, 52, 119
prejudice, anti-Semitic. *See* defining anti-Semitism
prejudice, other forms of. *See* comparison of anti-Semitism to other forms of racism and prejudice
projection theory, 103, 227n69
Protestant individualist conception of faith, 76–78

Protocols of the Elders of Zion, 42, 44, 51, 66, 76, 102, 136, 179, 195, 204
Psaki, Jen, 3

Ra'ad, Basem L., 209
race, 30, 56–84. *See also* anti-black racism; comparison of anti-Semitism to other forms of racism and prejudice
  anti-Arab discrimination, anti-Semitism viewed as including, 59–61
  demonization, bestialization, and dehumanization of Jews, 54, 66, 71, 73, 79–84
  eliding distinction between religion and, 66, 69–70, 73, 84
  hidden racial dimensions of religious anti-Semitism, 66, 70–76
  history of racial bigotry regarding Jews, 64–66
  hyphenation versus non-hyphenation of anti-Semitic, 61–62
  Jewish identity and, 124
  Jews, white versus non-white identity attributed to, 68–69, 77, 111, 117
  OCR investigations and, 24
  origins of "anti-Semitism" as term and, 56–59
  problem of race as concept, 62–64
  religion and (*See* religion)
  scare quotes around race, use of, 62–64, 69–70
Ramadan, Tariq, 2, 200
Rashi, 86–87
religion, 30, 56–84
  Christian religious Jew-hatred, 71–73, 74–75, 76

demonization, bestialization, and dehumanization of Jews, 54, 66, 71, 73, 79–84
doctrinal rivalry or disagreement, anti-Semitism distinguished from, 70–71
eliding distinction between race and, 66, 69–70, 73, 84
ethnic traits principle and, 182–185
hidden racial dimensions of religious anti-Semitism, 66, 70–76
history of religious bigotry regarding Jews, 66, 70–76
Jewish identity and, 124
Muslim religious Jew-hatred, 73–74
OCR investigations and, 24
problem of religion as concept, 76–79
Protestant individualist conception of faith, 76–78
race and (*See* race)
Renan, Ernest, 58
repetition, viewing anti-Semitism as, 99–105
Respublika, 164
right of return to Israel, 27, 134, 202, 203
rigid designators, 143, 145
ritual murder. *See* blood libel
Riva, Mira and Emanuel, 199–200
Rogan, Seth, 179
Rose, Jacqueline, 189
Rosenthal, Hannah, 167
Rossman-Benjamin, Tammi, 189
Rotteck-Welckerschen State Dictionary, 58
Rubin, Edward, 122
Rue Copernic synagogue bombing, Paris, 134
Russia, blood libel in, 101
Rutgers University study of unconscious anti-Semitism, 176–178, 180

Sacks, Jonathan, 144
St. Francis College vs. Al Khazraji, 78
Saleh, Safaa, 119
San Francisco State University, anti-Semitic incidents at, 36, 100, 175
Saramago, José, 75
Sarkozy, Nicholas, 33
Sartre, Jean-Paul, 35, 43, 44, 130
Saussure, Ferdinand, 117
scare quotes around race, use of, 62–64, 69–70
Schnitzler, Arthur, 188
Second Intifada, 6, 19, 147, 151
self-criticism and self-hatred, Jewish, 124–126, 185–190
self-defeating, eternalism viewed as, 92
self determination, right of, 158, 163
Semites other than Jews, discrimination against, 40, 59–61
Seneca, 98
Senesi, Vauro, 15
Shapiro, L., 92
Sharansky, Natan, 23, 155–159, 161, 167, 174, 202, 215, 249n38
Sharon, Ariel, 25, 42
Sherry, Suzanne, 121–122
Shoah. *See* Holocaust
Shoah (Lanzmann documentary), 117
Simon Wiesenthal Center, 22–23
Simpson, George E., 40
Sira, 74
socio-economics
  rise of Jews in late 19th-century Germany, 75, 97
  trauma or failure and prejudice, 104
Sontag, Susan, 47
sovereign conceit, 38
Spain, historical anti-Semitism in, 65, 188
Stark, Rodney, 120

State Department (U.S.)
   *Contemporary Global
      Anti-Semitism,* 123
   Office to Monitor and Combat
      Global Antisemitism, 164
   suspicions of U.N.
      anti-Semitism, 123
State Department definition
   anti-Israel/anti-Zionist sentiments
      and, 164, 166–169,
      173–174
   applied to anti-Semitic incidents,
      195, 198, 199, 201, 202
   BDS movement and, 208, 209
   conduct, focus on, 30
   development of, 9, 17, 20, 23
   general definition and, 194
   importance of adoption by
      civil rights enforcement
      agencies, 215
Steinbrink, Meier, 109
Steinschneider, Moritz, 58
Stern, Kenneth, 18, 20–21, 38,
   41–42, 154, 161, 162
Sternberg, Ernest, "Purifying the
   World," 119
Strauss, Leo, 9
Süddeutsche Zeitung, 4
Swiss Federal Commission Against
   Racism (FCR), 62
Szasz, Thomas, 48, 52, 53

tacitness principle, 32, 39–40, 175,
   176–178
Taeb, Mehdi, 156–157
Taguieff, Pierre-André, 63, 67
Tapia, Blanca, 22–23
Thanatos and *Eros,* 82
Theobald (Jewish convert in
   Norwich), 73
Theodorakis, Mikis, 75, 208
theozoomorphism, 81
3-D Definition/Test, 23, 155–159,
   161, 167, 174, 202, 215
Tikkun, 40

Title VI of Civil Rights Act of 1964
   (U.S.), 21, 24, 170, 172
Tobin, Gary, 243n38
Tobin, Jonathan, 21
Tolstoy, Leo, 35
Torquemada, Tomás de, 65
Toulouse Massacre, 1–2, 7, 32, 33, 34,
   133, 194, 198–200
true versus false statements,
   anti-Semitism of, 127–130
Truman National Security Project, 16
Tumin, Melvin, 132
Turkey, refusal of Turkish
   Jews to acknowledge
   anti-Semitism in, 10
two-stage process (incident and
   blaming the victim), 14–15

UCU (University and College Union),
   UK, 20, 32, 114, 127, 149,
   150, 151, 164–166, 182–183
unconscious anti-Semitism and
   tacitness principle, 32, 39–40,
   175, 176–178
United Kingdom
   academic associations in, 16,
      20, 32, 114, 127, 148–151,
      164–166, 182–183, 254n111
   blood libel in medieval England,
      73, 100–101
   Equality Act 2010, 182
   MCB (Muslim Council of
      Britain) boycott of Holocaust
      Memorial Day in, 114
   National Union of Students, 164
   Parliamentary Inquiry into
      Anti-Semitism, 114
   student test question on
      anti-Semitism, 5
United Nations
   anti-Israel condemnations and
      anti-Semitism at, 123,
      157, 242n10
   declaration of Zionism as racism
      (1975), 67

Economic and Social Council, 63
General Assembly, 123
Human Rights Council, 123
WCAR (World Conference against Racism) or Durban I, 151, 204, 206
United States. *See also entries at* American; State Department; State Department definition
anti-Semitic feeling in, 8
Commission on Civil Rights, 20, 164, 179–180
court cases dealing with anti-Semitism in, 217n18
Hollywood, disproportionate representation of Jews in, 128–129, 129–130, 244n39
Jewish assimilation in, 107
Kober case of accidental marriage to Nazi, 49–51
NSA, 134
OCR (Office for Civil Rights) investigations, 21, 24–27, 30, 32, 77, 169–174, 194, 200–202, 222n96, 251–252n76–77
poll tax in, 214
San Francisco State University, anti-Semitic incidents at, 36, 100, 175
Supreme Court definition of immutability, 183–184
Title VI of Civil Rights Act of 1964, 21, 24, 170, 172
University of California system, anti-Semitic incidents in, 21–22, 25–27, 32, 68, 170–174, 175–176, 189, 200–202, 222n96, 251n77, 252n80
universal viscosity, 144, 145
University and College Union (UCU), UK, 20, 32, 114, 127, 149, 150, 151, 164–166, 182–183, 254n111

University of Birmingham, linguistic study by, 60
University of California system, anti-Semitic incidents in, 21–22, 25–27, 32, 68, 170–174, 175–176, 189, 200–202, 222n96
U.S. Campaign for the Academic Boycott of Israel, 27, 212

ventilation theory, 103
Vespasian (Roman emperor), 83

Waldenegg, Georg Christoph Berger, 58
WCAR (World Conference against Racism) or Durban I, 151, 204, 206
Webster's Third New International Dictionary, 32, 146–150, 194. See also *Merriam-Webster* dictionaries
Weil, Gustaf, 58
Weinberg, Aryeh, 238n38
Weizmann, Chaim, 106
Whitaker, Alan, 127
whiteness, of Jews, 68–69, 77, 111, 117
white supremacism, 68–69
Wieseltier, Leon, 85, 86, 92
William of Norwich, 73, 100
Winkler, Beate, 152, 162
Winter, Cécile, "The Master-Signifier of the New Aryans," 116–117
Wise, Stephen S., 107
Wisse, Ruth, 12, 48, 92
Wistrich, Robert, 91, 100, 148, 227n69
Working Definition. *See* International Working Definition
World Conference against Racism (WCAR) or Durban I, 151, 204, 206

xenophobia, 7, 64, 106, 109, 111–112, 180

Yale University
  study showing
    correlation between
    anti-Israel views
    and anti-Semitism, 149–150
  YIISA (Yale Interdisciplinary
    Initiative for the Study of
    Antisemitism), 14
Yanay, Niza, 187
Yaqub, Muhammad Hussein, 135
Yehoshua, A. B., 124,
  125, 126, 143
Yellen, Janet, 195–196
Yinger, Milton, 40
Young-Bruehl, Elizabeth, 14–15
Yudof, Mark, 21

Zeit, Die, 5
ZfA (Centre for Research on
  Anti-Semitism), 152
Zionism
  diaspora, anti-Semitism viewed as
    related to, 106–107
  hatred of (*See* anti-Israel/
    anti-Zionist sentiments)
Zionist Organization of America
  (ZOA), 25, 26, 170–171
Žižek, Slavoj, 51–54, 105, 117–118,
  141–142, 143, 145, 228n91
ZOA (Zionist Organization
  of America), 25, 26,
  170–171, 251n77
Zoroastrianism, 74

www.ingramcontent.com/pod-product-compliance
Ingram Content Group UK Ltd.
Pitfield, Milton Keynes, MK11 3LW, UK
UKHW022155230426
12049UKWH00004BA/110